AUTOBIOGRAPHIC SKETCHES

LECTOR HOUSE PUBLIC DOMAIN WORKS

AUTOBIOGRAPHIC SKETCHES

THOMAS DE QUINCEY

ISBN: 978-93-90294-19-0

Published: -

LECTOR HOUSE LLP
E-MAIL: lectorpublishing@gmail.com

AUTOBIOGRAPHIC SKETCHES.

BY

THOMAS DE QUINCEY

(SELECTIONS, GRAVE AND GAY,
FROM WRITINGS PUBLISHED AND UNPUBLISHED)

EXTRACT FROM A LETTER

WRITTEN BY MR. DE QUINCEY TO THE AMERICAN EDITOR OF THIS WORKS.

LASSWADE, January 8, 1853

MY DEAR SIR:

I am on the point of revising and considerably altering, for republication in England, an edition of such amongst my writings as it may seem proper deliberately to avow. Not that I have any intention, or consciously any reason, expressly to disown any one thing that I have ever published; but some things have sufficiently accomplished their purpose when they have met the call of that particular transient occasion in which they arose; and others, it may be thought on review, might as well have been suppressed from the very first. Things immoral would of course fall within that category; of these, however, I cannot reproach myself with ever having published so much as one. But even pure levities, simply *as* such, and without liability to any worse objection, may happen to have no justifying principle of life within them; and if, any where, I find such a reproach to lie against a paper of mine, that paper I should wish to cancel. So that, upon the whole, my new and revised edition is likely to differ by very considerable changes from the original papers; and, consequently, to that extent is likely to differ from your existing Boston reprint.

These changes, as sure to be more or less advantageous to the collection, it is my wish to place at your disposal as soon as possible, in order that you may make what use of them you see fit, be it little or much. It may so happen that the public demand will give you no opportunity for using them at all. I go on therefore to mention, that over and above these changes, which may possibly strike you as sometimes mere caprices, pulling down in order to rebuild, or turning squares into rotundas, (*diruit, aedificat, mutat quadrata rotundis,*) it is my purpose to enlarge this edition by as many new papers as I find available for such a station. These I am anxious to put into the hands of your house, and, so far as regards the U.S., of *your* house exclusively; not with any view to further emolument, but as an acknowledgment of the services which you have already rendered me; viz., first, in having brought together so widely scattered a collection—a difficulty which in my own hands by too painful an experience I had found from nervous depression to be absolutely insurmountable; secondly, in having made me a participator in the pecuniary profits of the American edition, without solicitation or the shadow of any expectation on my part, without any legal claim that I could plead, or equitable warrant in established usage, solely and merely upon your own spontaneous motion. Some of these new papers, I hope, will not be without their value in the eyes of those who have taken an interest in the original series. But at all events, good or bad, they are now tendered to the appropriation of your individual house, the Messrs. TICKNOR, REED, & FIELDS, according to the amplest extent of any power to make such a transfer that I may be found to possess by law or custom in America.

I wish this transfer were likely to be of more value. But the veriest trifle, interpreted by the spirit in which I offer it, may express my sense of the liberality manifested throughout this transaction by your honorable house.

Ever believe me my dear sir,
Your faithful and obliged,
THOMAS DE QUINCEY.

PREFACE TO THE ENGLISH EDITION.

The miscellaneous writings which I propose to lay before the public in this body of selections are in part to be regarded as a republication of papers scattered through several British journals twenty or thirty years ago, which papers have been reprinted in a collective form by an American house of high character in Boston; but in part they are to be viewed as entirely new, large sections having been intercalated in the present edition, and other changes made, which, even to the old parts, by giving very great expansion, give sometimes a character of absolute novelty. Once, therefore, at home, with the allowance for the changes here indicated, and once in America, it may be said that these writings have been in some sense published. But *publication* is a great idea never even approximated by the utmost anxieties of man. Not the Bible, not the little book which, in past times, came next to the Bible in European diffusion and currency,[1] viz., the treatise "De Imitatione Christi," has yet in any generation been really published. Where is the *printed* book of which, in Coleridge's words, it may not be said that, after all efforts to publish itself, still it remains, for the world of possible readers, "as good as manuscript"? Not to insist, however, upon any romantic rigor in constructing this idea, and abiding by the ordinary standard of what is understood by *publication*, it is probable that, in many cases, my own papers must have failed in reaching even this. For they were printed as contributions to journals. Now, that mode of publication is unavoidably disadvantageous to a writer, except under unusual conditions. By its harsh peremptory punctuality, it drives a man into hurried writing, possibly into saying the thing that is not. They won't wait an hour for you in a magazine or a review; they won't wait for truth; you may as well reason with the sea, or a railway train, as in such a case with an editor; and, as it makes no difference whether that

[1] *"Next to the bible in currency."* —That is, next in the fifteenth century to the Bible of the nineteenth century. The diffusion of the "De Imitatione Christi" over Christendom (the idea of Christendom, it must be remembered, not then including any part of America) anticipated, in 1453, the diffusion of the Bible in 1853. But why? Through what causes? Elsewhere I have attempted to show that this enormous (and seemingly incredible) popularity of the "De Imitatione Christi" is virtually to be interpreted as a vicarious popularity of the Bible. At that time the Bible itself was a fountain of inspired truth every where sealed up; but a whisper ran through the western nations of Europe that the work of Thomas à Kempis contained some slender rivulets of truth silently stealing away into light from that interdicted fountain. This belief (so at least I read the case) led to the prodigious multiplication of the book, of which not merely the reimpressions, but the separate translations, are past all counting; though bibliographers *have* undertaken to count them. The book came forward as an answer to the sighing of Christian Europe for light from heaven. I speak of Thomas à Kempis as the author; but his claim was disputed. Gerson was adopted by France as the author; and other local saints by other nations.

sea which you desire to argue with is the Mediterranean or the Baltic, so, with that editor and his deafness, it matters not a straw whether he belong to a northern or a southern journal. Here is one evil of journal writing—viz., its overmastering precipitation. A second is, its effect at times in narrowing your publicity. Every journal, or pretty nearly so, is understood to hold (perhaps in its very title it makes proclamation of holding) certain fixed principles in politics, or possibly religion. These distinguishing features, which become badges of enmity and intolerance, all the more intense as they descend upon narrower and narrower grounds of separation, must, at the very threshold, by warning off those who dissent from them, so far operate to limit your audience. To take my own case as an illustration: these present sketches were published in a journal dedicated to purposes of political change such as many people thought revolutionary. I thought so myself, and did not go along with its politics. Inevitably that accident shut them out from the knowledge of a very large reading class. Undoubtedly this journal, being ably and conscientiously conducted, had some circulation amongst a neutral class of readers; and amongst its own class it was popular. But its own class did not ordinarily occupy that position in regard to social influence which could enable them rapidly to diffuse the knowledge of a writer. A reader whose social standing is moderate may communicate his views upon a book or a writer to his own circle; but his own circle is a narrow one. Whereas, in aristocratic classes, having more leisure and wealth, the intercourse is inconceivably more rapid; so that the publication of any book which interests *them* is secured at once; and this publishing influence passes downwards; but rare, indeed, is the inverse process of publication through an influence spreading upwards.

According to the way here described, the papers now presented to the public, like many another set of papers nominally published, were *not* so in any substantial sense. Here, at home, they may be regarded as still unpublished.[2] But, in such a case, why were not the papers at once detached from the journal, and reprinted? In the neglect to do this, some there are who will read a blamable carelessness in the author; but, in that carelessness, others will read a secret consciousness that the papers were of doubtful value. I have heard, indeed, that some persons, hearing of this republication, had interpreted the case thus: Within the last four or five years, a practice has arisen amongst authors of gathering together into volumes their own scattered contributions to periodical literature. Upon that suggestion, they suppose me suddenly to have remembered that I also had made such contributions; that mine might be entitled to their chance as well as those of others; and, accordingly, that on such a slight invitation *ab extra*, I had called back into life

---

[2] At the same time it must not be denied, that, if you lose by a journal in the way here described, you also gain by it. The journal gives you the benefit of its own separate audience, that might else never have heard your name. On the other hand, in such a case, the journal secures to you the special enmity of its own peculiar antagonists. These papers, for instance, of mine, not being political, were read possibly in a friendly temper by the regular supporters of the journal that published them. But some of my own political friends regarded me with displeasure for connecting myself at all with a reforming journal. And far more, who would have been liberal enough to disregard that objection, naturally lost sight of me when under occultation to *them* in a journal which they never saw.

what otherwise I had long since regarded as having already fulfilled its mission, and must doubtless have dismissed to oblivion.

I do not certainly know, or entirely believe, that any such thing was really said. But, however that may be, no representation can be more opposed to the facts. Never for an instant did I falter in my purpose of republishing most of the papers which I had written. Neither, if I myself had been inclined to forget them, should I have been allowed to do so by strangers. For it happens that, during the fourteen last years, I have received from many quarters in England, in Ireland, in the British colonies, and in the United States, a series of letters expressing a far profounder interest in papers written by myself than any which I could ever think myself entitled to look for. Had I, therefore, otherwise cherished no purposes of republication, it now became a duty of gratitude and respect to these numerous correspondents, that I should either republish the papers in question, or explain why I did not. The obstacle in fact had been in part the shifting state of the law which regulated literary property, and especially the property in periodical literature. But a far greater difficulty lay in the labor (absolutely insurmountable to myself) of bringing together from so many quarters the scattered materials of the collection. This labor, most fortunately, was suddenly taken off my hands by the eminent house of Messrs TICKNOR, REED, & FIELDS, Boston, U. S. To them I owe my acknowledgments, first of all, for that service: they have brought together a great majority of my fugitive papers in a series of volumes now amounting to twelve. And, secondly, I am bound to mention that they have made me a sharer in the profits of the publication, called upon to do so by no law whatever, and assuredly by no expectation of that sort upon my part.

Taking as the basis of my remarks this collective American edition, I will here attempt a rude general classification of all the articles which compose it. I distribute them grossly into three classes: *First*, into that class which proposes primarily to amuse the reader; but which, in doing so, may or may not happen occasionally to reach a higher station, at which the amusement passes into an impassioned interest. Some papers are merely playful; but others have a mixed character. These present *Autobiographic Sketches* illustrate what I mean. Generally, they pretend to little beyond that sort of amusement which attaches to any real story, thoughtfully and faithfully related, moving through a succession of scenes sufficiently varied, that are not suffered to remain too long upon the eye, and that connect themselves at every stage with intellectual objects. But, even here, I do not scruple to claim from the reader, occasionally, a higher consideration. At times, the narrative rises into a far higher key. Most of all it does so at a period of the writer's life where, of necessity, a severe abstraction takes place from all that could invest him with any alien interest; no display that might dazzle the reader, nor ambition that could carry his eye forward with curiosity to the future, nor successes, fixing his eye on the present; nothing on the stage but a solitary infant, and its solitary combat with grief—a mighty darkness, and a sorrow without a voice. But something of the same interest will be found, perhaps, to rekindle at a maturer age, when the characteristic features of the individual mind have been unfolded. And I contend that much more than amusement ought to settle upon any narrative of a life that is really *confidential*. It is singular—but many of my readers will know it for a truth—that vast numbers of people, though liberated from all reasonable motives to self-restraint, *cannot* be confidential—have it not in their power to lay aside reserve; and many, again, cannot be so with particular people. I have witnessed more than once the case, that a young female dancer, at a certain turn of a peculiar dance, could not—though she had died for it—sustain a free, fluent motion. Aerial chains fell upon her at one point; some invisible spell (who could say *what*?) froze her elasticity. Even as a horse, at noonday on an open heath, starts aside from something his rider cannot see; or as the flame within a Davy lamp feeds upon the poisonous gas up to the meshes that surround it, but there suddenly is arrested by barriers that no Aladdin will ever dislodge. It is because a man cannot see and measure these mystical forces which palsy him, that he cannot deal with them effectually. If he were able really to pierce the haze which so often envelops, even to himself, his own secret springs of action and reserve, there cannot be a life moving at all under intellectual impulses that would not, through that single force of absolute frankness, fall within the reach of a deep, solemn, and sometimes even of a thrilling interest. Without pretending to an interest of this quality, I have done what was possible on *my* part towards the readiest access to such an interest by perfect sincerity—saying every where nothing *but* the truth; and in any case forbearing to say the *whole* truth only through consideration for others.

Into the second class I throw those papers which address themselves purely to the understanding as an insulated faculty; or do so primarily. Let me call them by the general name of ESSAYS. These, as in other cases of the same kind, must have their value measured by two separate questions. A. What is the problem, and of what rank in dignity or in use, which the essay undertakes? And next, that point being settled, B. What is the success obtained? and (as a separate question) what is the executive ability displayed in the solution of the problem? This latter question is naturally no question for myself, as the answer would involve a verdict upon my own merit. But, generally, there will be quite enough in the answer to question A for establishing the value of any essay on its soundest basis. *Prudens interrogatio est dimidium scientiae.* Skilfully to frame your question, is half way towards insuring the true answer. Two or three of the problems treated in these essays I will here rehearse.

1. ESSENISM—The essay on this, where mentioned at all in print, has been mentioned as dealing with a question of pure speculative curiosity: so little suspicion is abroad of that real question which lies below. Essenism means simply this—Christianity before Christ, and consequently without Christ. If, therefore, Essenism could make good its pretensions, there at one blow would be an end of Christianity, which in that case is not only superseded as an idle repetition of a religious system already published, but also as a criminal plagiarism. Nor can the wit of man evade that conclusion. But even *that* is not the worst. When we contemplate the total orb of Christianity, we see it divide into two hemispheres: first, an ethical system, differing *centrally* from any previously made known to man; secondly, a mysterious and divine machinery for reconciling man to God; a teaching to be taught, but also a work to be worked. Now, the first we find again

in the ethics of the counterfeit Essenes—which ought not to surprise us at all; since it is surely an easy thing for him who pillages my thoughts *ad libitum* to reproduce a perfect resemblance in his own:[3] but what has become of the second, viz., not the teaching, but the operative working of Christianity? The ethical system is replaced by a stolen system; but what replaces the mysterious *agencies* of the Christian faith? In Essenism we find again a saintly scheme of ethics; but where is the scheme of mediation?

In the Roman church, there have been some theologians who have also seen reason to suspect the romance of "Essenismus." And I am not sure that the knowledge of this fact may not have operated to blunt the suspicions of the Protestant churches. I do not mean that such a fact would have absolutely deafened Protestant ears to the grounds of suspicion when loudly proclaimed; but it is very likely to have indisposed them towards listening. Meantime, so far as I am acquainted with these Roman Catholic demurs, the difference between *them* and my own is broad. They, without suspecting any subtle, fraudulent purpose, simply recoil from the romantic air of such a statement—which builds up, as with an enchanter's wand, an important sect, such as could not possibly have escaped the notice of Christ and his apostles. I, on the other hand, insist not only upon the revolting incompatibility of such a sect with the absence of all attention to it in the New Testament, but (which is far more important) the incompatibility of such a sect (as a sect elder than Christ) with the originality and heavenly revelation of Christianity. Here is my first point of difference from the Romish objectors. The second is this: not content with exposing the imposture, I go on, and attempt to show in what real circumstances, fraudulently disguised, it might naturally have arisen. In the real circumstances of the Christian church, when struggling with *Jewish* persecution at some period of the generation between the crucifixion and the siege of Jerusalem, arose probably that secret defensive society of Christians which suggested to Josephus his knavish forgery. We must remember that Josephus did not write until *after* the great ruins effected by the siege; that he wrote at Rome, far removed from the criticism of those survivors who could have exposed, or had a motive for exposing, his malicious frauds; and, finally, that he wrote under the patronage of the Flavian family: by his sycophancy he had won their protection, which would have overawed any Christian whatever from coming forward to unmask him, in the very improbable case of a work so large, costly, and, by its title, merely archaeological, finding its way, at such a period, into the hands of any poor hunted Christian.[4]

2. THE CAESARS.—This, though written hastily, and in a situation where I had no aid from books, is yet far from being what some people have supposed

[3] The crime of Josephus in relation to Christianity is the same, in fact, as that of Lauder in respect to Milton. It was easy enough to detect plagiarisms in the "Paradise Lost" from Latin passages fathered upon imaginary writers, when these passages had previously been forged by Lauder himself for the purpose of sustaining such a charge.

[4] It is a significant fact, that Dr. Strauss, whose sceptical spirit, left to its own disinterested motions, would have looked through and through this monstrous fable of Essenism, coolly adopted it, no questions asked, as soon as he perceived the value of it as an argument against Christianity.

it—a simple recapitulation, or *resumé*, of the Roman imperatorial history. It moves rapidly over the ground, but still with an exploring eye, carried right and left into the deep shades that have gathered so thickly over the one solitary road[5] traversing that part of history. Glimpses of moral truth, or suggestions of what may lead to it; indications of neglected difficulties, and occasionally conjectural solutions of such difficulties,—these are what this essay offers. It was meant as a specimen of fruits, gathered hastily and without effort, by a vagrant but thoughtful mind: through the coercion of its theme, sometimes it became ambitious; but I did not give to it an ambitious title. Still I felt that the meanest of these suggestions merited a valuation: derelicts they were, not in the sense of things willfully abandoned by my predecessors on that road, but in the sense of things blindly overlooked. And, summing up in one word the pretensions of this particular essay, I will venture to claim for it so much, at least, of originality as ought *not* to have been left open to any body in the nineteenth century.

3. CICERO.—This is not, as might be imagined, any literary valuation of Cicero; it is a new reading of Roman history in the most dreadful and comprehensive of her convulsions, in that final stage of her transmutations to which Cicero was himself a party—and, as I maintain, a most selfish and unpatriotic party. He was governed in one half by his own private interest as a *novus homo* dependent upon a wicked oligarchy, and in the other half by his blind hatred of Caesar; the grandeur of whose nature he could not comprehend, and the real patriotism of whose policy could never be appreciated by one bribed to a selfish course. The great mob of historians have but one way of constructing the great events of this era—they succeed to it as to an inheritance, and chiefly under the misleading of that *prestige* which is attached to the name of Cicero; on which account it was that I gave this title to my essay. Seven years after it was published, this essay, slight and imperfectly developed as is the exposition of its parts, began to receive some public countenance.

I was going on to abstract the principle involved in some other essays. But I forbear. These specimens are sufficient for the purpose of informing the reader that I do not write without a thoughtful consideration of my subject; and also, that to think reasonably upon any question has never been allowed by me as a sufficient ground for writing upon it, unless I believed myself able to offer some considerable novelty. Generally I claim (not arrogantly, but with firmness) the merit of rectification applied to absolute errors or to injurious limitations of the truth.

Finally, as a third class, and, in virtue of their aim, as a far higher class of compositions included in the American collection, I rank *The Confessions of an Opium Eater*, and also (but more emphatically) the *Suspiria de Profundis*. On these, as modes of impassioned prose ranging under no precedents that I am aware of in any literature, it is much more difficult to speak justly, whether in a hostile or a

---

[5] *"Solitary road."*—The reader must remember that, until the seventh century of our era, when Mahometanism arose, there was no *collateral* history. Why there was none, why no Gothic, why no Parthian history, it is for Rome to explain. We tax ourselves, and are taxed by others, with many an imaginary neglect as regards India; but assuredly we cannot be taxed with *that* neglect. No part of our Indian empire, or of its adjacencies, but has occupied the researches of our Oriental scholars.

friendly character. As yet, neither of these two works has ever received the least degree of that correction and pruning which both require so extensively; and of the *Suspiria*, not more than perhaps one third has yet been printed. When both have been fully revised, I shall feel myself entitled to ask for a more determinate adjudication on their claims as works of art. At present, I feel authorized to make haughtier pretensions in right of their *conception* than I shall venture to do, under the peril of being supposed to characterize their *execution*. Two remarks only I shall address to the equity of my reader. First, I desire to remind him of the perilous difficulty besieging all attempts to clothe in words the visionary scenes derived from the world of dreams, where a single false note, a single word in a wrong key, ruins the whole music; and, secondly, I desire him to consider the utter sterility of universal literature in this one department of impassioned prose; which certainly argues some singular difficulty suggesting a singular duty of indulgence in criticizing any attempt that even imperfectly succeeds. The sole Confessions, belonging to past times, that have at all succeeded in engaging the attention of men, are those of St. Augustine and of Rousseau. The very idea of breathing a record of human passion, not into the ear of the random crowd, but of the saintly confessional, argues an impassioned theme. Impassioned, therefore, should be the tenor of the composition. Now, in St. Augustine's Confessions is found one most impassioned passage, viz., the lamentation for the death of his youthful friend in the fourth book; one, and no more. Further there is nothing. In Rousseau there is not even so much. In the whole work there is nothing grandly affecting but the character and the inexplicable misery of the writer.

Meantime, by what accident, so foreign to my nature, do I find myself laying foundations towards a higher valuation of my own workmanship? O reader, I have been talking idly. I care not for any valuation that depends upon comparison with others. Place me where you will on the scale of comparison: only suffer me, though standing lowest in your catalogue, to rejoice in the recollection of letters expressing the most fervid interest in particular passages or scenes of the *Confessions*, and, by rebound from *them*, an interest in their author: suffer me also to anticipate that, on the publication of some parts yet in arrear of the *Suspiria*, you yourself may possibly write a letter to me, protesting that your disapprobation is just where it was, but nevertheless that you are disposed to shake hands with me—by way of proof that you like me better than I deserve.

CONTENTS

* THE NATION OF LONDON.. 97

CHAPTER VIII.

* DUBLIN.. 119

CHAPTER IX.

* FIRST REBELLION. 129

CHAPTER X.

* FRENCH INVASION OF IRELAND, AND SECOND REBELLION. 143

CHAPTER XI.

* TRAVELLING. 155

CHAPTER XII.

* MY BROTHER. 168

CHAPTER XIII.

* PREMATURE MANHOOD.. 186

AUTOBIOGRAPHIC SKETCHES.

CHAPTER I.

THE AFFLICTION OF CHILDHOOD.

About the close of my sixth year, suddenly the first chapter of my life came to a violent termination; that chapter which, even within the gates of recovered paradise, might merit a remembrance. "*Life is finished!*" was the secret misgiving of my heart; for the heart of infancy is as apprehensive as that of maturest wisdom in relation to any capital wound inflicted on the happiness. "*Life is finished! Finished it is!*" was the hidden meaning that, half unconsciously to myself, lurked within my sighs; and, as bells heard from a distance on a summer evening seem charged at times with an articulate form of words, some monitory message, that rolls round unceasingly, even so for me some noiseless and subterraneous voice seemed to chant continually a secret word, made audible only to my own heart—that "now is the blossoming of life withered forever." Not that such words formed themselves vocally within my ear, or issued audibly from my lips; but such a whisper stole silently to my heart. Yet in what sense could *that* be true? For an infant not more than six years old, was it possible that the promises of life had been really blighted, or its golden pleasures exhausted? Had I seen Rome? Had I read Milton? Had I heard Mozart? No. St. Peter's, the "Paradise Lost," the divine melodies of "Don Giovanni," all alike were as yet unrevealed to me, and not more through the accidents of my position than through the necessity of my yet imperfect sensibilities. Raptures there might be in arrear; but raptures are modes of *troubled* pleasure. The peace, the rest, the central security which belong to love that is past all understanding,—these could return no more. Such a love, so unfathomable,—such a peace, so unvexed by storms, or the fear of storms,—had brooded over those four latter years of my infancy, which brought me into special relations to my elder sister; she being at this period three years older than myself. The circumstances which attended the sudden dissolution of this most tender connection I will here rehearse. And, that I may do so more intelligibly, I will first describe that serene and sequestered position which we occupied in life.[6]

___

[6] As occasions arise in these Sketches, when, merely for the purposes of intelligibility, it becomes requisite to call into notice such personal distinctions in my family as otherwise might be unimportant, I here record the entire list of my brothers and sisters, according to their order of succession; and Miltonically I include myself; having surely as much logical right to count myself in the series of my own brothers as Milton could have to pronounce Adam the goodliest of his own sons. First and last, we counted as eight children, viz., four brothers and four sisters, though never counting more than six living at once, viz., 1. *William*, older than myself by more than five years; 2. *Elizabeth*; 3. *Jane*, who died in her fourth

Any expression of personal vanity, intruding upon impassioned records, is fatal to their effect—as being incompatible with that absorption of spirit and that self-oblivion in which only deep passion originates or can find a genial home. It would, therefore, to myself be exceedingly painful that even a shadow, or so much as a *seeming* expression of that tendency, should creep into these reminiscences. And yet, on the other hand, it is so impossible, without laying an injurious restraint upon the natural movement of such a narrative, to prevent oblique gleams reaching the reader from such circumstances of luxury or aristocratic elegance as surrounded my childhood, that on all accounts I think it better to tell him, from the first, with the simplicity of truth, in what order of society my family moved at the time from which this preliminary narrative is dated. Otherwise it might happen that, merely by reporting faithfully the facts of this early experience, I could hardly prevent the reader from receiving an impression as of some higher rank than did really belong to my family. And this impression might seem to have been designedly insinuated by myself.

My father was a merchant; not in the sense of Scotland, where it means a retail dealer, one, for instance, who sells groceries in a cellar, but in the English sense, a sense rigorously exclusive; that is, he was a man engaged in *foreign* commerce, and no other; therefore, in *wholesale* commerce, and no other—which last limitation of the idea is important, because it brings him within the benefit of Cicero's condescending distinction[7] as one who ought to be despised certainly, but not too intensely to be despised even by a Roman senator. He—this imperfectly despicable man—died at an early age, and very soon after the incidents recorded in this chapter, leaving to his family, then consisting of a wife and six children, an unburdened estate producing exactly sixteen hundred pounds a year. Naturally, therefore, at the date of my narrative,—whilst he was still living,—he had an income very much larger, from the addition of current commercial profits. Now, to any man who is acquainted with commercial life as it exists in England, it will readily occur that in an opulent English family of that class—opulent, though not emphatically *rich* in a mercantile estimate—the domestic economy is pretty sure to move upon a scale of liberality altogether unknown amongst the corresponding orders in foreign nations. The establishment of servants, for instance, in such houses, measured even *numerically* against those establishments in other nations, would somewhat surprise the foreign appraiser, simply as interpreting the relative station in society occupied by the English merchant. But this same establishment, when measured by the quality and amount of the provision made for its comfort and even elegant accommodation, would fill him with twofold astonishment, as interpreting equal-

---

year; 4. *Mary*; 5. myself, certainly not the goodliest man of men since born my brothers; 6. *Richard*, known to us all by the household name of *Pink*, who in his after years tilted up and down what might then be called his Britannic majesty's oceans (viz., the Atlantic and Pacific) in the quality of midshipman, until Waterloo in one day put an extinguisher on that whole generation of midshipmen, by extinguishing all further call for their services; 7. a second *Jane*; 8. *Henry*, a posthumous child, who belonged to Brazennose College, Oxford, and died about his twenty-sixth year.

[7] Cicero, in a well-known passage of his "Ethics", speaks of trade as irredeemably base, if petty, but as not so absolutely felonious if wholesale.

ly the social valuation of the English merchant, and also the social valuation of the English servant; for, in the truest sense, England is the paradise of household servants. Liberal housekeeping, in fact, as extending itself to the meanest servants, and the disdain of petty parsimonies, are peculiar to England. And in this respect the families of English merchants, as a class, far outrun the scale of expenditure prevalent, not only amongst the corresponding bodies of continental nations, but even amongst the poorer sections of our own nobility—though confessedly the most splendid in Europe; a fact which, since the period of my infancy, I have had many personal opportunities for verifying both in England and in Ireland. From this peculiar anomaly, affecting the domestic economy of English merchants, there arises a disturbance upon the usual scale for measuring the relations of rank. The equation, so to speak, between rank and the ordinary expressions of rank, which usually runs parallel to the graduations of expenditure, is here interrupted and confounded, so that one rank would be collected from the name of the occupation, and another rank, much higher, from the splendor of the domestic *ménage*. I warn the reader, therefore, (or, rather, my explanation has already warned him,) that he is not to infer, from any casual indications of luxury or elegance, a corresponding elevation of rank.

We, the children of the house, stood, in fact, upon the very happiest tier in the social scaffolding for all good influences. The prayer of Agur—"Give me neither poverty nor riches"—was realized for us. That blessing we had, being neither too high nor too low. High enough we were to see models of good manners, of self-respect, and of simple dignity; obscure enough to be left in the sweetest of solitudes. Amply furnished with all the nobler benefits of wealth, with *extra* means of health, of intellectual culture, and of elegant enjoyment, on the other hand, we knew nothing of its social distinctions. Not depressed by the consciousness of privations too sordid, not tempted into restlessness by the consciousness of privileges too aspiring, we had no motives for shame, we had none for pride. Grateful also to this hour I am, that, amidst luxuries in all things else, we were trained to a Spartan simplicity of diet—that we fared, in fact, very much less sumptuously than the servants. And if (after the model of the Emperor Marcus Aurelius) I should return thanks to Providence for all the separate blessings of my early situation, these four I would single out as worthy of special commemoration—that I lived in a rustic solitude; that this solitude was in England; that my infant feelings were moulded by the gentlest of sisters, and not by horrid, pugilistic brothers; finally, that I and they were dutiful and loving members of a pure, holy, and magnificent church.

* * * * *

The earliest incidents in my life, which left stings in my memory so as to be remembered at this day, were two, and both before I could have completed my second year; namely, 1st, a remarkable dream of terrific grandeur about a favorite nurse, which is interesting to myself for this reason—that it demonstrates my dreaming tendencies to have been constitutional, and not dependent upon laudanum;[8] and, 2dly, the fact of having connected a profound sense of pathos with

---

[8] It is true that in those days *paregoric elixir* was occasionally given to children in colds; and in this medicine there is a small proportion of laudanum. But no medicine was

the reappearance, very early in the spring, of some crocuses. This I mention as inexplicable: for such annual resurrections of plants and flowers affect us only as memorials, or suggestions of some higher change, and therefore in connection with the idea of death; yet of death I could, at that time, have had no experience whatever.

This, however, I was speedily to acquire. My two eldest sisters— eldest of three *then* living, and also elder than myself—were summoned to an early death. The first who died was Jane, about two years older than myself. She was three and a half, I one and a half, more or less by some trifle that I do not recollect. But death was then scarcely intelligible to me, and I could not so properly be said to suffer sorrow as a sad perplexity. There was another death in the house about the same time, namely, of a maternal grandmother; but, as she had come to us for the express purpose of dying in her daughter's society, and from illness had lived perfectly secluded, our nursery circle knew her but little, and were certainly more affected by the death (which I witnessed) of a beautiful bird, viz., a kingfisher, which had been injured by an accident. With my sister Jane's death (though otherwise, as I have said, less sorrowful than perplexing) there was, however, connected an incident which made a most fearful impression upon myself, deepening my tendencies to thoughtfulness and abstraction beyond what would seem credible for my years. If there was one thing in this world from which, more than from any other, nature had forced me to revolt, it was brutality and violence. Now, a whisper arose in the family that a female servant, who by accident was drawn off from her proper duties to attend my sister Jane for a day or two, had on one occasion treated her harshly, if not brutally; and as this ill treatment happened within three or four days of her death, so that the occasion of it must have been some fretfulness in the poor child caused by her sufferings, naturally there was a sense of awe and indignation diffused through the family. I believe the story never reached my mother, and possibly it was exaggerated; but upon me the effect was terrific. I did not often see the person charged with this cruelty; but, when I did, my eyes sought the ground; nor could I have borne to look her in the face; not, however, in any spirit that could be called anger. The feeling which fell upon me was a shuddering horror, as upon a first glimpse of the truth that I was in a world of evil and strife. Though born in a large town, (the town of Manchester, even then amongst the largest of the island,) I had passed the whole of my childhood, except for the few earliest weeks, in a rural seclusion. With three innocent little sisters for playmates, sleeping always amongst them, and shut up forever in a silent garden from all knowledge of poverty, or oppression, or outrage, I had not suspected until this moment the true complexion of the world in which myself and my sisters were living. Henceforward the character of my thoughts changed greatly; for so *representative* are some acts, that one single case of the class is sufficient to throw open before you the whole theatre of possibilities in that direction. I never heard that the woman accused of this cruelty took it at all to heart, even after the event

---

ever administered to any member of our nursery except under medical sanction; and this, assuredly, would not have been obtained to the exhibition of laudanum in a case such as mine. For I was then not more that twenty-one months old: at which age the action of opium is capricious, and therefore perilous.

which so immediately succeeded had reflected upon it a more painful emphasis. But for myself, that incident had a lasting revolutionary power in coloring my estimate of life.

So passed away from earth one of those three sisters that made up my nursery playmates; and so did my acquaintance (if such it could be called) commence with mortality. Yet, in fact, I knew little more of mortality than that Jane had disappeared. She had gone away; but perhaps she would come back. Happy interval of heaven-born ignorance! Gracious immunity of infancy from sorrow disproportioned to its strength! I was sad for Jane's absence. But still in my heart I trusted that she would come again. Summer and winter came again—crocuses and roses; why not little Jane?

Thus easily was healed, then, the first wound in my infant heart. Not so the second. For thou, dear, noble Elizabeth, around whose ample brow, as often as thy sweet countenance rises upon the darkness, I fancy a *tiara* of light or a gleaming aureola[9] in token of thy premature intellectual grandeur,—thou whose head, for its superb developments, was the astonishment of science,[10]—thou next, but after an interval of happy years, thou also wert summoned away from our nursery; and the night, which for me gathered upon that event, ran after my steps far into life; and perhaps at this day I resemble little for good or for ill that which else I should have been. Pillar of fire that didst go before me to guide and to quicken,—pillar of darkness, when thy countenance was turned away to God, that didst too truly reveal to my dawning fears the secret shadow of death,—by what mysterious gravitation was it that *my* heart had been drawn to thine? Could a child, six years old, place any special value upon intellectual forwardness? Serene and capacious as my sister's mind appeared to me upon after review, was *that* a charm for stealing away the heart of an infant? O, no! I think of it *now* with interest, because it lends, in a stranger's ear, some justification to the excess of my fondness. But then

[9] *"Aureola."*—The *aureola* is the name given in the "Legends of the Christian Saints" to that golden diadem or circlet of supernatural light (that *glory*, as it is commonly called in English) which, amongst the great masters of painting in Italy, surrounded the heads of Christ and of distinguished saints.

[10] *"The astonishment of science."*—Her medical attendants were Dr. Percival, a well-known literary physician, who had been a correspondent of Condorcet, D'Alembert, &c., and Mr. Charles White, the most distinguished surgeon at that time in the north of England. It was he who pronounced her head to be the finest in its development of any that he had ever seen—an assertion which, to my own knowledge, he repeated in after years, and with enthusiasm. That he had some acquaintance with the subject may be presumed from this, that, at so early a stage of such inquiries, he had published a work on human craniology, supported by measurement of heads selected from all varieties of the human species. Meantime, as it would grieve me that any trait of what might seem vanity should creep into this record, I will admit that my sister died of hydrocephalus; and it has been often supposed that the premature expansion of the intellect in cases of that class is altogether morbid—forced on, in fact, by the mere stimulation of the disease. I would, however, suggest, as a possibility, the very opposite order of relation between the disease and the intellectual manifestations. Not the disease may always have caused the preternatural growth of the intellect; but, inversely, this growth of the intellect coming on spontaneously, and outrunning the capacities of the physical structure, may have caused the disease.

it was lost upon me; or, if not lost, was perceived only through its effects. Hadst thou been an idiot, my sister, not the less I must have loved thee, having that capacious heart—overflowing, even as mine overflowed, with tenderness; stung, even as mine was stung, by the necessity of loving and being loved. This it was which crowned thee with beauty and power.

> "Love, the holy sense,
> Best gift of God, in thee was most intense."

That lamp of paradise was, for myself, kindled by reflection from the living light which burned so steadfastly in thee; and never but to thee, never again since *thy* departure, had I power or temptation, courage or desire, to utter the feelings which possessed me. For I was the shyest of children; and, at all stages of life, a natural sense of personal dignity held me back from exposing the least ray of feelings which I was not encouraged *wholly* to reveal.

It is needless to pursue, circumstantially, the course of that sickness which carried off my leader and companion. She (according to my recollection at this moment) was just as near to nine years as I to six. And perhaps this natural precedency in authority of years and judgment, united to the tender humility with which she declined to assert it, had been amongst the fascinations of her presence. It was upon a Sunday evening, if such conjectures can be trusted, that the spark of fatal fire fell upon that train of predispositions to a brain complaint which had hitherto slumbered within her. She had been permitted to drink tea at the house of a laboring man, the father of a favorite female servant. The sun had set when she returned, in the company of this servant, through meadows reeking with exhalations after a fervent day. From that time she sickened. In such circumstances, a child, as young as myself, feels no anxieties. Looking upon medical men as people privileged, and naturally commissioned, to make war upon pain and sickness, I never had a misgiving about the result. I grieved, indeed, that my sister should lie in bed; I grieved still more to hear her moan. But all this appeared to me no more than as a night of trouble, on which the dawn would soon arise. O moment of darkness and delirium, when the elder nurse awakened me from that delusion, and launched God's thunderbolt at my heart in the assurance that my sister MUST die! Rightly it is said of utter, utter misery, that it "cannot be *remembered*."[11] Itself, as a rememberable thing, is swallowed up in its own chaos. Blank anarchy and confusion of mind fell upon me. Deaf and blind I was, as I reeled under the revelation. I wish not to recall the circumstances of that time, when *my* agony was at its height, and hers, in another sense, was approaching. Enough it is to say that all was soon over; and, the morning of that day had at last arrived which looked down upon her innocent face, sleeping the sleep from which there is no awaking, and upon me sorrowing the sorrow for which there is no consolation.

On the day after my sister's death, whilst the sweet temple of her brain was yet unviolated by human scrutiny, I formed my own scheme for seeing her once more.

---

[11] "I stood in unimaginable trance
    And agony which cannot be remembered."

Speech of Alhadra, in Coleridge's Remorse

Not for the world would I have made this known, nor have suffered a witness to accompany me. I had never heard of feelings that take the name of "sentimental," nor dreamed of such a possibility. But grief, even in a child, hates the light, and shrinks from human eyes. The house was large enough to have two staircases; and by one of these I knew that about midday, when all would be quiet, (for the servants dined at one o'clock,) I could steal up into her chamber. I imagine that it was about an hour after high noon when I reached the chamber door: it was locked, but the key was not taken away. Entering, I closed the door so softly, that, although it opened upon a hall which ascended through all the stories, no echo ran along the silent walls. Then, turning round, I sought my sister's face. But the bed had been moved, and the back was now turned towards myself. Nothing met my eyes but one large window, wide open, through which the sun of midsummer, at midday, was showering down torrents of splendor. The weather was dry, the sky was cloudless, the blue depths seemed the express types of infinity; and it was not possible for eye to behold, or for heart to conceive, any symbols more pathetic of life and the glory of life.

Let me pause in approaching a remembrance so affecting for my own mind, to mention, that, in the "Opium Confessions," I endeavored to explain the reason why death, other conditions remaining the same, is more profoundly affecting in summer than in other parts of the year—so far, at least, as it is liable to any modification at all from accidents of scenery or season. The reason, as I there suggested, lies in the antagonism between the tropical redundancy of life in summer and the frozen sterilities of the grave. The summer we see, the grave we haunt with our thoughts; the glory is around us, the darkness is within us; and, the two coming into collision, each exalts the other into stronger relief. But, in my case, there was even a subtler reason why the summer had this intense power of vivifying the spectacle or the thoughts of death. And, recollecting it, I am struck with the truth, that far more of our deepest thoughts and feelings pass to us through perplexed combinations of *concrete* objects, pass to us as *involutes* (if I may coin that word) in compound experiences incapable of being disentangled, than ever reach us *directly*, and in their own abstract shapes. It had happened, that amongst our vast nursery collection of books was the Bible, illustrated with many pictures. And in long dark evenings, as my three sisters, with myself, sat by the firelight round the *guard*[12] of our nursery, no book was so much in request among us. It ruled us and swayed us as mysteriously as music. Our younger nurse, whom we all loved, would sometimes, according to her simple powers, endeavor to explain what we found obscure. We, the children, were all constitutionally touched with pensiveness: the fitful gloom and sudden lambencies of the room by firelight suited our evening state of feelings; and they suited, also, the divine revelations of power and mysterious beauty which awed us. Above all, the story of a just man,—man, and yet *not* man, real above all things, and yet shadowy above all things,—who had suffered the passion of death in Palestine, slept upon our minds like early dawn upon the waters. The nurse knew and explained to us the chief differences

---

[12] *"The guard."*—I know not whether the word is a local one in this sense. What I mean is a sort of fender, four or five feet high, which locks up the fire from too near an approach on the part of children.

in Oriental climates; and all these differences (as it happens) express themselves, more or less, in varying relations to the great accidents and powers of summer. The cloudless sunlights of Syria— those seemed to argue everlasting summer; the disciples plucking the ears of corn—that *must* be summer; but, above all, the very name of Palm Sunday (a festival in the English church) troubled me like an anthem. "Sunday!" what was *that*? That was the day of peace which masked another peace deeper than the heart of man can comprehend. "Palms!" what were they? *That* was an equivocal word; palms, in the sense of trophies, expressed the pomps of life; palms, as a product of nature, expressed the pomps of summer. Yet still even this explanation does not suffice; it was not merely by the peace and by the summer, by the deep sound of rest below all rest and of ascending glory, that I had been haunted. It was also because Jerusalem stood near to those deep images both in time and in place. The great event of Jerusalem was at hand when Palm Sunday came; and the scene of that Sunday was near in place to Jerusalem. What then was Jerusalem? Did I fancy it to be the *omphalos* (navel) or physical centre of the earth? Why should *that* affect me? Such a pretension had once been made for Jerusalem, and once for a Grecian city; and both pretensions had become ridiculous, as the figure of the planet became known. Yes; but if not of the earth, yet of mortality; for earth's tenant, Jerusalem, had now become the *omphalos* and absolute centre. Yet how? There, on the contrary, it was, as we infants understood, that mortality had been trampled under foot. True; but, for that very reason, there it was that mortality had opened its very gloomiest crater. There it was, indeed, that the human had risen on wings from the grave; but, for that reason, there also it was that the divine had been swallowed up by the abyss; the lesser star could not rise before the greater should submit to eclipse. Summer, therefore, had connected itself with death, not merely as a mode of antagonism, but also as a phenomenon brought into intricate relations with death by scriptual scenery and events.

Out of this digression, for the purpose of showing how inextricably my feelings and images of death were entangled with those of summer, as connected with Palestine and Jerusalem, let me come back to the bed chamber of my sister. From the gorgeous sunlight I turned around to the corpse. There lay the sweet childish figure; there the angel face; and, as people usually fancy, it was said in the house that no features had suffered any change. Had they not? The forehead, indeed,— the serene and noble forehead,—*that* might be the same; but the frozen eyelids, the darkness that seemed to steal from beneath them, the marble lips, the stiffening hands, laid palm to palm, as if repeating the supplications of closing anguish,— could these be mistaken for life? Had it been so, wherefore did I not spring to those heavenly lips with tears and never-ending kisses? But so it was *not*. I stood checked for a moment; awe, not fear, fell upon me; and, whilst I stood, a solemn wind began to blow—the saddest that ear ever heard. It was a wind that might have swept the fields of mortality for a thousand centuries. Many times since, upon summer days, when the sun is about the hottest, I have remarked the same wind arising and uttering the same hollow, solemn, Memnonian,[13] but saintly swell: it is in

---

[13] "*Memnonian*."—For the sake of many readers, whose hearts may go along earnestly with a record of infant sorrow, but whose course of life has not allowed them much leisure for study, I pause to explain—that the head of Memnon, in the British Museum,

this world the one great *audible* symbol of eternity. And three times in my life have I happened to hear the same sound in the same circumstances —namely, when standing between an open window and a dead body on a summer day.

Instantly, when my ear caught this vast Aeolian intonation, when my eye filled with the golden fulness of life, the pomps of the heavens above, or the glory of the flowers below, and turning when it settled upon the frost which overspread my sister's face, instantly a trance fell upon me. A vault seemed to open in the zenith of the far blue sky, a shaft which ran up forever. I, in spirit, rose as if on billows that also ran up the shaft forever; and the billows seemed to pursue the throne of God; but *that* also ran before us and fled away continually. The flight and the pursuit seemed to go on forever and ever. Frost gathering frost, some Sarsar wind of death, seemed to repel me; some mighty relation between God and death dimly struggled to evolve itself from the dreadful antagonism between them; shadowy meanings even yet continued to exercise and torment, in dreams, the decipher-ing oracle within me. I slept—for how long I cannot say: slowly I recovered my self-possession; and, when I woke, found myself standing, as before, close to my sister's bed.

I have reason to believe that a *very* long interval had elapsed during this wan-dering or suspension of my perfect mind. When I returned to myself, there was a foot (or I fancied so) on the stairs. I was alarmed; for, if any body had detected me, means would have been taken to prevent my coming again. Hastily, there-fore, I kissed the lips that I should kiss no more, and slunk, like a guilty thing, with stealthy steps from the room. Thus perished the vision, loveliest amongst all

---

that sublime head which wears upon its lips a smile coextensive with all time and all space, an Aeonian smile of gracious love and Pan-like mystery, the most diffusive and patheti-cally divine that the hand of man has created, is represented, on the authority of ancient traditions, to have uttered at sunrise, or soon after as the sun's rays had accumulated heat enough to rarefy the air within certain cavities in the bust, a solemn and dirge-like series of intonations; the simple explanation being, in its general outline, this— that sonorous currents of air were produced by causing chambers of cold and heavy air to press upon other collections of air, warmed, and therefore rarefied, and therefore yielding readily to the pressure of heavier air. Currents being thus established by artificial arrangements of tubes, a certain succession of notes could be concerted and sustained. Near the Red Sea lies a chain of sand hills, which, by a natural system of grooves inosculating with each other, become vocal under changing circumstances in the position of the sun, &c. I knew a boy who, upon observing steadily, and reflecting upon a phenomenon that met him in his daily experience, viz., that tubes, through which a stream of water was passing, gave out a very different sound according to the varying slenderness or fulness of the current, devised an instrument that yielded a rude hydraulic gamut of sounds; and, indeed, upon this simple phenomenon is founded the use and power of the stethoscope. For exactly as a thin thread of water, trickling through a leaden tube, yields a stridulous and plaintive sound compared with the full volume of sound corresponding to the full volume of water, on parity of prin-ciples, nobody will doubt that the current of blood pouring through the tubes of the human frame will utter to the learned ear, when armed with the stethoscope, an elaborate gamut or compass of music recording the ravages of disease, or the glorious plenitudes of health, as faithfully as the cavities within this ancient Memnonian bust reported this mighty event of sunrise to the rejoicing world of light and life; or, again, under the sad passion of the dying day, uttered the sweet requiem that belonged to its departure.

the shows which earth has revealed to me; thus mutilated was the parting which should have lasted forever; tainted thus with fear was that farewell sacred to love and grief, to perfect love and to grief that could not be healed.

O Abasuerus, everlasting Jew![14] fable or not a fable, thou, when first starting on thy endless pilgrimage of woe,—thou, when first flying through the gates of Jerusalem, and vainly yearning to leave the pursuing curse behind thee,—couldst not more certainly in the words of Christ have read thy doom of endless sorrow, than I when passing forever from my sister's room. The worm was at my heart; and, I may say, the worm that could not die. Man is doubtless *one* by some subtle *nexus*, some system of links, that we cannot perceive, extending from the new-born infant to the superannuated dotard; but, as regards many affections and passions incident to his nature at different stages, he is *not* one, but an intermitting creature, ending and beginning anew: the unity of man, in this respect, is coextensive only with the particular stage to which the passion belongs. Some passions, as that of sexual love, are celestial by one half of their origin, animal and earthly by the other half. These will not survive their own appropriate stage. But love, which is *altogether* holy, like that between two children, is privileged to revisit by glimpses the silence and the darkness of declining years; and, possibly, this final experience in my sister's bed room, or some other in which her innocence was concerned, may rise again for me to illuminate the clouds of death.

On the day following this which I have recorded came a body of medical men to examine the brain and the particular nature of the complaint, for in some of its symptoms it had shown perplexing anomalies. An hour after the strangers had withdrawn, I crept again to the room; but the door was now locked, the key had been taken away, and I was shut out forever.

Then came the funeral. I, in the ceremonial character of *mourner*, was carried thither. I was put into a carriage with some gentlemen whom I did not know. They were kind and attentive to me; but naturally they talked of things disconnected with the occasion, and their conversation was a torment. At the church, I was told to hold a white handkerchief to my eyes. Empty hypocrisy! What need had *he* of masks or mockeries, whose heart died within him at every word that was uttered? During that part of the service which passed within the church, I made an effort to attend; but I sank back continually into my own solitary darkness, and I heard little consciously, except some fugitive strains from the sublime chapter of St. Paul, which in England is always read at burials.[15]

Lastly came that magnificent liturgical service which the English church performs at the side of the grave; for this church does not forsake her dead so long as they continue in the upper air, but waits for her last "sweet and solemn[16] fare-

[14] *"Everlasting Jew."*—*Der ewige Jude*—which is the common German expression for "The Wandering Jew," and sublimer even than our own.

[15] First Epistle to Corinthians, chap. xv., beginning at ver. 20.

[16] This beautiful expression, I am pretty certain, must belong to Mrs. Trollope; I read it, probably, in a tale of hers connected with the backwoods of America, where the absence of such a farewell must unspeakably aggravate the gloom at any rate belonging to a household separation of that eternal character occurring amongst the shadows of those mighty

well" at the side of the grave. There is exposed once again, and for the last time, the coffin. All eyes survey the record of name, of sex, of age, and the day of departure from earth—records how shadowy! and dropped into darkness as if messages addressed to worms. Almost at the very last comes the symbolic ritual, tearing and shattering the heart with volleying discharges, peal after peal, from the final artillery of woe. The coffin is lowered into its home; it has disappeared from all eyes but those that look down into the abyss of the grave. The sacristan stands ready, with his shovel of earth and stones. The priest's voice is heard once more,—*earth to earth,*— and immediately the dread rattle ascends from the lid of the coffin; *ashes to ashes*—and again the killing sound is heard; *dust to dust*— and the farewell volley announces that the grave, the coffin, the face are sealed up forever and ever.

Grief! thou art classed amongst the depressing passions. And true it is that thou humblest to the dust, but also thou exaltest to the clouds. Thou shakest as with ague, but also thou steadiest like frost. Thou sickenest the heart, but also thou healest its infirmities. Among the very foremost of mine was morbid sensibility to shame. And, ten years afterwards, I used to throw my self-reproaches with regard to that infirmity into this shape, viz., that if I were summoned to seek aid for a perishing fellow-creature, and that I could obtain that aid only by facing a vast company of critical or sneering faces, I might, perhaps, shrink basely from the duty. It is true that no such case had ever actually occurred; so that it was a mere romance of casuistry to tax myself with cowardice so shocking. But, to feel a doubt, was to feel condemnation; and the crime that *might* have been was, in my eyes, the crime that *had* been. Now, however, all was changed; and for any thing which regarded my sister's memory, in one hour I received a new heart. Once in Westmoreland I saw a case resembling it. I saw a ewe suddenly put off and abjure her own nature, in a service of love—yes, slough it as completely as ever serpent sloughed his skin. Her lamb had fallen into a deep trench, from which all escape was hopeless without the aid of man. And to a man she advanced, bleating clamorously, until he followed her and rescued her beloved. Not less was the change in myself. Fifty thousand sneering faces would not have troubled me *now* in any office of tenderness to my sister's memory. Ten legions would not have repelled me from seeking her, if there had been a chance that she could be found. Mockery! it was lost upon me. Laughter! I valued it not. And when I was taunted insultingly with "my girlish tears," that word "*girlish*" had no sting for me, except as a verbal echo to the one eternal thought of my heart—that a girl was the sweetest thing which I, in my short life, had known; that a girl it was who had crowned the earth with beauty, and had opened to my thirst fountains of pure celestial love, from which, in this world, I was to drink no more.

Now began to unfold themselves the consolations of solitude, those consolations which only I was destined to taste; now, therefore, began to open upon me those fascinations of solitude, which, when acting as a co-agency with unresisted grief, end in the paradoxical result of making out of grief itself a luxury; such a luxury as finally becomes a snare, overhanging life itself, and the energies of life, with growing menaces. All deep feelings of a *chronic* class agree in this, that they seek

---

forests.

for solitude, and are fed by solitude. Deep grief, deep love, how naturally do these ally themselves with religious feeling! and all three—love, grief, religion—are haunters of solitary places. Love, grief, and the mystery of devotion,—what were these without solitude? All day long, when it was not impossible for me to do so, I sought the most silent and sequestered nooks in the grounds about the house or in the neighboring fields. The awful stillness oftentimes of summer noons, when no winds were abroad, the appealing silence of gray or misty afternoons,—these were fascinations as of witchcraft. Into the woods, into the desert air, I gazed, as if some comfort lay hid in *them*. I wearied the heavens with my inquest of beseeching looks. Obstinately I tormented the blue depths with my scrutiny, sweeping them forever with my eyes, and searching them for one angelic face that might, perhaps, have permission to reveal itself for a moment.

At this time, and under this impulse of rapacious grief, that grasped at what it could not obtain, the faculty of shaping images in the distance out of slight elements, and grouping them after the yearnings of the heart, grew upon me in morbid excess. And I recall at the present moment one instance of that sort, which may show how merely shadows, or a gleam of brightness, or nothing at all, could furnish a sufficient basis for this creative faculty.

On Sunday mornings I went with the rest of my family to church: it was a church on the ancient model of England, having aisles, galleries,[17] organ, all things ancient and venerable, and the proportions majestic. Here, whilst the congregation knelt through the long litany, as often as we came to that passage, so beautiful amongst many that are so, where God is supplicated on behalf of "all sick persons and young children," and that he would "show his pity upon all prisoners and captives," I wept in secret; and raising my streaming eyes to the upper windows of the galleries, saw, on days when the sun was shining, a spectacle as affecting as ever prophet can have beheld. The sides of the windows were rich with storied glass; through the deep purples and crimsons streamed the golden light; emblazonries of heavenly illumination (from the sun) mingling with the earthly emblazonries (from art and its gorgeous coloring) of what is grandest in man. *There* were the apostles that had trampled upon earth, and the glories of earth, out of celestial love to man. *There* were the martyrs that had borne witness to the truth through flames, through torments, and through armies of fierce, insulting faces. *There* were the saints who, under intolerable pangs, had glorified God by meek submission to his will. And all the time, whilst this tumult of sublime memorials held on as the deep chords from some accompaniment in the bass, I saw through the wide central field of the window, where the glass was *uncolored*, white, fleecy clouds sailing over the azure depths of the sky: were it but a fragment or a hint of such a cloud, immediately under the flash of my sorrow-haunted eye, it grew and shaped itself into visions of beds with white lawny curtains; and in the beds lay sick children, dying children, that were tossing in anguish, and weeping clamorously for death. God, for some mysterious reason, could not suddenly

[17] *"Galleries."*—These, though condemned on some grounds by the restorers of authentic church architecture, have, nevertheless, this one advantage—that, when the *height* of a church is that dimension which most of all expresses its sacred character, galleries expound and interpret that height.

release them from their pain; but he suffered the beds, as it seemed, to rise slowly through the clouds; slowly the beds ascended into the chambers of the air; slowly, also, his arms descended from the heavens, that he and his young children, whom in Palestine, once and forever, he had blessed, though they *must* pass slowly through the dreadful chasm of separation, might yet meet the sooner. These visions were self-sustained. These visions needed not that any sound should speak to me, or music mould my feelings. The hint from the litany, the fragment from the clouds,—those and the storied windows were sufficient. But not the less the blare of the tumultuous organ wrought its own separate creations. And oftentimes in anthems, when the mighty instrument threw its vast columns of sound, fierce yet melodious, over the voices of the choir,—high in arches, when it seemed to rise, surmounting and overriding the strife of the vocal parts, and gathering by strong coercion the total storm into unity,—sometimes I seemed to rise and walk triumphantly upon those clouds which, but a moment before, I had looked up to as mementoes of prostrate sorrow; yes, sometimes under the transfigurations of music, felt of grief itself as of a fiery chariot for mounting victoriously above the causes of grief.

God speaks to children, also, in dreams and by the oracles that lurk in darkness. But in solitude, above all things, when made vocal to the meditative heart by the truths and services of a national church, God holds with children "communion undisturbed." Solitude, though it may be silent as light, is, like light, the mightiest of agencies; for solitude is essential to man. All men come into this world *alone*; all leave it *alone*. Even a little child has a dread, whispering consciousness, that, if he should be summoned to travel into God's presence, no gentle nurse will be allowed to lead him by the hand, nor mother to carry him in her arms, nor little sister to share his trepidations. King and priest, warrior and maiden, philosopher and child, all must walk those mighty galleries alone. The solitude, therefore, which in this world appalls or fascinates a child's heart, is but the echo of a far deeper solitude, through which already he has passed, and of another solitude, deeper still, through which he *has* to pass: reflex of one solitude—prefiguration of another.

O burden of solitude, that cleavest to man through every stage of his being! in his birth, which *has* been—in his life, which *is*—in his death, which *shall* be— mighty and essential solitude! that wast, and art, and art to be; thou broodest, like the Spirit of God moving upon the surface of the deeps, over every heart that sleeps in the nurseries of Christendom. Like the vast laboratory of the air, which, seeming to be nothing, or less than the shadow of a shade, hides within itself the principles of all things, solitude for the meditating child is the Agrippa's mirror of the unseen universe. Deep is the solitude of millions who, with hearts welling forth love, have none to love them. Deep is the solitude of those who, under secret griefs, have none to pity them. Deep is the solitude of those who, fighting with doubts or darkness, have none to counsel them. But deeper than the deepest of these solitudes is that which broods over childhood under the passion of sorrow—bringing before it, at intervals, the final solitude which watches for it, and is waiting for it within the gates of death. O mighty and essential solitude, that wast, and art, and art to be, thy kingdom is made perfect in the grave; but even over those that keep watch outside the grave, like myself, an infant of six years old, thou stretchest out a sceptre of fascination.

* * * * *

DREAM ECHOES OF THESE INFANT EXPERIENCES.

[*Notice to the reader.*—The sun, in rising or setting, would produce little effect if he were defrauded of his rays and their infinite reverberations. "Seen through a fog," says Sara Coleridge, the noble daughter of Samuel Taylor Coleridge, "the golden, beaming sun looks like a dull orange, or a red billiard ball."—*Introd. to Biog. Lit.*, p. clxii. And, upon this same analogy, psychological experiences of deep suffering or joy first attain their entire fulness of expression when they are reverberated from dreams. The reader must, therefore, suppose me at Oxford; more than twelve years are gone by; I am in the glory of youth: but I have now first tampered with opium; and now first the agitations of my childhood reopened in strength; now first they swept in upon the brain with power, and the grandeur of recovered life.]

Once again, after twelve years' interval, the nursery of my childhood expanded before me: my sister was moaning in bed; and I was beginning to be restless with fears not intelligible to myself. Once again the elder nurse, but now dilated to colossal proportions, stood as upon some Grecian stage with her uplifted hand, and, like the superb Medea towering amongst her children in the nursery at Corinth,[18] smote me senseless to the ground. Again I am in the chamber with my sister's corpse, again the pomps of life rise up in silence, the glory of summer, the Syrian sunlights, the frost of death. Dream forms itself mysteriously within dream; within these Oxford dreams remoulds itself continually the trance in my sister's chamber—the blue heavens, the everlasting vault, the soaring billows, the throne steeped in the thought (but not the sight) of "*Who* might sit thereon;" the flight, the pursuit, the irrecoverable steps of my return to earth. Once more the funeral procession gathers; the priest, in his white surplus, stands waiting with a book by the side of an open grave; the sacristan is waiting with his shovel; the coffin has sunk; the *dust to dust* has descended. Again I was in the church on a heavenly Sunday morning. The golden sunlight of God slept amongst the heads of his apostles, his martyrs, his saints; the fragment from the litany, the fragment from the clouds, awoke again the lawny beds that went up to scale the heavens—awoke again the shadowy arms that moved downward to meet them. Once again arose the swell of the anthem, the burst of the hallelujah chorus, the storm, the trampling movement of the choral passion, the agitation of my own trembling sympathy, the tumult of the choir, the wrath of the organ. Once more I, that wallowed in the dust, became he that rose up to the clouds. And now all was bound up into unity; the first state and the last were melted into each other as in some sunny glorifying haze. For high in heaven hovered a gleaming host of faces, veiled with wings, around the pillows of the dying children. And such beings sympathize equally with sorrow that grovels and with sorrow that soars. Such beings pity alike the children that

[18] Euripides.

are languishing in death, and the children that live only to languish in tears.

* * * * *

DREAM ECHOES FIFTY YEARS LATER.

[In this instance the echoes, that rendered back the infant experience, might be interpreted by the reader as connected with a *real* ascent of the Brocken; which was not the case. It was an ascent through all its circumstances executed in dreams, which, under advanced stages in the development of opium, repeat with marvellous accuracy the longest succession of phenomena derived either from reading or from actual experience. That softening and spiritualizing haze which belongs at any rate to the action of dreams, and to the transfigurings worked upon troubled remembrances by retrospects so vast as those of fifty years, was in this instance greatly aided to my own feelings by the alliance with the ancient phantom of the forest mountain in North Germany. The playfulness of the scene is the very evoker of the solemn remembrances that lie hidden below. The half-sportive interlusory revealings of the symbolic tend to the same effect. One part of the effect from the symbolic is dependent upon the great catholic principle of the *Idem in alio.* The symbol restores the theme, but under new combinations of form or coloring; gives back, but changes; restores, but idealizes.]

Ascend with me on this dazzling Whitsunday the Brocken of North Germany. The dawn opened in cloudless beauty; it is a dawn of bridal June; but, as the hours advanced, her youngest sister April, that sometimes cares little for racing across both frontiers of May,—the rearward frontier, and the vanward frontier,—frets the bridal lady's sunny temper with sallies of wheeling and careering showers, flying and pursuing, opening and closing, hiding and restoring. On such a morning, and reaching the summits of the forest mountain about sunrise, we shall have one chance the more for seeing the famous Spectre of the Brocken.[19] Who and what is

---

[19] *"Spectre of the Brocken."*—This very striking phenomenon has been continually described by writers, both German and English, for the last fifty years. Many readers, however, will not have met with these descriptions; and on *their* account I add a few words in explanation, referring them for the best scientific comment on the case to Sir David Brewster's "Natural Magic." The spectre takes the shape of a human figure, or, if the visitors are more than one, then the spectres multiply; they arrange themselves on the blue ground of the sky, or the dark ground of any clouds that may be in the right quarter, or perhaps they are strongly relieved against a curtain of rock, at a distance of some miles, and always exhibiting gigantic proportions. At first, from the distance and the colossal size, every spectator supposes the appearances to be quite independent of himself. But very soon he is surprised to observe his own motions and gestures mimicked, and wakens to the conviction that the phantom is but a dilated reflection of himself. This Titan amongst the apparitions of earth is exceedingly capricious, vanishing abruptly for reasons best known to himself, and more coy in coming forward than the Lady Echo of Ovid. One reason why he is seen so seldom must be ascribed to the concurrence of conditions under which only the phenomenon can be manifested; the sun must be near to the horizon, (which, of itself, implies a time of day inconvenient to a person starting from a station as distant as Elbingerode;) the spectator must have his back to the sun; and the air must contain some vapor, but *partially* distributed. Coleridge ascended the Brocken on the Whitsunday of 1799, with a party of English students from Goettingen, but failed to see the phantom; afterwards in England (and under

he? He is a solitary apparition, in the sense of loving solitude; else he is not always solitary in his personal manifestations, but, on proper occasions, has been known to unmask a strength quite sufficient to alarm those who had been insulting him.

Now, in order to test the nature of this mysterious apparition, we will try two or three experiments upon him. What we fear, and with some reason, is, that, as he lived so many ages with foul pagan sorcerers, and witnessed so many centuries of dark idolatries, his heart may have been corrupted, and that even now his faith may be wavering or impure. We will try.

Make the sign of the cross, and observe whether he repeats it, (as on Whitsunday[20] he surely ought to do.) Look! he *does* repeat it; but these driving April showers perplex the images, and *that*, perhaps, it is which gives him the air of one who acts reluctantly or evasively. Now, again, the sun shines more brightly, and the showers have all swept off like squadrons of cavalry to the rear. We will try him again.

Pluck an anemone, one of these many anemones which once was called the sorcerer's flower,[21] and bore a part, perhaps, in this horrid ritual of fear; carry it to that stone which mimics the outline of a heathen altar, and once was called the sorcerer's altar;[22] then, bending your knee, and raising your right hand to God, say, "Father which art in heaven, this lovely anemone, that once glorified the worship of fear, has travelled back into thy fold; this altar, which once reeked with bloody rites to Cortho, has long been rebaptized into thy holy service. The darkness is gone; the cruelty is gone which the darkness bred; the moans have passed away which the victims uttered; the cloud has vanished which once sat continually upon

---

the three same conditions) he saw a much rarer phenomenon, which he described in the following lines:—

> "Such thou art as when
> The woodman winding westward up the glen
> At wintry dawn, when o'er the sheep-track's maze
> The viewless snow mist weaves a glistening haze,
> Sees full before him, gliding without tread,
> An image with a glory round its head;
> This shade he worships for its golden hues,
> And *makes* (not knowing) that which he pursues."

[20] *"On Whitsunday."*—It is singular, and perhaps owing to the temperature and weather likely to prevail in that early part of summer, that more appearances of the spectre have been witnessed on Whitsunday than on any other day.

[21] *"The sorcerer's flower,"* and *"The sorcerer's altar."*—These are names still clinging to the anemone of the Brocken, and to an altar- shaped fragment of granite near one of the summits; and there is no doubt that they both connect themselves, through links of ancient tradition, with the gloomy realities of paganism, when the whole Hartz and the Brocken formed for a very long time the last asylum to a ferocious but perishing idolatry.

[22] *"The sorcerer's flower,"* and *"The sorcerer's altar."*—These are names still clinging to the anemone of the Brocken, and to an altar- shaped fragment of granite near one of the summits; and there is no doubt that they both connect themselves, through links of ancient tradition, with the gloomy realities of paganism, when the whole Hartz and the Brocken formed for a very long time the last asylum to a ferocious but perishing idolatry.

their graves—cloud of protestation that ascended forever to thy throne from the tears of the defenceless, and from the anger of the just. And lo! we—I thy servant, and this dark phantom, whom for one hour on this thy festival of Pentecost I make *my* servant—render thee united worship in this thy recovered temple."

Lo! the apparition plucks an anemone, and places it on the altar; he also bends his knee, he also raises his right hand to God. Dumb he is; but sometimes the dumb serve God acceptably. Yet still it occurs to you, that perhaps on this high festival of the Christian church he may have been overruled by supernatural influence into confession of his homage, having so often been made to bow and bend his knee at murderous rites. In a service of religion he may be timid. Let us try him, therefore, with an earthly passion, where he will have no bias either from favor or from fear.

If, then, once in childhood you suffered an affliction that was ineffable,—if once, when powerless to face such an enemy, you were summoned to fight with the tiger that couches within the separations of the grave,—in that case, after the example of Judaea,[23] sitting under her palm tree to weep, but sitting with her head veiled, do you also veil your head. Many years are passed away since then; and perhaps you were a little ignorant thing at that time, hardly above six years old. But your heart was deeper than the Danube; and, as was your love, so was your grief. Many years are gone since that darkness settled on your head; many summers, many winters; yet still its shadows wheel round upon you at intervals, like these April showers upon this glory of bridal June. Therefore now, on this dove-like morning of Pentecost, do you veil your head like Judaea in memory of that transcendent woe, and in testimony that, indeed, it surpassed all utterance of words. Immediately you see that the apparition of the Brocken veils *his* head, after the model of Judaea weeping under her palm tree, as if he also had a human heart; and as if *he* also, in childhood, having suffered an affliction which was ineffable, wished by these mute symbols to breathe a sigh towards heaven in memory of that transcendent woe, and by way of record, though many a year after, that it was indeed unutterable by words.

---

[23] On the Roman coins.

CHAPTER II.

INTRODUCTION TO THE WORLD OF STRIFE.

So, then, one chapter in my life had finished. Already, before the completion of my sixth year, this first chapter had run its circle, had rendered up its music to the final chord—might seem even, like ripe fruit from a tree, to have detached itself forever from all the rest of the arras that was shaping itself within my loom of life. No Eden of lakes and forest lawns, such as the *mirage* suddenly evokes in Arabian sands,—no pageant of air-built battlements and towers, that ever burned in dream-like silence amongst the vapors of summer sunsets, mocking and repeating with celestial pencil "the fuming vanities of earth,"—could leave behind it the mixed impression of so much truth combined with so much absolute delusion. Truest of all things it seemed by the excess of that happiness which it had sustained: most fraudulent it seemed of all things, when looked back upon as some mysterious parenthesis in the current of life, "self-withdrawn into a wonderous depth," hurrying as if with headlong malice to extinction, and alienated by *every* feature from the new aspects of life that seemed to await me. Were it not in the bitter corrosion of heart that I was called upon to face, I should have carried over to the present no connecting link whatever from the past. Mere reality in this fretting it was, and the undeniableness of its too potent remembrances, that forbade me to regard this burned-out inaugural chapter of my life as no chapter at all, but a pure exhalation of dreams. Misery is a guaranty of truth too substantial to be refused; else, by its determinate evanescence, the total experience would have worn the character of a fantastic illusion.

Well it was for me at this period, if well it were for me to live at all, that from any continued contemplation of my misery I was forced to wean myself, and suddenly to assume the harness of life. Else under the morbid languishing of grief, and of what the Romans called *desiderium*, (the yearning too obstinate after one irrecoverable face,) too probably I should have pined away into an early grave. Harsh was my awaking; but the rough febrifuge which this awaking administered broke the strength of my sickly reveries through a period of more than two years; by which time, under the natural expansion of my bodily strength, the danger had passed over.

In the first chapter I have rendered solemn thanks for having been trained amongst the gentlest of sisters, and not under "horrid pugilistic brothers." Meantime, one such brother I had, senior by much to myself, and the stormiest of his class: him I will immediately present to the reader; for up to this point of my narrative he may be described as a stranger even to myself. Odd as it sounds, I had at this time both a brother and a father, neither of whom would have been able to challenge me as a relative, nor I *him*, had we happened to meet on the public roads.

In my father's case, this arose from the accident of his having lived abroad for a space that, measured against *my* life, was a very long one. First, he lived for months in Portugal, at Lisbon, and at Cintra; next in Madeira; then in the West Indies; sometimes in Jamaica, sometimes in St. Kitt's; courting the supposed benefit of hot climates in his complaint of pulmonary consumption. He had, indeed, repeatedly returned to England, and met my mother at watering-places on the south coast of Devonshire, &c. But I, as a younger child, had not been one of the party selected for such excursions from home. And now, at last, when all had proved unavailing, he was coming home to die amongst his family, in his thirty-ninth year. My mother had gone to await his arrival at the port (whatever port) to which the West India packet should bring him; and amongst the deepest recollections which I connect with that period, is one derived from the night of his arrival at Greenhay.

It was a summer evening of unusual solemnity. The servants, and four of us children, were gathered for hours, on the lawn before the house, listening for the sound of wheels. Sunset came—nine, ten, eleven o'clock, and nearly another hour had passed—without a warning sound; for Greenhay, being so solitary a house, formed a *terminus ad quem*, beyond which was nothing but a cluster of cottages, composing the little hamlet of Greenhill; so that any sound of wheels coming from the winding lane which then connected us with the Rusholme Road, carried with it, of necessity, a warning summons to prepare for visitors at Greenhay. No such summons had yet reached us; it was nearly midnight; and, for the last time, it was determined that we should move in a body out of the grounds, on the chance of meeting the travelling party, if, at so late an hour, it could yet be expected to arrive. In fact, to our general surprise, we met it almost immediately, but coming at so slow a pace, that the fall of the horses' feet was not audible until we were close upon them. I mention the case for the sake of the undying impressions which connected themselves with the circumstances. The first notice of the approach was the sudden emerging of horses' heads from the deep gloom of the shady lane; the next was the mass of white pillows against which the dying patient was reclining. The hearse-like pace at which the carriage moved recalled the overwhelming spectacle of that funeral which had so lately formed part in the most memorable event of my life. But these elements of awe, that might at any rate have struck forcibly upon the mind of a child, were for me, in my condition of morbid nervousness, raised into abiding grandeur by the antecedent experiences of that particular summer night. The listening for hours to the sounds from horses' hoofs upon distant roads, rising and falling, caught and lost, upon the gentle undulation of such fitful airs as might be stirring—the peculiar solemnity of the hours succeeding to sunset—the glory of the dying day—the gorgeousness which, by description, so well I knew of sunset in those West Indian islands from which my father was returning—the knowledge that he returned only to die—the almighty pomp in which this great idea of Death apparelled itself to my young sorrowing heart—the corresponding pomp in which the antagonistic idea, not less mysterious, of life, rose, as if on wings, amidst tropic glories and floral pageantries that seemed even *more* solemn and pathetic than the vapory plumes and trophies of mortality,—all this chorus of restless images, or of suggestive thoughts, gave to my father's return, which else had been fitted only to interpose one transitory red-letter day in the calendar of a child, the shadowy power of an ineffaceable agency among my dreams. This, indeed, was the one sole memorial which restores my father's image to me as a personal reality; otherwise he would have been for me a bare *nominis umbra*. He languished, indeed, for weeks upon a sofa; and, during that interval, it happened naturally, from my repose of manners, that I was a privileged visitor to him throughout his waking hours. I was also present at his bedside in the closing hour of his life, which exhaled quietly, amidst snatches of delirious conversation with some imaginary visitors.

My brother was a stranger from causes quite as little to be foreseen, but seeming quite as natural after they had really occurred. In an early stage of his career, he had been found wholly unmanageable. His genius for mischief amounted to inspiration; it was a divine *afflatus* which drove him in that direction; and such was his capacity for riding in whirlwinds and directing storms, that he made it his trade to create them, as a *nephelaegereta Zeus*, a cloud-compelling Jove, in order that he *might* direct them. For this, and other reasons, he had been sent to the Grammar School of Louth, in Lincolnshire—one of those many old classic institutions which form the peculiar[24] glory of England. To box, and to box under the severest restraint of honorable laws, was in those days a mere necessity of schoolboy life at *public* schools; and hence the superior manliness, generosity, and self-control of those generally who had benefited by such discipline—so systematically hostile to all meanness, pusillanimity, or indirectness. Cowper, in his "Tyrocinium," is far from doing justice to our great public schools. Himself disqualified, by a delicacy of temperament, for reaping the benefits from such a warfare, and having suffered too much in his own Westminster experience, he could not judge them from an impartial station; but I, though ill enough adapted to an atmosphere so stormy, yet having tried both classes of schools, public and private, am compelled in mere conscience to give my vote (and, if I had a thousand votes, to give *all* my votes) for the former.

Fresh from such a training as this, and at a time when his additional five or six years availed nearly to make *his* age the double of mine, my brother very naturally despised me; and, from his exceeding frankness, he took no pains to conceal that he did. Why should he? Who was it that could have a right to feel aggrieved by this contempt? Who, if not myself? But it happened, on the contrary, that I had a perfect craze for being despised. I doted on it, and considered contempt a sort of luxury that I was in continual fear of losing. Why not? Wherefore should any rational person shrink from contempt, if it happen to form the tenure by which he holds his repose in life? The cases which are cited from comedy of such a yearning after contempt, stand upon a footing altogether different: *there* the contempt is wooed

[24] *"Peculiar."*—Viz., as *endowed* foundations to which those resort who are rich and pay, and those also who, being poor, cannot pay, or cannot pay so much. This most honorable distinction amongst the services of England from ancient times to the interests of education—a service absolutely unapproached by any one nation of Christendom—is amongst the foremost cases of that remarkable class which make England, whilst often the most aristocratic, yet also, for many noble purposes, the most democratic of lands.

as a serviceable ally and tool of religious hypocrisy. But to me, at that era of life, it formed the main guaranty of an unmolested repose; and security there was not, on any lower terms, for the *latentis semita vitae.* The slightest approach to any favorable construction of my intellectual pretensions alarmed me beyond measure; because it pledged me in a manner with the hearer to support this first attempt by a second, by a third, by a fourth—O Heavens! there is no saying how far the horrid man might go in his unreasonable demands upon me. I groaned under the weight of his expectations; and, if I laid but the first round of such a staircase, why, then, I saw in vision a vast Jacob's ladder towering upwards to the clouds, mile after mile, league after league; and myself running up and down this ladder, like any fatigue party of Irish hodmen, to the top of any Babel which my wretched admirer might choose to build. But I nipped the abominable system of extortion in the very bud, by refusing to take the first step. The man could have no pretence, you know, for expecting me to climb the third or fourth round, when I had seemed quite unequal to the first. Professing the most absolute bankruptcy from the very beginning, giving the man no sort of hope that I would pay even one farthing in the pound, I never could be made miserable by unknown responsibilities.

Still, with all this passion for being despised, which was so essential to my peace of mind, I found at times an altitude—a starry altitude—in the station of contempt for me assumed by my brother that nettled me. Sometimes, indeed, the mere necessities of dispute carried me, before I was aware of my own imprudence, so far up the staircase of Babel, that my brother was shaken for a moment in the infinity of his contempt; and before long, when my superiority in some bookish accomplishments displayed itself, by results that could not be entirely dissembled, mere foolish human nature forced me into some trifle of exultation at these retributory triumphs. But more often I was disposed to grieve over them. They tended to shake that solid foundation of utter despicableness upon which I relied so much for my freedom from anxiety; and therefore, upon the whole, it was satisfactory to my mind that my brother's opinion of me, after any little transient oscillation, gravitated determinately back towards that settled contempt which had been the result of his original inquest. The pillars of Hercules, upon which rested the vast edifice of his scorn, were these two—1st, my physics; he denounced me for effeminacy; 2d, he assumed, and even postulated as a *datum,* which I myself could never have the face to refuse, my general idiocy. Physically, therefore, and intellectually, he looked upon me as below notice; but, *morally,* he assured me that he would give me a written character of the very best description, whenever I chose to apply for it. "You're honest," he said; "you're willing, though lazy; you *would* pull, if you had the strength of a flea; and, though a monstrous coward, you don't run away." My own demurs to these harsh judgments were not so many as they might have been. The idiocy I confessed; because, though positive that I was not uniformly an idiot, I felt inclined to think that, in a majority of cases, I really *was*; and there were more reasons for thinking so than the reader is yet aware of. But, as to the effeminacy, I denied it *in toto*; and with good reason, as will be seen. Neither did my brother pretend to have any experimental proofs of it. The ground he went upon was a mere *a priori* one, viz., that I had always been tied to the apron string of women or girls; which amounted at most to this—that, by training and the natural tendency of circumstances, I *ought* to be effeminate; that is, there was reason to expect beforehand that I *should* be so; but, then, the more merit in me, if, in spite of such reasonable presumptions, I really were *not*. In fact, my brother soon learned, by a daily experience, how entirely he might depend upon me for carrying out the most audacious of his own warlike plans—such plans, it is true, that I abominated; but *that* made no difference in the fidelity with which I tried to fulfil them.

This eldest brother of mine was in all respects a remarkable boy. Haughty he was, aspiring, immeasurably active; fertile in resources as Robinson Crusoe; but also full of quarrel as it is possible to imagine; and, in default of any other opponent, he would have fastened a quarrel upon his own shadow for presuming to run before him when going westwards in the morning, whereas, in all reason, a shadow, like a dutiful child, ought to keep deferentially in the rear of that majestic substance which is the author of its existence. Books he detested, one and all, excepting only such as he happened to write himself. And these were not a few. On all subjects known to man, from the Thirty-nine Articles of our English church down to pyrotechnics, legerdemain, magic, both black and white, thaumaturgy, and necromancy, he favored the world (which world was the nursery where I lived amongst my sisters) with his select opinions. On this last subject especially—of necromancy—he was very great: witness his profound work, though but a fragment, and, unfortunately, long since departed to the bosom of Cinderella, entitled "How to raise a Ghost; and when you've got him down, how to keep him down." To which work he assured us that some most learned and enormous man, whose name was a foot and a half long, had promised him an appendix, which appendix treated of the Red Sea and Solomon's signet ring, with forms of *mittimus* for ghosts that might be refractory, and probably a riot act, for any *émeute* amongst ghosts inclined to raise barricades; since he often thrilled our young hearts by supposing the case, (not at all unlikely, he affirmed,) that a federation, a solemn league and conspiracy, might take place amongst the infinite generations of ghosts against the single generation of men at any one time composing the garrison of earth. The Roman phrase for expressing that a man had died, viz., "*Abiit ad plures*" (He has gone over to the majority,) my brother explained to us; and we easily comprehended that any one generation of the living human race, even if combined, and acting in concert, must be in a frightful minority, by comparison with all the incalculable generations that had trot this earth before us. The Parliament of living men, Lords and Commons united, what a miserable array against the Upper and Lower House composing the Parliament of ghosts! Perhaps the Pre-Adamites would constitute one wing in such a ghostly army. My brother, dying in his sixteenth year, was far enough from seeing or foreseeing Waterloo; else he might have illustrated this dreadful duel of the living human race with its ghostly predecessors, by the awful apparition which at three o'clock in the afternoon, on the 18th of June, 1815, the mighty contest at Waterloo must have assumed to eyes that watched over the trembling interests of man. The English army, about that time in the great agony of its strife, was thrown into squares; and under that arrangement, which condensed and contracted its apparent numbers within a few black geometrical diagrams, how frightfully narrow, how spectral, did its slender quadrangels appear at a distance, to any philosophic spectators that knew about the amount of human interests confided to that army, and the hopes for Christendom that even then were trembling in the balance! Such a disproportion, it seems, might exist, in the case of a ghostly war, between the harvest of possible results and the slender band of reapers that were to gather it. And there was even a worse peril than any analogous one that has been *proved* to exist at Waterloo. A British surgeon, indeed, in a work of two octavo volumes, has endeavored to show that a conspiracy was traced at Waterloo, between two or three foreign regiments, for kindling a panic in the heat of battle, by flight, and by a sustained blowing up of tumbrils, under the miserable purpose of shaking the British steadiness. But the evidences are not clear; whereas my brother insisted that the presence of sham men, distributed extensively amongst the human race, and meditating treason against us all, had been demonstrated to the satisfaction of all true philosophers. Who were these shams and make- believe men? They were, in fact, people that had been dead for centuries, but that, for reasons best known to themselves, had returned to this upper earth, walked about amongst us, and were undistinguishable, except by the most learned of necromancers, from authentic men of flesh and blood. I mention this for the sake of illustrating the fact, of which the reader will find a singular instance in the foot note attached, that the same crazes are everlastingly revolving upon men.[25]

This hypothesis, however, like a thousand others, when it happened that they engaged no durable sympathy from his nursery audience, he did not pursue. For some time he turned his thoughts to philosophy, and read lectures to us every night upon some branch or other of physics. This undertaking arose upon some one of us envying or admiring flies for their power of walking upon the ceiling. "Poh!" he said, "they are impostors; they pretend to do it, but they can't do it as it ought to be done. Ah! you should see *me* standing upright on the ceiling, with my head downwards, for half an hour together, and meditating profoundly." My sister Mary remarked, that we should all be very glad to see him in that position. "If that's the case," he replied, "it's very well that all is ready, except as to a strap or two." Being an excellent skater, he had first imagined that, if held up until he

---

[25] Five years ago, during the carnival of universal anarchy equally amongst doers and thinkers, a closely-printed pamphlet was published with this title, "A New Revelation, or the Communion of the Incarnate Dead with the Unconscious Living. Important Fact, without trifling Fiction, by HIM." I have not the pleasure of knowing HIM; but certainly I must concede to HIM, that he writes like a man of extreme sobriety upon his extravagant theme. He is angry with Swedenborg, as might be expected, for his chimeras; some of which, however, of late years have signally altered their aspect; but. as to HIM, there is no chance that he should be occupied with chimeras, because (p. 6) "he has met with some who have acknowledged the fact of their having come from the dead" —*habes confitentem reum.* Few, however, are endowed with so much candor; and in particular, for the honor of literature, it grieves me to find, by p. 10, that the largest number of these shams, and perhaps the most uncandid, are to be looked for amongst "publishers and printers," of whom, it seems, "the great majority" are mere forgeries: a very few speak frankly about the matter, and say they don't care who knows it, which, to my thinking, is impudence, but by far the larger section doggedly deny it, and call a policeman, if you persist in charging them with being shams. Some differences there are between my brother and HIM, but in the great outline of their views they coincide.

had started, he might then, by taking a bold sweep ahead, keep himself in position through the continued impetus of skating. But this he found not to answer; because, as he observed, "the friction was too retarding from the plaster of Paris, but the case would be very different if the ceiling were coated with ice." As it was *not*, he changed his plan. The true secret, he now discovered, was this: he would consider himself in the light of a humming top; he would make an apparatus (and he made it) for having himself launched, like a top, upon the ceiling, and regularly spun. Then the vertiginous motion of the human top would overpower the force of gravitation. He should, of course, spin upon his own axis, and sleep upon his own axis—perhaps he might even dream upon it; and he laughed at "those scoundrels, the flies," that never improved in their pretended art, nor made any thing of it. The principle was now discovered; "and, of course," he said, if a man can keep it up for five minutes, what's to hinder him from doing so for five months?" "Certainly, nothing that I can think of," was the reply of my sister, whose scepticism, in fact, had not settled upon the five months, but altogether upon the five minutes. The apparatus for spinning him, however, perhaps from its complexity, would not work—a fact evidently owing to the stupidity of the gardener. On reconsidering the subject, he announced, to the disappointment of some amongst us, that, although the physical discovery was now complete, he saw a moral difficulty. It was not a *humming* top that was required, but a peg top. Now, this, in order to keep up the *vertigo* at full stretch, without which, to a certainty, gravitation would prove too much for him, needed to be whipped incessantly. But that was precisely what a gentleman ought not to tolerate: to be scourged unintermittingly on the legs by any grub of a gardener, unless it were father Adam himself, was a thing that he could not bring his mind to face. However, as some compensation, he proposed to improve the art of flying, which was, as every body must acknowledge, in a condition disgraceful to civilized society. As he had made many a fire balloon, and had succeeded in some attempts at bringing down cats by *parachutes*, it was not very difficult to fly downwards from moderate elevations. But, as he was reproached by my sister for never flying back again,—which, however, was a far different thing, and not even attempted by the philosopher in "Rasselas,"—(for

> "Revocare gradum, et *superas* evadere ad auras
> Hic labor, hoc opus est,")

he refused, under such poor encouragement, to try his winged parachutes any more, either "aloft or alow," till he had thoroughly studied Bishop Wilkins[26] on the art of translating right reverend gentlemen to the moon; and, in the mean time, he resumed his general lectures on physics. From these, however, he was speedily

[26] Charles II., notoriously wrote a book on the possibility of a voyage to the moon, which, in a bishop, would be called a translation to the moon, and perhaps it was *his* name in combination with *his* book that suggested the "Adventures of Peter Wilkins." It is unfair, however, to mention him in connection with that single one of his works which announces an extravagant purpose. He was really a scientific man, and already in the time of Cromwell (about 1656) had projected that Royal Society of London which was afterwards realized and presided over by Isaac Barrow and Isaac Newton. He was also a learned man, but still with a veil of romance about him, as may be seen in his most elaborate work— "The Essay towards a Philosophic or Universal Language."

driven, or one might say shelled out, by a concerted assault of my sister Mary's. He had been in the habit of lowering the pitch of his lectures with ostentatious condescension to the presumed level of our poor understandings. This supercil-iousness annoyed my sister; and accordingly, with the help of two young female visitors, and my next younger brother,—in subsequent times a little middy on board many a ship of H. M., and the most predestined rebel upon earth against all assumptions, small or great, of superiority,—she arranged a mutiny, that had the unexpected effect of suddenly extinguishing the lectures forever. He had hap-pened to say, what was no unusual thing with him, that he flattered himself he had made the point under discussion tolerably clear; "clear," he added, bowing round the half circle of us, the audience, "to the meanest of capacities;" and then he re-peated, sonorously, "clear to the most excruciatingly mean of capacities." Upon which, a voice, a female voice,—but whose voice, in the tumult that followed, I did not distinguish,—retorted, "No, you haven't; it's as dark as sin; "and then, with-out a moment's interval, a second voice exclaimed, "Dark as night;" then came my young brother's insurrectionary yell, "Dark as midnight;" then another female voice chimed in melodiously, "Dark as pitch;" and so the peal continued to come round like a catch, the whole being so well concerted, and the rolling fire so well sustained, that it was impossible to make head against it; whilst the abruptness of the interruption gave to it the protecting character of an oral "round robin," it be-ing impossible to challenge any one in particular as the ringleader. Burke's phrase of "the swinish multitude," applied to mobs, was then in every body's mouth; and, accordingly, after my brother had recovered from his first astonishment at this audacious mutiny, he made us several sweeping bows that looked very much like tentative rehearsals of a sweeping *fusillade,* and then addressed us in a very brief speech, of which we could distinguish the words *pearls* and *swinish multitude,* but uttered in a very low key, perhaps out of some lurking consideration for the two young strangers. We all laughed in chorus at this parting salute; my brother himself condescended at last to join us; but there ended the course of lectures on natural philosophy.

As it was impossible, however, that he should remain quiet, he announced to us, that for the rest of his life he meant to dedicate himself to the intense cultivation of the tragic drama. He got to work instantly; and very soon he had composed the first act of his "Sultan Selim;" but, in defiance of the metre, he soon changed the ti-tle to "Sultan Amurath," considering *that* a much fiercer name, more bewhiskered and beturbaned. It was no part of his intention that we should sit lolling on chairs like ladies and gentleman that had paid opera prices for private boxes. He expect-ed every one of us, he said, to pull an oar. We were to *act* the tragedy. But, in fact, we had many oars to pull. There were so many characters, that each of us took four at the least, and the future middy had six. He, this wicked little middy,[27] caused the greatest affliction to Sultan Amurath, forcing him to order the amputation of

---

[27] *"Middy."* —I call him so simply to avoid confusion, and by way of anticipation; else he was too young at this time to serve in the navy. Afterwards he did so for many years, and saw every variety of service in every class of ships belonging to our navy. At one time, when yet a boy, he was captured by pirates, and compelled to sail with them; and the end of his adventurous career was, that for many a year he has been lying at the bottom of the Atlantic.

his head six several times (that is, once in every one of his six parts) during the first act. In reality, the sultan, though otherwise a decent man, was too bloody. What by the bowstring, and what by the cimeter, he had so thinned the population with which he commenced business, that scarcely any of the characters remained alive at the end of act the first. Sultan Amurath found himself in an awkward situation. Large arrears of work remained, and hardly any body to do it but the sultan himself. In composing act the second, the author had to proceed like Deucalion and Pyrrha, and to create an entirely new generation. Apparently this young generation, that ought to have been so good, took no warning by what had happened to their ancestors in act the first: one must conclude that they were quite as wicked, since the poor sultan had found himself reduced to order them all for execution in the course of this act the second. To the brazen age had succeeded an iron age; and the prospects were becoming sadder and sadder as the tragedy advanced. But here the author began to hesitate. He felt it hard to resist the instinct of carnage. And was it right to do so? Which of the felons whom he had cut of prematurely could pretend that a court of appeal would have reversed his sentence? But the consequences were distressing. A new set of characters in every act brought with it the necessity of a new plot; for people could not succeed to the arrears of old actions, or inherit ancient motives, like a landed estate. Five crops, in fact, must be taken off the ground in each separate tragedy, amounting, in short, to five tragedies involved in one.

Such, according to the rapid sketch which at this moment my memory furnishes, was the brother who now first laid open to me the gates of war. The occasion was this. He had resented, with a shower of stones, an affront offered to us by an individual boy, belonging to a cotton factory: for more than two years afterwards this became the *teterrima causa* of a skirmish or a battle as often as we passed the factory; and, unfortunately, *that* was twice a day on every day except Sunday. Our situation in respect to the enemy was as follows: Greenhay, a country house newly built by my father, at that time was a clear mile from the outskirts of Manchester; but in after years Manchester, throwing out the *tentacula* of its vast expansions, absolutely enveloped Greenhay; and, for any thing I know, the grounds and gardens which then insulated the house may have long disappeared. Being a modest mansion, which (including hot walls, offices, and gardener's house) had cost only six thousand pounds, I do not know how it should have risen to the distinction of giving name to a region of that great town; however, it *has* done so;[28] and at this time, therefore, after changes so great, it will be difficult for the *habitué* of that region to understand how my brother and myself could have a solitary road to traverse between Greenhay and Princess Street, then the termination, on that side, of Manchester. But so it was. Oxford *Street*, like its namesake in London, was then called the Oxford *Road*; and during the currency of our acquaintance with it, arose the first three houses in its neighborhood; of which the third was built for the Rev. S. H., one of our guardians, for whom his friends had also built the Church of St. Peter's—not a bowshot from the house. At present, however, he resided in

---

[28] "Green *heys*," with slight variation in the spelling, is the name given to that district of which Greenhay formed the original nucleus. Probably it was the solitary situation of the house which (failing any other grounds of denomination) raised it to this privilege.

Salford, nearly two miles from Greenhay; and to him we went over daily, for the benefit of his classical instructions. One sole cotton factory had then risen along the line of Oxford Street; and this was close to a bridge, which also was a new creation; for previously all passengers to Manchester went round by Garrat. This factory became to us the *officina gentium*, from which swarmed forth those Goths and Vandals that continually threatened our steps; and this bridge became the eternal arena of combat, we taking good care to be on the right side of the bridge for retreat, *i.e.*, on the town side, or the country side, accordingly as we were going out in the morning, or returning in the afternoon. Stones were the implements of warfare; and by continual practice both parties became expert in throwing them.

The origin of the feud it is scarcely requisite to rehearse, since the particular accident which began it was not the true efficient cause of our long warfare, but simply the casual occasion. The cause lay in our aristocratic dress. As children of an opulent family, where all provisions were liberal, and all appointments elegant, we were uniformly well dressed; and, in particular, we wore troussers, (at that time unheard of, except among sailors,) and we also wore Hessian boots—a crime that could not be forgiven in the Lancashire of that day, because it expressed the double offence of being aristocratic and being outlandish. We were aristocrats, and it was vain to deny it; could we deny our boots? whilst our antagonists, if not absolutely *sans culottes*, were slovenly and forlorn in their dress, often unwashed, with hair totally neglected, and always covered with flakes of cotton. Jacobins they were not, as regarded any sympathy with the Jacobinism that then desolated France; for, on the contrary, they detested every thing French, and answered with brotherly signals to the cry of "Church and king," or "King and constitution." But, for all that, as they were perfectly independent, getting very high wages, and these wages in a mode of industry that was then taking vast strides ahead, they contrived to reconcile this patriotic anti-Jacobinism with a personal Jacobinism of that sort which is native to the heart of man, who is by natural impulse (and not without a root of nobility, though also of base envy) impatient of inequality, and submits to it only through a sense of its necessity, or under a long experience of its benefits.

It was on an early day of our new *tyrocinium*, or perhaps on the very first, that, as we passed the bridge, a boy happening to issue from the factory[29] sang out to us derisively, "Hollo, bucks!" In this the reader may fail to perceive any atrocious insult commensurate to the long war which followed. But the reader is wrong. The word *"dandies"*[30] which was what the villain meant, had not then been born, so that he could not have called us by that name, unless through the spirit of prophecy. *Buck* was the nearest word at hand in his Manchester vocabulary: he gave all he could, and let us dream the rest. But in the next moment he discovered our boots, and he consummated his crime by saluting us as "Boots! boots!" My brother made a dead stop, surveyed him with intense disdain, and bade him draw near,

---

[29] *"Factory."*—Such was the designation technically at that time. At present, I believe that a building of that class would be called a "mill."

[30] This word, however, exists in *Jack-a-dandy*—a very old English word. But what does *that* mean?

that he might "give his flesh to the fowls of the air." The boy declined to accept this liberal invitation, and conveyed his answer by a most contemptuous and plebian gesture,[31] upon which my brother drove him in with a shower of stones.

During this inaugural flourish of hostilities, I, for my part, remained inactive, and therefore apparently neutral. But this was the last time that I did so: for the moment, indeed, I was taken by surprise. To be called a *buck* by one that had it in his choice to have called me a coward, a thief, or a murderer, struck me as a most pardonable offence; and as to *boots*, that rested upon a flagrant fact that could not be denied; so that at first I was green enough to regard the boy as very considerate and indulgent. But my brother soon rectified my views; or, if any doubts remained, he impressed me, at least, with a sense of my paramount duty to himself, which was threefold. First, it seems that I owed military allegiant to *him*, as my commander-in-chief, whenever we "took the field;" secondly, by the law of nations, I, being a cadet of my house, owed suit and service to him who was its head; and he assured me, that twice in a year, on *my* birthday and on *his*, he had a right, strictly speaking, to make me lie down, and to set his foot upon my neck; lastly, by a law not so rigorous, but valid amongst gentlemen, — viz., "by the *comity* of nations," — it seems I owed eternal deference to one so much older than myself, so much wiser, stronger, braver, more beautiful, and more swift of foot. Something like all this in tendency I had already believed, though I had not so minutely investigated the modes and grounds of my duty. By temperament, and through natural dedication to despondency, I felt resting upon me always too deep and gloomy a sense of obscure duties attached to life, that I never *should* be able to fulfil; a burden which I could not carry, and which yet I did not know how to throw off. Glad, therefore, I was to find the whole tremendous weight of obligations — the law and the prophets — all crowded into this one pocket command, "Thou shalt obey thy brother as God's vicar upon earth." For now, if, by any future stone levelled at him who had called me a "buck," I should chance to draw blood, perhaps I might not have committed so serious a trespass on any rights which he could plead; but if I *had*, (for on this subject my convictions were still cloudy,) at any rate, the duty I might have violated in regard to this general brother, in right of Adam, was cancelled when it came into collision with my paramount duty to this liege brother of my own individual house.

From this day, therefore, I obeyed all my brother's military commands with the utmost docility; and happy it made me that every sort of doubt, or question, or opening for demur was swallowed up in the unity of this one papal principle, discovered by my brother, viz., that all rights and duties of casuistry were transferred from me to himself. *His* was the judgment — *his* was the responsibility; and to me belonged only the sublime obligation of unconditional faith in *him*. That faith I realized. It is true that he taxed me at times, in his reports of particular fights, with "horrible cowardice," and even with "a cowardice that seemed inexplicable, except on the supposition of treachery." But this was only a *façon de parler* with

[31] Precisely, however, the same gesture, plebian as it was, by which the English commandant at Heligoland replied to the Danes when civilly inviting him to surrender. Southey it was, on the authority of Lieutenant Southey, his brother, who communicated to me this anecdote.

him: the idea of secret perfidy, that was constantly moving under ground, gave an interest to the progress of the war, which else tended to the monotonous. It was a dramatic artifice for sustaining the interest, where the incidents might happen to be too slightly diversified. But that he did not believe his own charges was clear, because he never repeated them in his "General History of the Campaigns," which was a *resumé*, or recapitulating digest, of his daily reports.

We fought every day, and, generally speaking, *twice* every day; and the result was pretty uniform, viz., that my brother and I terminated the battle by insisting upon our undoubted right to run away. *Magna Charta*, I should fancy, secures that great right to every man; else, surely, it is sadly defective. But out of this catastrophe to most of our skirmishes, and to all our pitched battles except one, grew a standing schism between my brother and myself. My unlimited obedience had respect to action, but not to opinion. Loyalty to my brother did not rest upon hypocrisy: because I was faithful, it did not follow that I must be false in relation to his capricious opinions. And these opinions sometimes took the shape of acts. Twice, at the least, in every week, but sometimes every night, my brother insisted on singing "Te Deum" for supposed victories which he had won; and he insisted also on my bearing a part in these "Te Deums." Now, as I knew of no such victories, but resolutely asserted the truth,—viz., that we ran away,—a slight jar was thus given to the else triumphal effect of these musical ovations. Once having uttered my protest, however, willingly I gave my aid to the chanting; for I loved unspeakably the grand and varied system of chanting in the Romish and English churches. And, looking back at this day to the ineffable benefits which I derived from the church of my childhood, I account among the very greatest those which reached me through the various chants connected with the "O, Jubilate," the "Magnificat," the "Te Deum," the "Benedicite," &c. Through these chants it was that the sorrow which laid waste my infancy, and the devotion which nature had made a necessity of my being, were profoundly interfused: the sorrow gave reality and depth to the devotion; the devotion gave grandeur and idealization to the sorrow. Neither was my love for chanting altogether without knowledge. A son of my reverend guardian, much older than myself, who possessed a singular faculty of producing a sort of organ accompaniment with one half of his mouth, whilst he sang with the other half, had given me some instructions in the art of chanting; and, as to my brother, he, the hundred-handed Briareus, could do all things; of course, therefore, he could chant.

Once having begun, it followed naturally that the war should deepen in bitterness. Wounds that wrote memorials in the flesh, insults that rankled in the heart,—these were not features of the case likely to be forgotten by our enemies, and far less by my fiery brother. I, for my part, entered not into any of the passions that war may be supposed to kindle, except only the chronic passion of anxiety. *Fear* it was not; for experience had taught me that, under the random firing of our undisciplined enemies, the chances were not many of being wounded. But the uncertainties of the war; the doubts in every separate action whether I could keep up the requisite connection with my brother, and, in case I could not, the utter darkness that surrounded my fate; whether, as a trophy won from Israel, I should be dedicated to the service of some Manchester Dagon, or pass through fire to Moloch,—all these contingencies, for me that had no friend to consult, ran too violently into the master current of my constitutional despondency ever to give way under any casual elation of success. Success, however, we really had at times; in slight skirmishes pretty often; and once, at least, as the reader will find to his mortification, if he is wicked enough to take the side of the Philistines, a most smashing victory in a pitched battle. But even then, and whilst the hurrahs were yet ascending from our jubilating lips, the freezing remembrance came back to my heart of that deadly depression which, duly at the coming round of the morning and evening watches, travelled with me like my shadow on our approach to the memorable bridge. A bridge of sighs[32] too surely it was for me; and even for my brother it formed an object of fierce yet anxious jealousy, that he could not always disguise, as we first came in sight of it; for, if it happened to be occupied in strength, there was an end of all hope that we could attempt the passage; and *that* was a fortunate solution of the difficulty, as it imposed no evil beyond a circuit; which, at least, was safe, if the world should choose to call it inglorious. Even this shade of ignominy, however, my brother contrived to color favorably, by calling us—that is, me and himself—"a corps of observation;" and he condescendingly explained to me, that, although making "a lateral movement," he had his eye upon the enemy, and "might yet come round upon his left flank in a way that wouldn't, perhaps, prove very agreeable." This, from the nature of the ground, never happened. We crossed the river at Garrat, out of sight from the enemy's position; and, on our return in the evening, when we reached that point of our route from which the retreat was secure to Greenhay, we took such revenge for the morning insult as might belong to extra liberality in our stone donations. On this line of policy there was, therefore, no cause for anxiety; but the common case was, that the numbers

---

[32] *"Bridge of sighs."*—Two men of memorable genius, Hood last, and Lord Byron by many years previously, have so appropriated this phrase, and reissued it as English currency, that many readers suppose it to be theirs. But the genealogies of fine expressions should be more carefully preserved. The expression belongs originally to Venice. This *jus postliminii* becomes of real importance in many cases, but especially in the case of Shakspeare. Could one have believed it possible beforehand? And yet it is a fact that he is made to seem a robber of the lowest order, by mere dint of suffering robbery. Purely through their own jewelly splendor have many hundreds of his phrases forced themselves into usage so general, under the vulgar infirmity of seeking to strengthen weak prose by shreds of poetic quotation, that at length the majority of careless readers come to look upon these phrases as belonging to the language, and traceable to no distinct proprietor any more than proverbs: and thus, on afterwards observing them in Shakspeare, they regard him in the light of one accepting alms (like so many meaner persons) from the common treasury of the universal mind, on which treasury, meantime, he had himself conferred these phrases as original donations of his own. Many expressions in the "Paradise Lost," in "Il Penseroso," and in "L'Allegro," are in the same predicament. And thus the almost incredible case is realized which I have described, viz., that simply by having suffered a robbery through two centuries, (for the first attempt at plundering Milton was made upon his juvenile poems,) have Shakspeare and Milton come to be taxed as robbers. N. B.—In speaking of Hood as having appropriated the phrase *Bridge of Sighs,* I would not be understood to represent him as by possibility aiming at any concealment. He was as far above such a meanness by his nobility of heart, as he was raised above all need for it by the overflowing opulence of his genius.

might not be such as to justify this caution, and yet quite enough for mischief. To my brother, however, stung and carried headlong into hostility by the martial instincts of his nature, the uneasiness of doubt or insecurity was swallowed up by his joy in the anticipation of victory, or even of contest; whilst to myself, whose exultation was purely official and ceremonial, as due by loyalty from a cadet to the head of his house, no such compensation existed. The enemy was no enemy in *my* eyes; his affronts were but retaliations; and his insults were so inapplicable to my unworthy self, being of a calibre exclusively meant for the use of my brother, that from me they recoiled, one and all, as cannon shot from cotton bags.

The ordinary course of our day's warfare was this: between nine and ten in the morning occurred our first transit, and, consequently, our earliest opportunity for doing business. But at this time the great sublunary interest of breakfast, which swallowed up all nobler considerations of glory and ambition, occupied the work people of the factory, (or what in the pedantic diction of this day are termed the "operatives,") so that very seldom any serious business was transacted. Without any formal armistice, the paramount convenience of such an arrangement silently secured its own recognition. Notice there needed none of truce, when the one side yearned for breakfast, and the other for a respite: the groups, therefore, on or about the bridge, if any at all, were loose in their array, and careless. We passed through them rapidly, and, on my part, uneasily; exchanging a few snarls, perhaps, but seldom or ever snapping at each other. The tameness was almost shocking of those who, in the afternoon, would inevitably resume their natural characters of tiger cats and wolves. Sometimes, however, my brother felt it to be a duty that we should fight in the morning; particularly when any expression of public joy for a victory,—bells ringing in the distance,—or when a royal birthday, or some traditional commemoration of ancient feuds, (such as the 5th of November,) irritated his martial propensities. Some of these being religious festivals, seemed to require of us an *extra* homage, for which we knew not how to find any natural or significant expression, except through sharp discharges of stones, that being a language older than Hebrew or Sanscrit, and universally intelligible. But, excepting these high days of religious solemnity, when a man is called upon to show that he is not a pagan or a miscreant in the eldest of senses, by thumping, or trying to thump, somebody who is accused or accusable of being heterodox, the great ceremony of breakfast was allowed to sanctify the hour. Some natural growls we uttered, but hushed them soon, regardless

> "Of the sweeping whirlpool's sway,
> That, hushed in grim repose, looked for his evening prey."

That came but too surely. Yes, evening never forgot to come; this odious necessity of fighting never missed its road back, or fell asleep, or loitered by the way, more than a bill of exchange or a tertian fever. Five times a week (Saturday sometimes, and Sunday always, were days of rest) the same scene rehearsed itself in pretty nearly the same succession of circumstances. Between four and five o'clock we had crossed the bridge to the safe, or Greenhay side; then we paused, and waited for the enemy. Sooner or later a bell rang, and from the smoky hive issued the hornets that night and day stung incurably my peace of mind. The order and procession of the incidents after this were odiously monotonous. My brother occupied the main high road, precisely at the point where a very gentle rise of the ground attained its summit; for the bridge lay in a slight valley, and the main military position was fifty or eighty yards above the bridge: then—but having first examined my pockets, in order to be sure that my stock of ammunition, stones, fragments of slate, with a reasonable proportion of brickbats, was all correct and ready for action—he detached me about forty yards to the right, my orders being invariable, and liable to no doubts or "quibbling." Detestable in *my* ears was that word "*quibbling*," by which, for a thousand years, if the war had happened to last so long, he would have fastened upon me the imputation of meaning, or wishing, at least, to do what he called "pettifogulizing"—that is, to plead some distinction, or verbal demur, in bar of my orders, under some colorable pretence that, according to their literal construction, they really did not admit of being fulfilled, or perhaps that they admitted it too much as being capable of fulfilment in two senses, either of them a practicable sense. True it was that my eye was preternaturally keen for flaws of language, not from pedantic exaction of superfluous accuracy, but, on the contrary, from too conscientious a wish to escape the mistakes which language not rigorous is apt to occasion. So far from seeking to "pettifogulize"—*i.e.*, to find evasions for any purpose in a trickster's minute tortuosities of construction—exactly in the opposite direction, from mere excess of sincerity, most unwillingly I found, in almost every body's words, an unintentional opening left for double interpretations. Undesigned equivocation prevails every where;[33] and it is not the cavilling hair splitter, but, on the contrary, the single-eyed servant of truth, that is most likely to insist upon the limitation of expressions too wide or too vague, and upon the decisive election between meanings potentially double. Not in order to resist or evade my brother's directions, but for the very opposite purpose—viz., that I might fulfil them to the letter; thus and no otherwise it happened that I showed so much scrupulosity about the exact value and position of his words, as finally to draw upon myself the vexatious reproach of being habitually a "pettifogulizer."

Meantime, our campaigning continued to rage. Overtures of pacification were never mentioned on either side. And I, for *my* part, with the passions only of peace at my heart, did the works of war faithfully and with distinction. I presume so, at least, from the results. It is true, I was continually falling into treason, without exactly knowing how I got into it, or how I got out of it. My brother also, it is true, sometimes assured me that he could, according to the rigor of martial justice, have me hanged on the first tree we passed; to which my prosaic answer had been, that of trees there *were* none in Oxford Street—[which, in imitation of Von Troil's famous chapter on the snakes of Lapland, the reader may accept, if he pleases, as

---

[33] Geometry (it has been said) would not evade disputation, if a man could find his interest in disputing it: such is the spirit of cavil. But I, upon a very opposite ground, assert that there is not one page of prose that could be selected from the best writer in the English language (far less in the German) which, upon a sufficient interest arising, would not furnish matter, simply through its defects in precision, for a suit in Chancery. Chancery suits do not arise, it is true, because the doubtful expressions do not touch any interest of property; but what *does* arise is this—that something more valuable than a pecuniary interest is continually suffering, viz., the interests of truth.

a complete course of lectures on the "dendrology" of Oxford Street.] But, notwithstanding such little stumblings in my career, I continued to ascend in the service; and, I am sure, it will gratify my friendly readers to hear, that, before my eighth birthday, I was promoted to the rank of major general. Over this sunshine, however, soon swept a train of clouds. Three times I was taken prisoner, and with different results. The first time I was carried to the rear, and not molested in any way. Finding myself thus ignominiously neglected, I watched my opportunity; and, by making a wide circuit, easily effected my escape. In the next case, a brief council was held over me; but I was not allowed to hear the deliberations; the result only being communicated to me—which result consisted in a message not very complimentary to my brother, and a small present of kicks to myself. This present was paid down without any discount, by means of a general subscription amongst the party surrounding me—that party, luckily, not being very numerous; besides which, I must, in honesty, acknowledge myself, generally speaking, indebted to their forbearance. They were not disposed to be too hard upon me. But, at the same time, they clearly did not think it right that I should escape altogether from tasting the calamities of war. And this translated the estimate of my guilt from the public jurisdiction to that of the individual, sometimes capricious and harsh, and carrying out the public award by means of legs that ranged through all gradations of weight and agility. One kick differed exceedingly from another kick in dynamic value; and, in some cases, this difference was so distressingly conspicuous as to imply special malice, unworthy, I conceive, of all generous soldiership.

On returning to our own frontiers, I had an opportunity of displaying my exemplary greenness. That message to my brother, with all its *virus* of insolence I repeated as faithfully for the spirit as, and as literally for the expressions, as my memory allowed me to do; and in that troublesome effort, simpleton that I was, fancied myself exhibiting a soldier's loyalty to his commanding officer. My brother thought otherwise: he was more angry with me than with the enemy. I ought, he said, to have refused all participation in such *sans cullotes* insolence; to carry it was to acknowledge it as fit to be carried. One, grows wiser every day; and on this particular day I made a resolution that, if again made prisoner, I would bring no more "jaw" (so my brother called it) from the Philistines. If these people *would* send "jaw," I settled that, henceforwards, it must go through the post office.

In my former captures, there had been nothing special or worthy of commemoration in the circumstances. Neither was there in the third, excepting that, by accident, in the second stage of the case, I was delivered over to the custody of young women and girls; whereas the ordinary course would have thrown me upon the vigilant attentions (relieved from monotony by the experimental kicks) of boys. So far, the change was very much for the better. I had a feeling myself, on first being presented to my new young mistresses, of a distressing sort. Having always, up to the completion of my sixth year, been a privileged pet, and almost, I might say, ranking amongst the sanctities of the household, with all its female sections, whether young or old, (an advantage which I owed originally to a long illness, an ague, stretching over two entire years of my infancy,) naturally I had learned to appreciate the indulgent tenderness of women; and my heart thrilled with love and gratitude, as often as they took me up into their arms and kissed me. Here it would have been as every where else; but, unfortunately, my introduction to these young women was in the very worst of characters. I had been taken in arms — in arms against their own brothers, cousins, sweethearts, and on pretexts too frivolous to mention. If asked the question, it would be found that I should not myself deny the fact of being at war with their whole order. What was the meaning of *that*? What was it to which war pledged a man? It pledged him, in case of opportunity, to burn, ravage, and depopulate the houses and lands of the enemy; which enemy was these fair girls. The warrior stood committed to universal destruction. Neither sex nor age, neither the smiles of unoffending infancy nor the gray hairs of the venerable patriarch, neither the sanctity of the matron nor the loveliness of the youthful bride, would confer any privilege with the warrior, consequently not with me.

Many other hideous features in the military character will be found in books innumerable — levelled at those who make war, and therefore at myself. And it appears finally by these books, that, as one of my ordinary practices, I make a wilderness, and call it a pacification; that I hold it a duty to put people to the sword; which done, to plough up the foundations of their hearths and altars, and then to sow the ground with salt.

All this passing through my brain, when suddenly one young woman snatched me up in her arms, and kissed me: from *her*, I was passed round to others of the party, who all in turn caressed me, with no allusion to that warlike mission against them and theirs, which only had procured me the honor of an introduction to themselves in the character of captive. The too palpable fact that I was not the person meant by nature to exterminate their families, or to make wildernesses, and call them pacifications, had withdrawn from their minds the counterfact — that whatever had been my performances, my intentions had been hostile, and that in such a character only I could have become their prisoner. Not only did these young people kiss me, but I (seeing no military reason against it) kissed *them*. Really, if young women will insist on kissing major generals, they must expect that the generals will retaliate. One only of the crowd adverted to the character in which I came before them: to be a lawful prisoner, it struck her too logical mind that I must have been caught in some aggressive practices. "Think," she said, "of this little dog fighting, and fighting our Jack." "But," said another in a propitiatory tone, "perhaps he'll not do so any more." I was touched by the kindness of her suggestion, and the sweet, merciful sound of that same *"Not do so any more"* which really was prompted, I fear, much more by that charity in her which hopeth all things than by any signs of amendment in myself. Well was it for me that no time was allowed for an investigation into my morals by point-blank questions as to my future intentions. In which case it would have appeared too undeniably, that the same sad necessity which had planted me hitherto in a position of hostility to their estimable families would continue to persecute me; and that, on the very next day, duty to my brother, howsoever it might struggle with gratitude to themselves, would range me in martial attitude, with a pocketful of stones, meant, alas! for the exclusive use of their respectable kinsmen. Whilst I was preparing myself, however, for this painful exposition, my female friends observed issuing from the factory a crowd of boys not likely at all to improve my prospects. Instantly setting me down on my feet, they formed a sort of *cordon sanitaire* behind me, by stretching out their petticoats or aprons, as in dancing, so as to touch; and then crying out, "Now, little dog, run for thy life," prepared themselves (I doubt not) for rescuing me, should my recapture be effected.

But this was not effected, although attempted with an energy that alarmed me, and even perplexed me with a vague thought (far too ambitious for my years) that one or two of the pursuing party might be possessed by some demon of jealousy, as eye witnesses to my revelling amongst the lips of that fair girlish bevy, kissing and being kissed, loving and being loved; in which case, from all that ever I had read about jealousy, (and I had read a great deal—viz., "Othello," and Collins's "Ode to the Passions,") I was satisfied that, if again captured, I had very little chance for my life. That jealousy was a green-eyed monster, nobody could know better than I did. "O, my lord, beware of jealousy!" Yes; and my lord couldn't possibly have more reason for bewaring of it than myself; indeed, well it would have been had his lordship run away from all the ministers of jealousy—Iago, Cassio, and embroidered handkerchiefs—at the same pace of six miles an hour which kept me ahead of my infuriated pursuers. Ah, that maniac, white as a leper with flakes of cotton, can I ever forget him—*him* that ran so far in advance of his party? What passion but jealousy could have sustained him in so hot a chase? There were some lovely girls in the fair company that had so condescendingly caressed me; but, doubtless, upon that sweet creature his love must have settled, who suggested, in her soft, relenting voice, a penitence in me that, alas! had not dawned, saying, "*Yes; but perhaps he will not do so any more.*" Thinking, as I ran, of her beauty, I felt that this jealous demoniac must fancy himself justified in committing seven times seven murders upon me, if he should have it in his power. But, thank Heaven, if jealousy can run six miles an hour, there are other passions—as, for instance, panic—that can run, upon occasion, six and a half; so, as I had the start of him, (you know, reader,) and not a very short start,—thanks be to the expanded petticoats of my dear female friends!—naturally it happend that the green-eyed monster came in second best. Time, luckily, was precious with *him*; and, accordingly, when he had chased me into the by-road leading down to Greenhay, he turned back. For the moment, therefore, I found myself suddenly released from danger. But this counted for nothing. The same scene would probably revolve upon me continually; and, on the next rehearsal, Green-eyes might have better luck. It saddened me, besides, to find myself under the political necessity of numbering amongst the Philistines, and as daughters of Gath, so many kind-hearted girls, whom, by personal proof, I knew to be such. In the profoundest sense, I was unhappy; and, not from any momentary accident of distress, but from deep glimpses which now, and heretofore, had opened themselves, as occasions arose, into the inevitable conflicts of life. One of the saddest among such conflicts is the necessity, wheresoever it occurs, of adopting—though the heart should disown—the enmities of one's own family, or country, or religious sect. In forms how afflicting must that necessity have sometimes occurred during the Parliamentary war! And, in after years, amongst our beautiful old English metrical romances, I found the same impassioned complaint uttered by a knight, Sir Ywain, as early as A.D. 1240—

> "But now, where'er I stray or go,
> My heart SHE has that is my foe!"

I knew—I anticipated to a certainty—that my brother would not hear of any merit belonging to the factory population whom every day we had to meet in battle; on the contrary, even submission on *their* part, and willingness to walk penitentially through the *Furcae Caudinae*, would hardly have satisfied his sense of their criminality. Often, indeed, as we came in view of the factory, he would shake his fist at it, and say, in a ferocious tone of voice, *"Delenda est Carthago!"* And certainly, I thought to myself, it must be admitted by every body, that the factory people are inexcusable in raising a rebellion against my brother. But still rebels were men, and sometimes were women; and rebels, that stretch out their petticoats like fans for the sake of screening one from the hot pursuit of enemies with fiery eyes, (green or otherwise,) really are not the sort of people that one wishes to hate.

Homewards, therefore, I drew in sadness, and little doubting that *hereafter* I might have verbal feuds with my brother on behalf of my fair friends, but not dreaming how much displeasure I had already incurred by my treasonable collusion with their caresses. That part of the affair he had seen with his own eyes, from his position on the field; and then it was that he left me indignantly to my fate, which, by my first reception, it was easy to see would not prove very gloomy. When I came into our own study, I found him engaged in preparing a *bulletin*, (which word was just then travelling into universal use,) reporting briefly the events of the day. The art of drawing, as I shall again have occasion to mention, was amongst his foremost accomplishments; and round the margin of the border ran a black border, ornamented with cyprus and other funereal emblems. When finished, it was carried into the room of Mrs. Evans. This Mrs. Evans was an important person in our affairs. My mother, who never chose to have any direct communication with her servants, always had a housekeeper for the regulation of all domestic business; and the housekeeper, for some years, was this Mrs. Evans. Into her private parlor, where she sat aloof from the under servants, my brother and I had the *entrée* at all times, but upon very different terms of acceptance: he as a favorite of the first class; *I*, by sufferance, as a sort of gloomy shadow that ran after *his* person, and could not well be shut out if *he* were let in. Him she admired in the very highest degree; myself, on the contrary, she detested, which made me unhappy. But then, in some measure, she made amends for this, by despising me in extremity; and for *that* I was truly thankful—I need not say *why*, as the reader already knows. Why she detested me, so far as I know, arose in part out of my thoughtfulness indisposed to garrulity, and in part out of my savage, Orson-like sincerity. I had a great deal to say, but then I could say it only to a very few people, amongst whom Mrs. Evans was certainly not one; and, when I *did* say any thing, I fear that dire ignorance prevented my laying the proper restraints upon my too liberal candor; and *that* could not prove acceptable to one who thought nothing of working for any purpose, or for no purpose, by petty tricks, or even falsehoods— all which I held in stern abhorrence that I was at no pains to conceal. The *bulletin* on this occasion, garnished with this pageantry of woe, cypress wreaths, and arms reversed, was read aloud to Mrs. Evans, indirectly, therefore, to me. It communicated with Spartan brevity, the sad intelligence (but not sad to Mrs. E.) "that the major general had forever disgraced himself, by submitting to the .... caresses of the enemy." I leave a blank for the epithet affixed to "caresses," not because there *was* any blank, but, on the contrary, because my brother's wrath had boiled over in such a hubble-bubble of epithets, some only half erased, some doubtfully erased, that it was impossible, out of the various readings, to pick out the true classical text. "Infamous," "disgusting," and "odious" struggled for precedency; and *infamous* they might be; but on the other affixes I held my own private opinions. For some days my brother's displeasure continued to roll in reverberating thunders; but at length it growled itself to rest; and at last he descended to mild expostulations with me, showing clearly, in a series of general orders, what frightful consequences must ensue, if major generals (as a general principle) should allow themselves to be kissed by the enemy.

About this time my brother began to issue, instead of occasional bulletins, through which hitherto he had breathed his opinions into the ear of the public, (viz., of Mrs. Evans,) a regular gazette, which, in imitation of the London Gazette, was published twice a week. I suppose that no creature ever led such a life as *I* did in that gazette. Run up to the giddiest heights of promotion on on day, for merits which I could not myself discern, in a week or two I was brought to a court martial for offenses equally obscure. I was cashiered; I was restored "on the intercession of a distinguished lady;" (Mrs. Evans, to wit;) I was threatened with being drummed out of the army, to the music of the "Rogue's March;" and then, in the midst of all this misery and degradation, upon the discovery of some supposed energy that I had manifested, I was decorated with the Order of the Bath. My reading had been extensive enough to give me some vague aerial sense of the honor involved in such a decoration, whilst I was profoundly ignorant of the channels through which it could reach an individual, and of the sole fountain from which it could flow. But, in this enormity of disproportion between the cause and the effect, between the agency and the result, I saw nothing more astonishing than I had seen in many other cases confessedly true. Thousands of vast effects, by all that I had heard, linked themselves to causes apparently trivial. The dreadful taint of scrofula, according to the belief of all Christendom, fled at the simple touch of a Stuart[34] sovereign: no miracle in the Bible, from Jordan or from Bethesda, could be more sudden or more astoundingly victorious. By my own experience, again, I knew that a *styan* (as it is called) upon the eyelid could be easily reduced, though not instantaneously, by the slight application of any golden trinket. Warts upon the fingers of children I had myself known to vanish under the *verbal* charm of a gypsy woman, without any medicinal application whatever. And I well knew, that

---

[34] *"Of a Stuart sovereign,"* and by no means of a Stuart only. Queen Anne, the last Stuart who sat on the British throne, was the last of *our princes* who touched for the *king's evil,* (as scrofula was generally called until lately;) but the Bourbon houses, on the thrones of France, Spain, and Naples, as well as the house of Savoy, claimed and exercised the same supernatural privilege down to a much later period than the year 1714—the last of Queen Anne: according to their own and the popular faith, they could have cleansed Naaman the Syrian, and Gehazi too.

almost all nations believed in the dreadful mystery of the *evil eye*; some requiring, as a condition of the evil agency, the co-presence of malice in the agent; but others, as appeared from my father's Portuguese recollections, ascribing the same horrid power to the eye of certain select persons, even though innocent of all malignant purpose, and absolutely unconscious of their own fatal gift, until awakened to it by the results. Why, therefore, should there be any thing to shock, or even to surprise, in the power claimed by my brother, as an attribute inalienable from primogeniture in certain select families, of conferring knightly honors? The red ribbon of the Bath he certainly *did* confer upon me; and once, in a paroxysm of imprudent liberality, he promised me at the end of certain months, supposing that I swerved from my duty by no atrocious delinquency, the Garter itself. This, I knew, was a far loftier distinction than the Bath. Even then it was so; and since those days it has become much more so; because the long roll of martial services in the great war with Napoleon compelled our government greatly to widen the basis of the Bath. This promise was never fulfilled; but not for any want of clamorous persecution on my part addressed to my brother's wearied ear and somewhat callous sense of honor. Every fortnight, or so, I took care that he should receive a "refresher," as lawyers call it, — a new and revised brief, — memorializing my pretensions. These it was my brother's policy to parry, by alleged instances of recent misconduct on my part. But all such offences, I insisted, were thoroughly washed away by subsequent services in moments of peril, such as he himself could not always deny. In reality, I believe his real motive for withholding the Garter was, that he had nothing better to bestow upon himself.

"Now, look here," he would say, appealing to Mrs. Evans; "I suppose there's a matter of half a dozen kings on the continent, that would consent to lose three of their fingers, if by such a sacrifice they could purchase the blue ribbon; and here is this little scamp, conceiting himself entitled to it before he has finished two campaigns. "But I was not the person to be beaten off in this fashion. I took my stand upon the promise. A promise *was* a promise, even if made to a scamp; and then, besides — but there I hesitated; awful thoughts interposed to check me; else I wished to suggest that, perhaps, some two or three among that half dozen kings might also be scamps. However, I reduced the case to this plain dilemma: These six kings had received a promise, or they had not. If they had not, my case was better than theirs; if they *had*, then, said I, "all seven of us" — I was going to add, "are sailing in the same boat," or something to that effect, though not so picturesquely expressed; but I was interrupted by his deadly frown at my audacity in thus linking myself on as a seventh to this *attelage* of kings, and that such an absolute grub should dream of ranking as one in a bright pleiad of pretenders to the Garter. I had not particularly thought of that; but now, that such a demur was offered to my consideration, I thought of reminding him that, in a certain shadowy sense, I also might presume to class myself as a king, the meaning of which was this: Both my brother and myself, for the sake of varying our intellectual amusements, occupied ourselves at times in governing imaginary kingdoms. I do not mention this as any thing unusual; it is a common resource of mental activity and of aspiring energies amongst boys. Hartley Coleridge, for example, had a kingdom which he governed for many years; whether well or ill, is more than I can say. Kindly, I am sure, he would govern it; but, unless a machine had been invented for enabling him to write without effort, (as was really done for our fourth George during the pressure of illness,) I fear that the public service must have languished deplorably for want of the royal signature. In sailing past his own dominions, what dolorous outcries would have saluted him from the shore—"Hollo, royal sir! here's the deuse to pay: a perfect lock there is, as tight as locked jaw, upon the course of our public business; throats there are to be cut, from the product of ten jail deliveries, and nobody dares to cut them, for want of the proper warrant; archbishoprics there are to be filled; and, because they are *not* filled, the whole nation is running helter skelter into heresy—and all in consequence of your majesty's sacred laziness." *Our* governments were less remissly administered; since each of us, by continued reports of improvements and gracious concessions to the folly or the weakness of our subjects, stimulated the zeal of his rival. And here, at least, there seemed to be no reason why I should come into collision with my brother. At any rate, I took pains *not* to do so. But all was in vain. My destiny was, to live in one eternal element of feud.

My own kingdom was an island called Gombroon. But in what parallel of north or south latitude it lay, I concealed for a time as rigorously as ancient Rome through every century concealed her real name.[35] The object in this provisional concealment was, to regulate the position of my own territory by that of my brother's; for I was determined to place a monstrous world of waters between us as the only chance (and a very poor one it proved) for compelling my brother to keep the peace. At length, for some reason unknown to me, and much to my astonishment, he located his capital city in the high latitude of 65 deg. N. That fact being once published and settled, instantly I smacked my little kingdom of Gombroon down into the tropics, 10 deg., I think, south of the line. Now, at least, I was on the right side of the hedge, or so I flattered myself; for it struck me that my brother never would degrade himself by fitting out a costly nautical expedition against poor little Gombroon; and how else could he get at me? Surely the very fiend himself, if he happened to be in a high arctic latitude, would not indulge his malice so far as to follow its trail into the tropic of Capricorn. And what was to be got by such a freak? There was no Golden Fleece in Gombroon. If the fiend or my brother fancied *that*, for once they were in the wrong box; and there was no variety of vegetable produce, for I never denied that the poor little island was only 270 miles in circuit. Think, then, of sailing through 75 deg. of latitude only to crack such a miserable little filbert as that. But my brother stunned me by explaining, that, although his capital lay in lat. 65 deg. N., not the less his dominions swept southwards through a matter of 80 or 90 deg.; and as to the tropic of Capricorn, much of it was his own private property. I was aghast at hearing *that*. It seemed that vast horns and promontories ran down from all parts of his dominions towards any

---

[35] One reason, I believe, why it was held a point of wisdom in ancient days that the metropolis of a warlike state should have a secret name hidden from the world, lay in the pagan practice of *evocation*, applied to the tutelary deities of such a state. These deities might be lured by certain rites and briberies into a transfer of their favors to the besieging army. But, in order to make such an evocation effectual, it was necessary to know the original and secret name of the beleaguered city; and this, therefore, was religiously concealed.

country whatsoever, in either hemisphere,—empire or republic, monarchy, polyarchy, or anarchy,—that he might have reasons for assaulting.

Here in one moment vanished all that I had relied on for protection: distance I had relied on, and suddenly I was found in close neighborhood to my most formidable enemy. Poverty I had rolled on, and *that* was not denied: he granted the poverty, but it was dependent on the barbarism of the Gombroonians. It seems that in the central forests of Gombroonia there were diamond mines, which my people, from their low condition of civilization, did not value, nor had any means of working. Farewell, therefore, on *my* side, to all hopes of enduring peace, for here was established, in legal phrase, *a lien* forever upon my island, and not upon its margin, but its very centre, in favor of any invaders better able than the natives to make its treasures available. For, of old, it was an article in my brother's code of morals, that, supposing a contest between any two parties, of which one possessed an article, whilst the other was better able to use it, the rightful property vested in the latter. As if you met a man with a musket, then you might justly challenge him to a trial in the art of making gunpowder; which if you *could* make, and he could *not*, in that case the musket was *de jure* yours. For what shadow of a right had the fellow to a noble instrument which he could not "maintain" in a serviceable condition, and "feed" with its daily rations of powder and shot? Still, it may be fancied that, since all the relations between us as independent sovereigns (whether of war, or peace, or treaty) rested upon our own representations and official reports, it was surely within my competence to deny or qualify as much as within his to assert. But, in reality, the *law* of the contest between us, as suggested by some instinct of propriety in my own mind, would not allow me to proceed in such a method. What he said was like a move at chess or draughts, which it was childish to dispute. The move being made, my business was—to face it, to parry it, to evade it, and, if I could, to overthrow it. I proceeded as a lawyer who moves as long as he can, not by blank denial of facts, (or *coming to an issue,*) but by *demurring, (i.e.,* admitting the allegations of fact, but otherwise interpreting their construction.) It was the understood necessity of the case that I must passively accept my brother's statements so far as regarded their verbal expression; and, if *I* would extricate my poor islanders from their troubles, it must be by some distinction or evasion lying *within* this expression, or not blankly contradicting it.

"How, and to what extent," my brother asked, "did I raise taxes upon my subjects?" My first impulse was to say, that I did not tax them at all, for I had a perfect horror of doing so; but prudence would not allow of my saying *that*; because it was too probable he would demand to know how, in that case, I maintained a standing army; and if I once allowed it to be supposed that I had none, there was an end forever to the independence of my people. Poor things! they would have been invaded and dragooned in a month. I took some days, therefore, to consider that point; but at last replied, that my people, being maritime, supported themselves mainly by a herring fishery, from which I deducted a part of the produce, and afterwards sold it for manure to neighboring nations. This last hint I borrowed from the conversation of a stranger who happened to dine one day at Greenhay, and mentioned that in Devonshire, or at least on the western coast of that county, near Ilfracombe, upon any excessive take of herrings, beyond what the markets could absorb, the surplus was applied to the land as a valuable dressing. It might be inferred from this account, however, that the arts must be in a languishing state amongst a people that did not understand the process of salting fish; and my brother observed derisively, much to my grief, that a wretched ichthyophagous people must make shocking soldiers, weak as water, and liable to be knocked over like ninepins; whereas, in *his* army, not a man ever ate herrings, pilchards, mackerels, or, in fact, condescended to any thing worse than surloins of beef.

At every step I had to contend for the honor and independence of my islanders; so that early I came to understand the weight of Shakspeare's sentiment—

"Uneasy lies the head that wears a crown!"

O reader, do not laugh! I lived forever under the terror of two separate wars in two separate worlds: one against the factory boys, in a real world of flesh and blood, of stones and brickbats, of flight and pursuit, that were any thing but figurative; the other in a world purely aerial, where all the combats and the sufferings were absolute moonshine. And yet the simple truth is, that, for anxiety and distress of mind, the reality (which almost every morning's light brought round) was as nothing in comparison of that dream kingdom which rose like a vapor from my own brain, and which apparently by *fiat* of my will could be forever dissolved. Ah! but no; I had contracted obligations to Gombroon; I had submitted my conscience to a yoke; and in secret truth my will had no such autocratic power. Long contemplation of a shadow, earnest study for the welfare of that shadow, sympathy with the wounded sensibilities of that shadow under accumulated wrongs, these bitter experiences, nursed by brooding thought, had gradually frozen that shadow into a rigor of reality far denser than the material realities of brass or granite. Who builds the most durable dwellings? asks the laborer in "Hamlet;" and the answer is, The gravedigger. He builds for corruption; and yet *his* tenements are incorruptible: "the houses which *he* makes last to doomsday."[36] Who is it that seeks for concealment? Let him hide himself[37] in the unsearchable chambers of light,—of light

---

[36] Hamlet, Act v., scene 1.

[37] *"Hide himself in—light."*—The greatest scholar, by far, that this island ever produced, viz., Richard Bentley, published (as is well known) a 4to volume that in some respects is the very worst 4to now extant in the world—viz., a critical edition of the. "Paradise Lost." I observe, in the "Edinburgh Review," (July, 1851, No. 191, p. 15,) that a learned critic supposes Bentley to have meant this edition as a "practical jest." Not at all. Neither could the critic have fancied such a possibility, if he had taken the trouble (which *I* did many a year back) to examine it. A jest book it certainly is, and the most prosperous of jest books, but undoubtedly never meant for such by the author. A man whose lips are livid with anger does not jest, and does not understand jesting. Still, the Edinburgh Reviewer is right about the proper functions of the book, though wrong about the intentions of the author. The fact is, the man was maniacally in error, and always in error, as regarded the ultimate or poetic truth of Milton; but, as regarded truth reputed and truth *apparent*, he often had the air of being furiously in the right; an example of which I will cite. Milton, in the First Book of the "Paradise Lost," had said,—

"That from the *secret* top
Of Oreb or of Sinai didst inspire;"

which at noonday, more effectually than any gloom, conceals the very brightest stars,—rather than in labyrinths of darkness the thickest. What criminal is that who wishes to abscond from public justice? Let him hurry into the frantic publicities of London, and by no means into the quiet privacies of the country. So, and upon the analogy of these cases, we may understand that, to make a strife overwhelming by a thousand fold to the feelings, it must not deal with gross material interests, but with such as rise into the world of dreams, and act upon the nerves through spiritual, and not through fleshly torments. Mine, in the present case, rose suddenly, like a rocket, into their meridian altitude, by means of a hint furnished to my brother from a Scotch advocate's reveries.

This advocate, who by his writings became the remote cause of so much affliction to my childhood, and struck a blow at the dignity of Gombroon, that neither my brother nor all the forces of Tigrosylvania (my brother's kingdom) ever could have devised, was the celebrated James Burnett, better known to the English public by his judicial title of Lord Monboddo. The Burnetts of Monboddo, I have often heard, were a race distinguished for their intellectual accomplishments through several successive generations; and the judge in question was eminently so. It did him no injury that many people regarded him as crazy. In England, at the beginning of the last century, we had a saying,[38] in reference to the Harveys of Lord Bristol's family, equally distinguished for wit, beauty, and eccentricity, that at the creation there had been three kinds of people made, viz., men, women, and Harveys; and by all accounts, something of the same kind might plausibly have been said in Scotland about the Burnetts. Lord Monboddo's nieces, of whom one perished by falling from a precipice, (and, as I have heard, through mere absence of mind, whilst musing upon a book which she carried in her hand,) still survive in the affection of many friends, through the interest attached to their intellectual gifts; and Miss Burnett, the daughter of the judge, is remembered in all the memorials of Burns the poet, as the most beautiful, and otherwise the most interesting, of his female aristocratic friends in Edinburgh. Lord Monboddo himself trod an eccentric path in literature and philosophy; and our tutor, who spent his whole life in reading, withdrawing himself in that way from the anxieties incident to a narrow income and a large family, found, no doubt, a vast fund of interesting sug-

---

upon which Bentley comments in effect thus: "How!—the exposed summit of a mountain *secret*? Why, it's like Charing Cross—always the least secret place in the whole county." So one might fancy; since the summit of a mountain, like Plinlimmon or Cader Idris in Wales, like Skiddaw or Helvellyn in England, constitutes a central object of attention and gaze for the whole circumjacent district, measured by a radius sometimes of 15 to 20 miles. Upon this consideration, Bentley instructs us to substitute as the true reading—"That on the *sacred* top," &c. Meantime, an actual experiment will demonstrate that there is no place so absolutely secret and hidden as the exposed summit of a mountain, 3500 feet high, in respect to an eye stationed in the valley immediately below. A whole party of men, women, horses, and even tents, looked at under those circumstances, is absolutely invisible unless by the aid of glasses: and it becomes evident that a murder might be committed on the bare open summit of such a mountain with more assurance of absolute secrecy than any where else in the whole surrounding district.

[38] Which "*saying*" is sometimes ascribed, I know not how truly, to Lady Mary Wortley Montagu.

gestions in Lord M.'s "Dissertations on the Origin of Language;" but to us he communicated only one section of the work. It was a long passage, containing some very useful illustrations of a Greek idiom; useful I call them, because four years afterwards, when I had made great advances in my knowledge of Greek, they so appeared to me.[39] But then, being scarcely seven years old, as soon as our tutor had finished his long extract from the Scottish judge's prelection, I could express my thankfulness for what I had received only by composing my features to a deeper solemnity and sadness than usual—no very easy task, I have been told; otherwise, I really had not the remotest conception of what his lordship meant. I knew very well the thing called a *tense*; I knew even then by name the *Aoristus Primus*, as a respectable tense in the Greek language. It (or shall we say *he*?) was known to the whole Christian world by this distinction of *Primus*; clearly, therefore, there must be some low, vulgar tense in the background, pretending also to the name of Aorist, but universally scouted as the *Aoristus Secundus*, or Birmingham counterfeit. So that, unable as I was, from ignorance, to go along with Lord M.'s appreciation of his pretensions, still, had it been possible to meet an Aoristus Primus in the flesh, I should have bowed to him submissively, as to one apparently endowed with the mysterious rights of primogeniture. Not so my brother.

Aorist, indeed! Primus or Secundus, what mattered it? Paving stones were

[39] It strikes me, upon second thoughts, that the particular idiom, which Lord Monboddo illustrated as regarded the Greek language, merits a momentary notice; and for this reason—that it plays a part not at all less conspicuous or less delicate in the Latin. Here is an instance of its use in Greek, taken from the well-known night scene in the "Iliad:"—

— — —*gaethaese de poimenos aetor,*

And the heart of the shepherd *rejoices*; where the verb *gaethaese* is in the indefinite or aorist tense, and is meant to indicate a condition of feeling not limited to any time whatever—past, present, or future. In Latin, the force and elegance of this usage are equally impressive, if not more so. At this moment, I remember two cases of this in Horace:- -

1. "Rarò antecedentem scelestum
Deseruit pede poena claudo;"
2. "saepe Diespiter
Neglectus incesto *addidit* integrum."

That is—"oftentimes the supreme ruler, when treated with neglect, confounds or unites (not *has united*, as the tyro might fancy) the impure man with the upright in one common fate."

Exceedingly common is this usage in Latin poetry, when the object is to generalize a remark—as not connected with one mode of time more than another. In reality, all three modes of time—past, present, future—are used (though not equally used) in all languages for this purpose of generalization. Thus,—

1. The *future*; as, Sapiens dominabitur astris;
2. The *present*; as, Fortes fortuna juvat;
3. The *past*; as in the two cases cited from Horace.

But this practice holds equally in English: as to the future and the present, nobody will doubt it; and here is a case from the past: "The fool *hath said* in his heart, There is no God;" not meaning, that in some past time he has said so, but that generally in all times he *does* say so, and *will* say so.

something, brickbats were something; but an old superannuated tense! That any grown man should trouble himself about *that!* Indeed there *was* something extraordinary there. For it is not amongst the ordinary functions of lawyers to take charge of Greek; far less, one might suppose, of lawyers of Scotland, where the *general* system of education has moved for two centuries upon a principle of slight regard to classical literature. Latin literature was very much neglected, and Greek nearly altogether. The more was the astonishment at finding a rare delicacy of critical instinct, as well as of critical sagacity, applied to the Greek idiomatic niceties by a Scottish lawyer, viz., that the same eccentric judge, first made known to us by our tutor.

To the majority of readers, meantime, at this day, Lord M. is memorable chiefly for his craze about the degeneracy of us poor moderns, when compared with the men of pagan antiquity; which craze itself might possibly not have been generally known, except in connection with the little skirmish between him and Dr. Johnson, noticed in Boswell's account of the doctor's Scottish tour. "Ah, doctor," said Lord M., upon some casual suggestion of that topic, "poor creatures are we of this eighteenth century; our fathers were better men than we!" "O, no, my lord," was Johnson's reply; "we are quite as strong as our forefathers, and a great deal wiser! "Such a craze, however, is too widely diffused, and falls in with too obstinate a preconception[40] in the human race, which has in every age hypochondri-

---

[40] *"Too obstinate a preconception."* —Until the birth of geology, and fossil paleontology, concurring with vast strides ahead in the science of comparative anatomy, it is a well-established fact, that oftentimes the most scientific museum admitted as genuine fragments of the human osteology what in fact belonged to the gigantic brutes of our earth in her earliest stages of development. This mistake would go some way in accounting for the absurd disposition in all generations to view themselves as abridged editions of their forefathers. Added to which, as a separate cause of error, there can be little doubt, that intermingled with the human race there has at most periods of the world been a separate and Titanic race, such as the Anakim amongst the peoples of Palestine, the Cyclopean race diffused over the Mediterranean in the elder ages of Greece, and certain tribes amongst the Alps, known to Evelyn in his youth (about Cromwell's time) by an unpleasant travelling experience. These gigantic races, however, were no arguments for a degeneration amongst the rest of mankind. They were evidently a variety of man, coexistent with the ordinary races, but liable to be absorbed and gradually lost by intermarriage amongst other tribes of the ordinary standard. Occasional exhumations of such Titan skeletons would strengthen the common prejudice. They would be taken, not for a local variety, but for an antediluvian or prehistoric type, from which the present races of man had arisen by gradual degeneration.

These cases of actual but misinterpreted experience, at the same time that they naturally must tend to fortify the popular prejudice, would also, by accounting for it, and ingrafting it upon a reasonable origin, so far tend to take from it the reproach of a prejudice. Though erroneous, it would yet seem to us, in looking back upon it, a rational and even an inevitable opinion, having such plausible grounds to stand upon; plausible, I mean, until science and accurate examination of the several cases had begun to read them into a different construction. Yet, on the other hand, in spite of any colorable excuses that may be pleaded for this prejudice, it is pretty plain that, after all, there is in human nature a deep-laid predisposition to an obstinate craze of this nature. Else why is it that, in every age alike, men have asserted or even assumed the downward tendency of the human race in all that regards *moral* qualities. For the *physical* degeneration of man there really were some

acally regarded itself as under some fatal necessity of dwindling, much to have challenged public attention. As real paradoxes (spite of the idle meaning attached usually to the word *paradox*) have often no falsehood in them, so here, on the contrary, was a falsehood which had in it nothing paradoxical. It contradicted all the indications of history and experience, which uniformly had pointed in the very opposite direction; and so far it ought to have been paradoxical, (that is, revolting to popular opinion,) but was *not* so; for it fell in with prevailing opinions, with the oldest, blindest, and most inveterate of human superstitions. If extravagant, yet to the multitude it did not *seem* extravagant. So natural a craze, therefore, however baseless, would never have carried Lord Monboddo's name into that meteoric notoriety and atmosphere of astonishment which soon invested it in England. And, in that case, my childhood would have escaped the deadliest blight of mortification and despondency that could have been incident to a most morbid temperament concurring with a situation of visionary (yes! if you please, of fantastic) but still of most real distress.

How much it would have astonished Lord Monboddo to find himself made answerable, virtually made answerable, by the evidence of secret tears, for the misery of an unknown child in Lancashire. Yet night and day these silent memorials of suffering were accusing him as the founder of a wound that could not be healed. It happened that the several volumes of his work lay for weeks in the study of our tutor. Chance directed the eye of my brother, one day, upon that part of the work in which Lord M. unfolds his hypothesis that originally the human race had been a variety of the ape. On which hypothesis, by the way, Dr. Adam Clarke's substitution of *ape* for *serpent*, in translating the word *nachash*, (the brute tempter of Eve,) would have fallen to the ground, since this would simply have been the case of one human being tempting another. It followed inevitably, according to Lord M., however painful it might be to human dignity, that in this, their early stage of brutality, men must have had tails. My brother mused upon this revery, and, in a few days, published an extract from some scoundrel's travels in Gombroon,

apparent (though erroneous) arguments; but, for the moral degeneration, no argument at all, small or great. Yet a bigotry of belief in this idle notion has always prevailed amongst moralists, pagan alike and Christian. Horace, for example, informs us that

> "Aetas parentum, pejor avis, tulit
> Nos nequiores—mox daturos
> Progeniem vitiosiorem."

The last generation was worse, it seems, than the penultimate, as the present is worst than the last. We, however, of the present, bad as we may be, shall be kept in countenance by the coming generation, which will prove much worse than ourselves. On the same precedent, all the sermons through the last three centuries, if traced back through decennial periods, so as to form thirty successive strata, will be found regularly claiming the precedency in wickedness for the immediate period of the writer. Upon which theories, as men ought physically to have dwindled long ago into pygmies, so, on the other hand, morally they must by this time have left Sodom and Gomorrah far behind. What a strange animal must man upon this scheme offer to our contemplation; shrinking in size, by graduated process, through every century, until at last he would not rise an inch from the ground; and, on the other hand, as regards villany, towering evermore and more up to the heavens. What a dwarf! what a giant! Why, the very crows would combine to destroy such a little monster.

according to which the Gombroonians had not yet emerged from this early condition of apedom. They, it seems, were still *homines caudati*. Overwhelming to me and stunning was the ignominy of this horrible discovery. Lord M. had not overlooked the natural question—In what way did men get rid of their tails? To speak the truth, they never *would* have got rid of them had they continued to run wild; but growing civilization introduced arts, and the arts introduced sedentary habits. By these it was, by the mere necessity of continually sitting down, that men gradually wore off their tails. Well, and what should hinder the Gombroonians from sitting down? *Their* tailors and shoemakers would and could, I hope, sit down, as well as those of Tigrosylvania. Why not? Ay, but my brother had insisted already that they *had* no tailors, that they *had* no shoemakers; which, *then*, I did not care much about, as it merely put back the clock of our history—throwing us into an earlier, and therefore, perhaps, into a more warlike stage of society. But, as the case stood now, this want of tailors, &c., showed clearly that the process of sitting down, so essential to the ennobling of the race, had not commenced. My brother, with an air of consolation, suggested that I might even now, without an hour's delay, compel the whole nation to sit down for six hours a day, which would always "make a beginning." But the truth would remain as before, viz., that I was the king of a people that had tails; and the slow, slow process by which, in a course of many centuries, their posterity might rub them off,—a hope of vintages never to be enjoyed by any generations that are yet heaving in sight,—*that* was to me the worst form of despair.

Still there was one resource: if I "didn't like it," meaning the state of things in Gombroon, I might "abdicate." Yes, I knew *that*. I might abdicate; and, once having cut the connection between myself and the poor abject islanders, I might seem to have no further interest in the degradation that affected them. After such a disruption between us, what was it to me if they had even three tails apiece? Ah, *that* was fine talking; but this connection with my poor subjects had grown up so slowly and so genially, in the midst of struggles so constant against the encroachments of my brother and his rascally people; we had suffered so much together; and the filaments connecting them with my heart were so aerially fine and fantastic, but for that reason so inseverable, that I abated nothing of my anxiety on their account; making this difference only in my legislation and administrative cares, that I pursued them more in a spirit of despondency, and retreated more shyly from communicating them. It was in vain that my brother counselled me to dress my people in the Roman toga, as the best means of concealing their ignominious appendages: if he meant this as comfort, it was none to me; the disgrace lay in the fact, not in its publication; and in my heart, though I continued to honor Lord Monboddo (whom I heard my guardian also daily delighting to honor) as a good Grecian, yet secretly I cursed the Aoristus Primus, as the indirect occasion of a misery which was not and could not be comprehended.

From this deep degradation of myself and my people, I was drawn off at intervals to contemplate a different mode of degradation affecting two persons, twin sisters, whom I saw intermittingly; sometimes once a week, sometimes frequently on each separate day. You have heard, reader, of pariahs. The pathos of that great idea possibly never reached you. Did it ever strike you how far that idea had extended? Do not fancy it peculiar to Hindostan. Before Delhi was, before Agra, or Lahore, might the pariah say, I was. The most interesting, if only as the most mysterious, race of ancient days, the Pelasgi, that overspread, in early times of Greece, the total Mediterranean,—a race distinguished for beauty and for intellect, and sorrowful beyond all power of man to read the cause that could lie deep enough for so imperishable an impression,—*they* were pariahs. The Jews that, in the twenty-eighth chapter of Deuteronomy, were cursed in a certain contingency with a sublimer curse than ever rang through the passionate wrath of prophecy, and that afterwards, in Jerusalem, cursed themselves, voluntarily taking on their own heads, and on the heads of their children's children forever and ever, the guilt of innocent blood,—*they* are pariahs to this hour. Yet for *them* there has ever shone a sullen light of hope. The gypsies, for whom no conscious or acknowledged hope burns through the mighty darkness that surrounds them,—they are pariahs of pariahs. Lepers were a race of mediaeval pariahs, rejected of men, that now have gone to rest. But travel into the forests of the Pyrenees, and there you will find their modern representatives in the Cagots. Are these Pyrenean Cagots pagans? Not at all, They are good Christians. Wherefore, then, that low door in the Pyrenean churches, through which the Cagots are forced to enter, and which, obliging them to stoop almost to the ground, is a perpetual memento of their degradation? Wherefore is it that men of pure Spanish blood will hold no intercourse with the Cagot? Wherefore is it that even the shadow of a Cagot, if it falls across a fountain, is held to have polluted that fountain? All this points to some dreadful taint of guilt, real or imputed, in ages far remote.[41]

But in ages far nearer to ourselves, nay, in our own generation and our own land, are many pariahs, sitting amongst us all, nay, oftentimes sitting (yet not recognized for what they really are) at good men's tables. How general is that sensuous dulness, that deafness of the heart, which the Scriptures attribute to human beings! "Having ears, they hear not; and, seeing, they do not understand." In the very act of facing or touching a dreadful object, they will utterly deny its existence. Men say to me daily, when I ask them, in passing, "Any thing in this morning's paper?" "O, no; nothing at all." And, as I never had any other answer, I am bound to suppose that there never *was* any thing in a daily newspaper; and, therefore, that the horrible burden of misery and of change, which a century accumulates as its *facit* or total result, has not been distributed at all amongst its thirty-six thou-

[41] The names and history of the Pyrenean Cagots are equally obscure. Some have supposed that, during the period of the Gothic warfare with the Moors, the Cagots were a Christian tribe that betrayed the Christian cause and interests at a critical moment. But all is conjecture. As to the name, Southey has somewhere offered a possible interpretation of it; but it struck me as far from felicitous, and not what might have been expected from Southey, whose vast historical research and commanding talent should naturally have unlocked this most mysterious of modern secrets, if any unlocking does yet lie within the resources of human skill and combining power, now that so many ages divide us from the original steps of the case. I may here mention, as a fact accidentally made known to myself, and apparently not known to Southey, that the Cagots, under a name very slightly altered, are found in France also, as well as Spain, and in provinces of France that have no connection at all with Spain.

sand five hundred and twenty-five days: every day, it seems, was separately a blank day, yielding absolutely nothing—what children call a deaf nut, offering no kernel; and yet the total product has caused angels to weep and tremble. Meantime, when I come to look at the newspaper with my own eyes, I am astonished at the misreport of my informants. Were there no other section in it than simply that allotted to the police reports, oftentimes I stand aghast at the revelations there made of human life and the human heart; at its colossal guilt, and its colossal misery; at the suffering which oftentimes throws its shadow over palaces, and the grandeur of mute endurance which sometimes glorifies a cottage. Here transpires the dreadful truth of what is going on forever under the thick curtains of domestic life, close behind us, and before us, and all around us. Newspapers are evanescent, and are too rapidly recurrent, and people see nothing great in what is familiar, nor can ever be trained to read the silent and the shadowy in what, for the moment, is covered with the babbling garrulity of daylight. I suppose now, that, in the next generation after that which is here concerned, had any neighbor of our tutor been questioned on the subject of a domestic tragedy, which travelled through its natural stages in a leisurely way, and under the eyes of good Dr. S——, he would have replied, "Tragedy! O, sir, nothing of the kind! You have been misled; the gentleman must lie under a mistake: perhaps it was in the next street." No, it was *not* in the next street; and the gentleman does not lie under a mistake, or, in fact, lie at all. The simple truth is, blind old neighbor, that you, being rarely in the house, and, *when* there, only in one particular room, saw no more of what was hourly going on than if you had been residing with the Sultan of Bokhara. But I, a child between seven and eight years old, had access every where. I was privileged, and had the *entree* even of the female apartments; one consequence of which was, that I put *this* and *that* together. A number of syllables, that each for itself separately might have meant nothing at all, did yet, when put together, through weeks and months, read for *my* eyes into sentences, as deadly and significant as *Tekel, upharsin*. And another consequence was, that, being, on account of my age, nobody at all, or very near it, I sometimes witnessed things that perhaps it had not been meant for any body to witness, or perhaps some half-conscious negligence overlooked my presence. "Saw things! What was it now? Was it a man at midnight, with a dark lantern and a six-barrel revolver?" No, *that* was not in the least like what I saw: it was a great deal more like what I will endeavor to describe. Imagine two young girls, of what exact age I really do not know, but apparently from twelve to fourteen, twins, remarkably plain in person and features, unhealthy, and obscurely reputed to be idiots. Whether they really were such was more than I knew, or could devise any plan for learning. Without dreaming of any thing unkind or uncourteous, my original impulse had been to say, "If you please, are you idiots?" But I felt that such a question had an air of coarseness about it, though, for my own part, I had long reconciled myself to being called an idiot by my brother. There was, however, a further difficulty: breathed as a gentle murmuring whisper, the question might possibly be reconciled to an indulgent ear as confidential and tender. Even to take a liberty with those you love is to show your trust in their affection; but, alas! these poor girls were deaf; and to have shouted out, "Are you idiots, if you please?" in a voice that would have rung down three flights of stairs, promised (as I felt, without exactly seeing why) a dreadful exaggeration to whatever incivility might, at any rate, attach to the question; and some *did* attach, that was clear, even if warbled through an air of Cherubini's and accompanied on the flute. Perhaps they were *not* idiots, and only seemed to be such from the slowness of apprehension naturally connected with deafness. That I saw them but seldom, arose from their peculiar position in the family. Their father had no private fortune; his income from the church was very slender; and, though considerably increased by the allowance made for us, his two pupils, still, in a great town, and with so large a family, it left him little room for luxuries. Consequently, he never had more than two servants, and at times only one. Upon this plea rose the scheme of the mother for employing these two young girls in menial offices of the household economy. One reason for that was, that she thus indulged her dislike for them, which she took no pains to conceal; and thus, also, she withdrew them from the notice of strangers. In this way, it happened that I saw them myself but at uncertain intervals. Gradually, however, I came to be aware of their forlorn condition, to pity them, and to love them. The poor twins were undoubtedly plain to the degree which is called, by unfeeling people, ugliness. They were also deaf, as I have said, and they were scrofulous; one of them was disfigured by the small pox; they had glimmering eyes, red, like the eyes of ferrets, and scarcely half open; and they did not walk so much as stumble along. There, you have the worst of them. Now, hear something on the other side. What first won my pity was, their affection for each other, united to their constant sadness; secondly, a notion which had crept into my head, probably derived from something said in my presence by elder people, that they were destined to an early death; and, lastly, the incessant persecutions of their mother. This lady belonged, by birth, to a more elevated rank than that of her husband, and she was remarkably well bred as regarded her manners. But she had probably a weak understanding; she was shrewish in her temper; was a severe economist; a merciless exactor of what she viewed as duty; and, in persecuting her two unhappy daughters, though she yielded blindly to her unconscious dislike of them, as creatures that disgraced her, she was not aware, perhaps, of ever having put forth more expressions of anger and severity than were absolutely required to rouse the constitutional torpor of her daughters' nature; and where disgust has once rooted itself, and been habitually expressed in tones of harshness, the mere sight of the hateful object mechanically calls forth the eternal tones of anger, without distinct consciousness or separate intention in the speaker. Loud speaking, besides, or even shouting, was required by the deafness of the two girls. From anger so constantly discharging its thunders, naturally they did not show open signs of recoiling; but that they felt it deeply, may be presumed from their sensibility to kindness. My own experience showed *that*; for, as often as I met them, we exchanged kisses; and my wish had always been to beg them, if they really *were* idiots, not to mind it, since I should not like them the less on that account. This wish of mine never came to utterance; but not the less they were aware, by my manner of salutation, that one person at least, amongst those who might be considered strangers, did not find any thing repulsive about them; and the pleasure they felt was expressed broadly upon their kindling faces.

Such was the outline of their position; and, that being explained, what I saw was simply this: it composed a silent and symbolic scene, a momentary interlude in dumb show, which interpreted itself, and settled forever in my recollection, as if it had prophesied and interpreted the event which soon followed. They were resting from toil, and both sitting down. This had lasted for perhaps ten or fifteen minutes. Suddenly from below stairs the voice of angry summons rang up to their ears. Both rose, in an instant, as if the echoing scourge of some avenging Tisiphone were uplifted above their heads; both opened their arms; flung them round each other's necks; and then, unclasping them, parted to their separate labors. This was my last rememberable interview with the two sisters; in a week both were corpses. They had died, I believe, of scarlatina, and very nearly at the same moment.

* * * * *

But surely it was no matter for grief, that the two scrofulous idiots were dead and buried. O, no! Call them idiots at your pleasure, serfs or slaves, strulbrugs[42] or pariahs; *their* case was certainly not worsened by being booked for places in the grave. Idiocy, for any thing I know, may, in that vast kingdom, enjoy a natural precedency; scrofula and leprosy may have some mystic privilege in a coffin; and the pariahs of the upper earth may form the aristocracy of the dead. That the idiots, real or reputed, were at rest,—that their warfare was accomplished,—might, if a man happened to know enough, be interpreted as a glorious festival. The sisters were seen no more upon staircases or in bed rooms, and deadly silence had succeeded to the sound of continual uproars. Memorials of *them* were none surviving on earth. Not *they* it was that furnished mementoes of themselves. The mother it was, the father it was—that mother who by persecution had avenged the wounds offered to her pride; that father, who had tolerated this persecution; she it was, he it was, that by the altered glances of her haunted eye, that by the altered character of his else stationary habits, had revived for me a spectacle, once real, of visionary twin sisters, moving forever up and down the stairs—sisters, patient, humble, silent, that snatched convulsively at a loving smile, or loving gesture, from a

---

[42] *"Strulbrugs."*—Hardly *strulbrugs,* will be the thought of the learned reader, who knows that *young* women could not be strulbrugs; since the true strulbrug was one who, from base fear of dying, had lingered on into an old age, omnivorous of every genial or vital impulse. The strulbrug of Swift (and Swift, being his horrid creator, ought to understand his own horrid creation) was a wreck, a shell, that had been burned hollow, and cancered by the fierce furnace of life. His clockwork was gone, or carious; only some miserable fragment of a pendulum continued to oscillate paralytically from mere incapacity of any thing so abrupt, and therefore so vigorous, as a decided HALT! However, the use of this dreadful word may be reasonably extended to the young who happen to have become essentially old in misery. Intensity of a suffering existence may compensate the want of extension; and a boundless depth of misery may be a transformed expression for a boundless duration of misery. The most aged person, to all appearance, that ever came under my eyes, was an infant—hardly eight months old. He was the illegitimate son of a poor idiot girl, who had herself been shamefully ill treated; and the poor infant, falling under the care of an enraged grandmother, who felt herself at once burdened and disgraced, was certainly not better treated. He was dying, when I saw him, of a lingering malady, with features expressive of frantic misery; and it seemed to me that he looked at the least three centuries old. One might have fancied him one of Swift's strulbrugs, that, through long attenuation and decay, had dwindled back into infancy, with one organ only left perfect—the organ of fear and misery.

child, as at some message of remembrance from God, whispering to them, "You are not forgotten"—sisters born apparently for the single purpose of suffering, whose trials, it is true, were over, and could not be repeated, but (alas for her who had been their cause!) could not be recalled. Her face grew thin, her eye sunken and hollow, after the death of her daughters; and, meeting her on the staircase, I sometimes fancied that she did not see me so much as something beyond me. Did any misfortune befall her after this double funeral? Did the Nemesis that waits upon the sighs of children pursue her steps? Not apparently: externally, things went well; her sons were reasonably prosperous; her handsome daughter—for she had a more youthful daughter, who really *was* handsome—continued to improve in personal attractions; and some years after, I have heard, she married happily. But from herself, so long as I continued to know her, the altered character of countenance did not depart, nor the gloomy eye, that seemed to converse with secret and visionary objects.

This result from the irrevocable past was not altogether confined to herself. It is one evil attached to chronic and domestic oppression, that it draws into its vortex, as unwilling, or even as loathing, coöperators, others who either see but partially the wrong they are abetting, or, in cases where they do see it, are unable to make head against it, through the inertia of their own nature, or through the coercion of circumstances. Too clearly, by the restless irritation of his manner for some time after the children's death, their father testified, in a language not fully, perhaps, perceived by himself, or meant to be understood by others, that to his inner conscience he also was not clear of blame. Had he, then, in any degree sanctioned the injustice which sometimes he must have witnessed? Far from it; he had been roused from his habitual indolence into energetic expressions of anger; he had put an end to the wrong, when it came openly before him. I had myself heard him say on many occasions, with patriarchal fervor, "Woman, they are your children, and God made them. Show mercy to *them*, as you expect it for yourself." But he must have been aware, that, for any three instances of tyrannical usage that fell under his notice, at least five hundred would escape it. That was the sting of the case—that was its poisonous aggravation. But with a nature that sought for peace before all things, in this very worst of its aggravations was found a morbid cure— the effectual temptation to wilful blindness and forgetfulness. The sting became the palliation of the wrong, and the poison became its anodyne. For together with the five hundred hidden wrongs, arose the necessity that they must be hidden. Could he be pinned on, morning, noon, and night, to his wife's apron? And if not, what else should he do by angry interferences at chance times than add special vindictive impulses to those of general irritation and dislike? Some truth there was in this, it cannot be denied: innumerable cases arise, in which a man the most just is obliged, in some imperfect sense, to connive at injustice; his chance experience must convince him that injustice is continually going on; and yet, in any attempt to intercept it or to check it, he is met and baffled by the insuperable obstacles of household necessities. Dr. S. therefore surrendered himself, as under a coercion that was none of *his* creating, to a passive acquiescence and a blindness that soothed his constitutional indolence; and he reconciled his feelings to a tyranny which he tolerated, under some self-flattering idea of submitting with resignation to a calamity that he suffered.

Some years after this, I read "Agamemnon" of Aeschylus; and then, in the prophetic horror with which Cassandra surveys the regal abode in Mycenae, destined to be the scene of murders so memorable through the long traditions of the Grecian stage, murders that, many centuries after all the parties to them—perpetrators, sufferers, avengers—had become dust and ashes, kindled again into mighty life through a thousand years upon the vast theaters of Athens and Rome, I retraced the horrors, not prophetic but memorial, with which I myself had invested that humble dwelling of Dr. S.; and read again, repeated in visionary proportions, the sufferings which there had darkened the days of people known to myself through two distinct successions—not, as was natural to expect, of parents first and then children, but inversely of children and parents. Manchester was not Mycenae. No, but by many degrees nobler. In some of the features most favorable to tragic effects, it was so; and wanted only these idealizing advantages for withdrawing mean details which are in the gift of distance and hazy antiquity. Even at that day Manchester was far larger, teeming with more and with stronger hearts; and it contained a population the most energetic even in the *modern* world—how much more so, therefore, by comparison with any race in *ancient* Greece, inevitably rendered effeminate by dependence too generally upon slaves. Add to this superior energy in Lanceshire, the immeasurably profounder feelings generated by the mysteries which stand behind Christianity, as compared with the shallow mysteries that stood behind paganism, and it would be easy to draw the inference, that, in the capacity for the infinite and impassioned, for horror and for pathos, Mycenae could have had no pretentions to measure herself against Manchester. Not that I had drawn such an inference myself. Why should I? there being nothing to suggest the points in which the two cities differed, but only the single one in which they agreed, viz., the dusky veil that overshadowed in both the noonday tragedies haunting their household recesses; which veil was raised only to the gifted eyes of a Cassandra, or to the eyes that, like my own, had experimentally become acquainted with them as facts. Pitiably mean is he that measures the relations of such cases by the scenical apparatus of purple and gold. That which never *has* been apparelled in royal robes, and hung with theatrical jewels, is but suffering from an accidental fraud, having the same right to them that any similar misery can have, or calamity upon an equal scale. These proportions are best measured from the fathoming ground of a real uncounterfeit sympathy.

I have mentioned already that we had four male guardians, (a fifth being my mother.) These four were B., E., G., and H. The two consonants, B. and G., gave us little trouble. G., the wisest of the whole band, lived at a distance of more than one hundred miles: him, therefore, we rarely saw; but B., living within four miles of Greenbay, washed his hands of us by inviting us, every now and then, to spend a few days at his house.

At this house, which stood in the country, there was a family of amiable children, who were more skilfully trained in their musical studies than at that day was usual. They sang the old English glees and madrigals, and correctly enough for me, who, having, even at that childish age, a preternatural sensibility to music, had also, as may be supposed, the most entire want of musical knowledge. No blunders could do much to mar *my* pleasure. There first I heard the concertos of Corelli; but also, which far more profoundly affected me, a few selections from Jomelli and Cimarosa. With Handel I had long been familiar, for the famous chorus singers of Lancashire sang continually at churches the most effective parts from his chief oratorios. Mozart was yet to come; for, except perhaps at the opera in London, even at this time, his music was most imperfectly diffused through England. But, above all, a thing which to my dying day I could never forget, at the house of this guardian I heard sung a long canon of Cherubini's. Forty years later I heard it again, and better sung; but at that time I needed nothing better. It was sung by four male voices, and rose into a region of thrilling passion, such as my heart had always dimly craved and hungered after, but which now first interpreted itself, as a physical possibility, to my ear.

My brother did not share my inexpressible delight; his taste ran in a different channel; and the arrangements of the house did not meet his approbation; particularly this, that either Mrs. B. herself, or else the governess, was always present when the young ladies joined our society, which my brother considered particularly vulgar, since natural propriety and decorum should have whispered to an old lady that a young gentleman might have "things" to say to her daughters which he could not possibly intend for the general ear of eavesdroppers—things tending to the confidential or the sentimental, which none but a shameless old lady would seek to participate; by that means compelling a young man to talk as loud as if he were addressing a mob at Charing Cross, or reading the Riot Act. There were other out-of-door amusements, amongst which a swing—which I mention for the sake of illustrating the passive obedience which my brother levied upon me, either through my conscience, as mastered by his doctrine of primogeniture, or, as in this case, through my sensibility to shame under his taunts of cowardice. It was a most ambitious swing, ascending to a height beyond any that I have since seen in fairs or public gardens. Horror was at my heart regularly as the swing reached its most aerial altitude; for the oily, swallow-like fluency of the swoop downwards threatened always to make me sick, in which it is probable that I must have relaxed my hold of the ropes, and have been projected, with fatal violence, to the ground. But, in defiance of all this miserable panic, I continued to swing whenever he tauntingly invited me. It was well that my brother's path in life soon ceased to coincide with my own, else I should infallibly have broken my neck in confronting perils which brought me neither honor nor profit, and in accepting defiances which, issue how they might, won self-reproach from myself, and sometimes a gayety of derision from *him*. One only of these defiances I declined. There was a horse of this same guardian B.'s, who always, after listening to Cherubini's music, grew irritable to excess; and, if any body mounted him, would seek relief to his wounded feelings in kicking, more or less violently, for an hour. This habit endeared him to my brother, who acknowledged to a propensity of the same amiable kind; protesting that an abstract desire of kicking seized him always after hearing good performers on particular instruments, especially the bagpipes. Of kicking? But of kicking what or *whom*? I fear of kicking the venerable public collectively, creditors without exception, but also as many of the debtors as might be found at large; doctors of medicine more especially, but with no absolute immunity for the majority of their patients; Jacobins, but not the less anti-Jacobins; every Calvinist, which seems reasonable; but then also, which is intolerable, every Arminian. Is philosophy able to account for this morbid affection, and particularly when it takes the restricted form (as sometimes it does, in the bagpipe case) of seeking furiously to kick the piper, instead of paying him? In this case, my brother was urgent with me to mount *en croupe* behind himself. But weak as I usually was, this proposal I resisted as an immediate suggestion of the fiend; for I had heard, and have since known proofs of it, that a horse, when he is ingeniously vicious, sometimes has the power, in lashing out, of curving round his hoofs, so as to lodge them, by way of indorsement, in the small of his rider's back; and, of course, he would have an advantage for such a purpose, in the case of a rider sitting on the crupper. That sole invitation I persisted in declining.

A young gentleman had joined us as a fellow-student under the care of our tutor. He was an only son; indeed, the only child of an amiable widow, whose love and hopes all centred in *him*. He was destined to inherit several separate estates, and a great deal had been done to spoil him by indulgent aunts; but his good natural disposition defeated all these efforts; and, upon joining us, he proved to be a very amiable boy, clever, quick at learning, and abundantly courageous. In the summer months, his mother usually took a house out in the country, sometimes on one side of Manchester, sometimes on another. At these rusticating seasons, he had often much farther to come than ourselves, and on that account he rode on horseback. Generally it was a fierce mountain pony that he rode; and it was worth while to cultivate the pony's acquaintance, for the sake of understanding the extent to which the fiend can sometimes incarnate himself in a horse. I do not trouble the reader with any account of his tricks, and drolleries, and scoundrelisms; but this I may mention, that he had the propensity ascribed many centuries ago to the Scandinavian horses for sharing and practically asserting his share in the angry passions of a battle. He would fight, or attempt to fight, on his rider's side, by biting, rearing, and suddenly wheeling round, for the purpose of lashing out when he found himself within kicking range.[43] This little monster was coal black; and, in virtue of his carcass, would not have seemed very formidable; but his head made amends—it was the head of a buffalo, or of a bison, and his vast jungle of mane was the mane of a lion. His eyes, by reason of this intolerable and unshorn mane, one did not often see, except as lights that sparkled in the rear of a thicket; but, once seen they were not easily forgotten, for their malignity was diabolic. A few miles more of less being a matter of indifference to one who was so well mounted, O. would sometimes ride out with us to the field of battle; and, by manoeuvring so as to menace the enemy of the flanks, in skirmishes he did good service. But at length came a day of pitched battle. The enemy had mustered in unusual strength, and would certainly have accomplished the usual result of putting us to flight with more than usual ease, but, under the turn which things took, their very numbers aided their overthrow, by deepening their confusion. O. had, on this occasion, accompanied us; and, as he had hitherto taken no very decisive

[43] This was a manoeuvre regularly taught to the Austrian cavalry in the middle of the last century; as a ready way of opening the doors of cottages.

part in the war, confining himself to distant "demonstrations," the enemy did not much regard his presence in the field. This carelessness threw them into a dense mass, upon which my brother's rapid eye saw instantly the opportunity offered for operating most effectually by a charge. O. saw it too; and, happening to have his spurs on, he complied cheerfully with my brother's suggestion. He had the advantage of a slight descent: the wicked pony went down "with a will;" his echoing hoofs drew the general gaze upon him; his head, his leonine mane, his diabolic eyes, did the rest; and in a moment the whole hostile array had broken, and was in rapid flight across the brick fields. I leave the reader to judge whether "Te Deum" would be sung on that night. A Gazette Extraordinary was issued; and my brother had really some reason for his assertion, "that in conscience he could not think of comparing Cannae to this smashing defeat;" since at Cannae many brave men had refused to fly—the consul himself, Terentius Varro, amongst them; but, in the present rout, there was no Terentius Varro—*every body* fled.

The victory, indeed, considered in itself, was complete. But it had consequences which we had not looked for. In the ardor of our conflict, neither my brother nor myself had remarked a stout, square-built man, mounted on an uneasy horse, who sat quietly in his saddle as spectator of the battle, and, in fact, as the sole non-combatant present. This man, however, had been observed by O., both before and after his own brilliant charge; and, by the description, there could be no doubt that it had been our guardian B., as also, by the description of the horse, we could as little doubt that he had been mounted on Cherubini. My brother's commentary was in a tone of bitter complaint, that so noble an opportunity should have been lost for strengthening O.'s charge. But the consequences of this incident were graver than we anticipated. A general board of our guardians, vowels and consonants, was summoned to investigate the matter. The origin of the feud, or "war," as my brother called it, was inquired into. As well might the war of Troy or the purser's accounts from the Argonautic expedition have been overhauled. Ancient night and chaos had closed over the "incunabula belli;" and that point was given up in despair. But what hindered a general pacification, no matter in how many wrongs the original dispute had arisen? Who stopped the way which led to peace? Not we, was our firm declaration; we were most pacifically inclined, and ever had been; we were, in fact, little saints. But the enemy could not be brought to any terms of accommodation. "That we will try," said the vowel amongst our guardians, Mr. E. He, being a magistrate, had naturally some weight with the proprietors of the cotton factory. The foremen of the several floors were summoned, and gave it as their humble opinion that we, the aristocratic party in the war, were as bad as the *sans culottes*—"not a pin to choose between us." Well, but no matter for the past: could any plan be devised for a pacific future? Not easily. The workspeople were so thoroughly independent of their employers, and so careless of their displeasure, that finally this only settlement was available as wearing any promise of permanence, viz., that we should alter our hours, so as not to come into collision with the exits or returns of the boys.

Under this arrangement, a sort of hollow armistice prevailed for some time; but it was beginning to give way, when suddenly an internal change in our own home put an end to the war forever. My brother, amongst his many accomplishments, was distinguished for his skill in drawing. Some of his sketches had been shown to Mr. De Loutherbourg, an academician well known in those days, esteemed even in these days, after he has been dead for forty or fifty years, and personally a distinguished favorite with the king, (George III.) He pronounced a very flattering opinion upon my brother's promise of excellence. This being known, a fee of a thousand guineas was offered to Mr. L. by the guardians; and finally that gentleman took charge of my brother as a pupil. Now, therefore, my brother, King of Tigrosylvania, scourge of Gombroon, separated from me; and, as it turned out, forever. I never saw him again; and, at Mr. De L.'s house in Hammersmith, before he had completed his sixteenth year, he died of typhus fever. And thus it happened that a little gold dust skilfully applied put an end to wars that else threatened to extend into a Carthaginian length. In one week's time

> "Hi motus animorum atque haec certamina tanta
> Pulveris exigui jactu compressa quiêrunt."

* * * * *

Here I had terminated this chapter, as at a natural pause, which, whilst shutting out forever my eldest brother from the reader's sight and from my own, necessarily at the same moment worked a permanent revolution in the character of my daily life. Two such changes, and both so abrupt, indicated imperiously the close of one era and the opening of another. The advantages, indeed, which my brother had over me in years, in physical activities of every kind, in decision of purpose, and in energy of will,—all which advantages, besides, borrowed a ratification from an obscure sense, on my part, of duty as incident to what seemed an appointment of Providence,—inevitably *had* controlled, and for years to come *would have* controlled, the free spontaneous movements of a contemplative dreamer like myself. Consequently, this separation, which proved an eternal one, and contributed to deepen my constitutional propensity to gloomy meditation, had for me (partly on that account, but much more through the sudden birth of perfect independence which so unexpectedly it opened) the value of a revolutionary experience. A new date, a new starting point, a redemption (as it might be called) into the golden sleep of halcyon quiet, after everlasting storms, suddenly dawned upon me; and not as any casual intercalation of holidays that would come to an end, but, for any thing that appeared to the contrary, as the perpetual tenor of my future career. No longer was the factory a Carthage for me: if any obdurate old Cato there were who found his amusement in denouncing it with a daily *"Delenda est,"* take notice, (I said silently to myself,) that I acknowledge no such tiger for a friend of mine. Nevermore was the bridge across the Irwell a bridge of sighs for me. And the meanest of the factory population—thanks be to their discrimination—despised my pretensions too entirely to waste a thought or a menace upon a cipher so abject.

This change, therefore, being so sudden and so total, ought to signalize itself externally by a commensurate break in the narrative. A new chapter, at the least, with a huge interspace of blank white paper, or even a new book, ought rightfully to solemnize so profound a revolution. And virtually it shall. But, according to the general agreement of antiquity, it is not felt as at all disturbing to the unity of that event which winds up the "Iliad," viz., the death of Hector, that Homer expands it circumstantially into the whole ceremonial of his funeral obsequies; and upon that same principle I—when looking back to this abrupt close of all connection with, my brother, whether in my character of major general or of potentate trembling daily for my people—am reminded that the very last morning of this connection had its own separate distinction from all other mornings, in a way that entitles it to its own separate share in the general commemoration. A shadow fell upon this particular morning as from a cloud of danger, that lingered for a moment over our heads, might seem even to muse and hesitate, and then sullenly passed away into distant quarters. It is noticeable that a danger which approaches, but wheels away,—which threatens, but finally forbears to strike,—is more interesting by much on a distant retrospect than the danger which accomplishes its mission. The Alpine precipice, down which many pilgrims have fallen, is passed without much attention; but that precipice, within one inch of which a traveller has passed unconsciously in the dark, first tracing his peril along the snowy margin on the next morning, becomes invested with an attraction of horror for all who hear the story. The dignity of mortal danger ever after consecrates the spot; and, in this particular case which I am now recalling, the remembrance of such a danger consecrates the day.

That day was amongst the most splendid in a splendid June: it was—to borrow the line of Wordsworth—

"One of those heavenly days which cannot die;"

and, early as it was at that moment, we children, all six of us that then survived, were already abroad upon the lawn. There were two lawns at Greenhay in the shrubbery that invested three sides of the house: one of these, which ran along one side of the house, extended to a little bridge traversed by the gates of entrance. The central gate admitted carriages: on each side of this was a smaller gate for foot passengers; and, in a family containing so many as six children, it may be supposed that often enough one or other of the gates was open; which, most fortunately, on this day was not the case. Along the margin of this side lawn ran a little brook, which had been raised to a uniform level, and kept up by means of a wear at the point where it quitted the premises; after which it resumed its natural character of wildness, as it trotted on to the little hamlet of Greenhill. This brook my brother was at one time disposed to treat as Remus treated the infant walls of Rome; but, on maturer thoughts, having built a fleet of rafts, he treated it more respectfully; and this morning, as will be seen, the breadth of the little brook did us "yeoman's service." Me at one time he had meant to put on board this fleet, as his man Friday; and I had a fair prospect of first entering life in the respectable character of supercargo. But it happened that the current carried his rafts and himself over the wear; which, he assured us, was no accident, but a lesson by way of practice in the art of contending with the rapids of the St. Lawrence and other Canadian streams. However, as the danger had been considerable, he was prohibited from trying such experiments with me. On the centre of the lawn stood my eldest surviving sister, Mary, and my brother William. Round *him*, attracted (as ever) by his inexhaustible opulence of thought and fun, stood, laughing and dancing, my youngest sister, a second Jane, and my youngest brother Henry, a posthumous child, feeble, and in his nurse's arms, but on this morning showing signs of unusual animation and of sympathy with the glorious promise of the young June day. Whirling round on his heel, at a little distance, and utterly abstracted from all around him, my next brother, Richard, he that had caused so much affliction by his incorrigible morals to the Sultan Amurath, pursued his own solitary thoughts—whatever those might be. And, finally, as regards myself, it happened that I was standing close to the edge of the brook, looking back at intervals to the group of five children and two nurse maids who occupied the centre of the lawn; time, about an hour before *our* breakfast, or about two hours before the world's breakfast,— *i.e.,* a little after seven,—when as yet in shady parts of the grounds the dazzling jewelry of the early dews had not entirely exhaled. So standing, and so occupied, suddenly we were alarmed by shouts as of some great mob manifestly in rapid motion, and probably, at this instant taking the right-angled turn into the lane connecting Greenhay with the Oxford Road. The shouts indicated hostile and headlong pursuit: within one minute another right-angled turn in the lane itself brought the uproar fully upon the ear; and it became evident that some imminent danger—of what nature it was impossible to guess—must be hastily nearing us. We were all rooted to the spot; and all turned anxiously to the gates, which happily seemed to be closed. Had this been otherwise, we should have had no time to apply any remedy whatever, and the consequences must probably have involved us all. In a few seconds, a powerful dog, not much above a furlong ahead of his pursuers, wheeled into sight. We all saw him pause at the gates; but, finding no ready access through the iron lattice work that protected the side battlements of the little bridge, and the pursuit being so hot, he resumed his course along the outer margin of the brook. Coming opposite to myself, he made a dead stop. I had thus an opportunity of looking him steadily in the face; which I did, without more fear than belonged naturally to a case of so much hurry, and to me, in particular, of mystery. I had never heard of hydrophobia. But necessarily connecting the furious pursuit with the dog that now gazed at me from the opposite side of the water, and feeling obliged to presume that he had made an assault upon somebody or other, I looked searchingly into his eyes, and observed that they seemed glazed, and as if in a dreamy state, but at the same time suffused with some watery discharge, while his mouth was covered with masses of white foam. He looked most earnestly at myself and the group beyond me; but he made no effort whatever to cross the brook, and apparently had not the energy to attempt it by a flying leap. My brother William, who did not in the least suspect the real danger, invited the dog to try his chance in a leap—assuring him that, if he succeeded, he would knight him on the spot. The temptation of a knighthood, however, did not prove sufficient. A very few seconds brought his pursuers within sight; and steadily, without sound or gesture of any kind, he resumed his flight in the only direction open to him, viz., by a field path across stiles to Greenhill. Half an hour later he would have met a bevy of children going to a dame's school, or carrying milk to rustic neighbors. As it was, the early morning kept the road clear in front. But behind immense was the body of agitated pursuers. Leading the chase came, probably, half a troop of light cavalry, all on foot, nearly all in their stable dresses, and armed generally with pitchforks, though some eight or ten carried carabines. Half mingled with these, and very little in the rear, succeeded a vast miscellaneous mob, that had gathered on the chase as it hurried through the purlieus of Deansgate, and all that populous suburb of Manchester. From some of these, who halted to recover breath, we obtained an explanation of the affair. About a mile and a half from Greenhay stood some horse barracks, occupied usually by an entire regiment of cavalry. A large dog—one of a multitude that haunted the barracks—had for some days manifested an increasing sullenness, snapping occasionally at dogs and horses, but finally at men. Upon this, he had been tied up; but in some way he had this morning liberated himself: two troop horses he had immediately bitten; and had made attacks upon several of the men, who fortunately parried these attacks by means of the pitchforks standing ready to their hands. On this evidence, coupled with the knowledge of his previous illness, he was summarily condemned as mad; and the general pursuit commenced, which brought all parties (hunters and game) sweeping so wildly past the quiet grounds of Greenhay. The sequel of the affair was this: none of the carabineers succeeded in getting a shot at the dog; in consequence of which, the chase lasted for 17 miles nominally; but, allowing for all the doublings and headings back of the dog, by computation for about 24; and finally, in a state of utter exhaustion, he was run into and killed, somewhere in Cheshire. Of the two horses whom he had bitten, both treated alike, one died in a state of furious hydrophobia some two months later, but the other (though the more seriously wounded of the two) manifested no symptoms whatever of constitutional derangement. And thus it happened that for me this general event of separation from my eldest brother, and the particular morning on which it occurred, were each for itself separately and equally memorable. Freedom won, and death escaped, almost in the same hour,—freedom from a yoke of such secret and fretful annoyance as none could measure but myself, and death probably through the fiercest of torments,—these double cases of deliverance, so sudden and so *unlooked for*, signalized by what heraldically might have been described as a two-headed memorial, the establishment of an *epoch* in my life. Not only was the chapter of INFANCY thus solemnly finished forever, and the record closed, but—which cannot often happen—the chapter was closed pompously and conspicuously by what the early printers through the 15th and 16th centuries would have called a bright and illuminated colophon.

CHAPTER III.
INFANT LITERATURE.

"The child," says Wordsworth, *"is father of the man;"* thus calling into conscious notice the fact, else faintly or not at all perceived, that whatsoever is seen in the maturest adult, blossoming and bearing fruit, must have preëxisted by way of germ in the infant. Yes; all that is now broadly emblazoned in the man once was latent—seen or not seen—as a vernal bud in the child. But not, therefore, is it true inversely, that all which preëxists in the child finds its development in the man. Rudiments and tendencies, which *might* have found, sometimes by accidental, *do* not find, sometimes under the killing frost of counter forces, *cannot* find, their natural evolution. Infancy, therefore, is to be viewed, not only as part of a larger world that waits for its final complement in old age, but also as a separate world itself; part of a continent, but also a distinct peninsula. Most of what he has, the grown-up man inherits from his infant self; but it does not follow that he always enters upon the whole of his natural inheritance.

Childhood, therefore, in the midst of its intellectual weakness, and sometimes even by means of this weakness, enjoys a limited privilege of strength. The heart in this season of life is apprehensive, and, where its sensibilities are profound, is endowed with a special power of listening for the tones of truth—hidden, struggling, or remote; for the knowledge being then narrow, the interest is narrow in the objects of knowledge; consequently the sensibilities are not scattered, are not multiplied, are not crushed and confounded (as afterwards they are) under the burden of that distraction which lurks in the infinite littleness of details.

That mighty silence which infancy is thus privileged by nature and by position to enjoy coöperates with another source of power,—almost peculiar to youth and youthful circumstances,—which Wordsworth also was the first person to notice. It belongs to a profound experience of the relations subsisting between ourselves and nature—that not always are we called upon to seek; sometimes, and in childhood above all, we are sought.

> "Think you, 'mid all this mighty sum
> Of things forever speaking,
> That noting *of itself* will come,
> But we must still be seeking?"

And again:—

> "Nor less I deem that there are powers
> Which *of themselves* our minds impress;

> And we can feed this mind of ours
> In a wise passiveness."

These cases of infancy, reached at intervals by special revelations, or creating for itself, through it privileged silence of heart, authentic whispers of truth, or beauty, or power, have some analogy to those other cases, more directly supernatural, in which (according to the old traditional faith of our ancestors) deep messages of admonition reached an individual through sudden angular deflexions of words, uttered or written, that had not been originally addressed to himself. Of these there were two distinct classes—those where the person concerned had been purely passive; and, secondly, those in which he himself had to some extent coöperated. The first class have been noticed by Cowper, the poet, and by George Herbert, the well-known pious brother of the still better-known infidel, Lord Herbert, (of Cherbury,) in a memorable sonnet; scintillations they are of what seems nothing less than providential lights oftentimes arresting our attention, from the very centre of what else seems the blank darkness of chance and blind accident. "Books lying open, millions of surprises,"—these are among the cases to which Herbert (and to which Cowper) alludes,—books, that is to say, left casually open without design or consciousness, from which some careless passer-by, when throwing the most negligent of glances upon the page, has been startled by a solitary word lying, as it were, in ambush, waiting and lurking for *him*, and looking at him steadily as an eye searching the haunted places of his conscience. These cases are in principle identical with those of the *second* class, where the inquirer himself coöperated, or was not entirely passive; cases such as those which the Jews called Bath-col, or daughter of a voice, (the echo augury,[44]) viz., where a man, perplexed in judgment and sighing for some determining counsel, suddenly heard from a stranger in some unlooked-for quarter words not meant for himself, but clamorously applying to the difficulty besetting him. In these instances, the mystical word, that carried a secret meaning and message to one sole ear in the world, was unsought for: *that* constituted its virtue and its divinity; and to arrange means wilfully for catching at such casual words, would have defeated the purpose. A well-known variety of augury, conducted upon this principle, lay in the "Sortes Biblicae," where the Bible was the oracular book consulted, and far more

---

[44] *"Echo augury."*—The daughter of a voice meant an echo, the original sound being viewed as the mother, and the reverberation, or secondary sound, as the daughter. Analogically, therefore, the direct and original meaning of any word, or sentence, or counsel, was the mother meaning but the secondary, or mystical meaning, created by the peculiar circumstances for one separate and peculiar ear, the daughter meaning, or echo meaning. This mode of augury, through secondary interpretations of chance words, is not, as some readers may fancy, an old, obsolete, or merely Jewish form of seeking the divine pleasure. About a century ago, a man so famous, and by repute so unsuperstitious, as Dr. Doddridge, was guided in a primary act of choice, influencing his whole after life, by a few chance words from a child reading aloud to his mother. With the other mode of augury viz., that noticed by Herbert, where not the ear but the eye presides, catching at some word that chance has thrown upon the eye in some book left open by negligence, or opened at random by one's self, Cowper, the poet, and his friend Newton, with scores of others that could be mentioned, were made acquainted through practical results and personal experiences that in *their* belief were memorably important.

extensively at a later period in the "Sortes Virgilianae,"[45] where the Aeneid was the oracle consulted.

Something analogous to these spiritual transfigurations of a word or a sentence, by a bodily organ (eye or ear) that has been touched with virtue for evoking the spiritual echo lurking in its recesses, belongs, perhaps, to every impassioned mind for the kindred result of forcing out the peculiar beauty, pathos, or grandeur that may happen to lodge (unobserved by ruder forms of sensibility) in special passages scattered up and down literature. Meantime, I wish the reader to understand that, in putting forward the peculiar power with which my childish eye detected a grandeur or a pomp of beauty not seen by others in some special instances, I am not arrogating more than it is lawful for every man the very humblest to arrogate, viz., an individuality of mental constitution so far applicable to special and exceptionable cases as to reveal in *them* a life and power of beauty which others (and sometimes which *all* others) had missed.

The first case belongs to the march (or boundary) line between my eighth and ninth years; the others to a period earlier by two and a half years. But I notice the latest case before the others, as it connected itself with a great epoch in the movement of my intellect. There is a dignity to every man in the mere historical assigning, if accurately he can assign, the first dawning upon his mind of any godlike faculty or apprehension, and more especially if that first dawning happened to connect itself with circumstances of individual or incommunicable splendor. The passage which I am going to cite first of all revealed to me the immeasurableness of the morally sublime. What was it, and where was it? Strange the reader will think it, and strange[46] it is, that a case of colossal sublimity should first emerge from such a writer as Phaedrus, the Aesopian fabulist. A great mistake it was, on the part of Doctor S., that the second book in the Latin language which I was

---

[45] "*Sortes Virgilianae.*" —Upon what principle could it have been that Virgil was adopted as the oracular fountain in such a case? An author so limited even as to bulk, and much more limited as regards compass of thought and variety or situation or character, was about the worst that pagan literature offered. But I myself once threw out a suggestion, which (if it is sound) exposes a motive in behalf of such a choice that would be likely to overrule the strong motives against it. That motive was, unless my whole speculation is groundless, the very same which led Dante, in an age of ignorance, to select Virgil as his guide in Hades. The seventh son of a seventh son has always traditionally been honored as the depositary of magical and other supernatural gifts. And the same traditional privilege attached to any man whose maternal grandfather was a sorcerer. Now, it happened that Virgil's maternal grandfather bore the name of *Magus*. This, by the ignorant multitude in Naples, &c., who had been taught to reverence his tomb, was translated from its true acception as a proper name, to a false one as an appellative: it was supposed to indicate, not the name, but the profession of the old gentleman. And thus, according to the belief of the *lazzaroni*, that excellent Christian, P. Virgilius Maro, had stepped by mere succession and right of inheritance into his wicked old grandpapa's infernal powers and knowledge, both of which he exercised, doubtless, for centuries without blame, and for the benefit of the faithful.

[46] "*Strange,*" &c.—Yet I remember that, in "The Pursuits of Literature,"—a satirical poem once universally famous,—the lines about Mnemosyne and her daughters, the Pierides, are cited as exhibiting matchless sublimity. Perhaps, therefore, if carefully searched, this writer may contain other jewels not yet appreciated.

summoned to study should have been Phaedrus—a writer ambitious of investing the simplicity, or rather homeliness, of Aesop with aulic graces and satiric brilliancy. But so it was; and Phaedrus naturally towered into enthusiasm when he had occasion to mention that the most intellectual of all races amongst men, viz., the Athenians, had raised a mighty statue to one who belonged to the same class in a social sense as himself, viz., the class of slaves, and rose above that class by the same intellectual power applying itself to the same object, viz., the moral apologue. These were the two lines in which that glory of the sublime, so stirring to my childish sense, seemed to burn as in some mighty pharos:—

> "Aesopo statuam ingentem posuere Attici;
> Servumque collocârunt eternâ in basi:"

A colossal statue did the Athenians raise to Aesop; and a poor pariah slave they planted upon an everlasting pedestal. I have not scrupled to introduce the word *pariah*, because in that way only could I decipher to the reader by what particular avenue it was that the sublimity which I fancy in the passage reached my heart. This sublimity originated in the awful chasm, in the abyss that no eye could bridge, between the pollution of slavery,—the being a man, yet without right or lawful power belonging to a man,—between this unutterable degradation and the starry altitude of the slave at that moment when, upon the unveiling of his everlasting statue, all the armies of the earth might be conceived as presenting arms to the emancipated man, the cymbals and kettledrums of kings as drowning the whispers of his ignominy, and the harps of all his sisters that wept over slavery yet joining in one choral gratulation to the regenerated slave. I assign the elements of what I did in reality feel at that time, which to the reader may seem extravagant, and by no means of what it was reasonable to feel. But, in order that full justice may be done to my childish self, I must point out to the reader another source of what strikes me as real grandeur. Horace, that exquisite master of the lyre, and that most shallow of critics, it is needless to say that in those days I had not read. Consequently I knew nothing of his idle canon, that the opening of poems must be humble and subdued. But my own sensibility told me how much of additional grandeur accrued to these two lines as being the immediate and all-pompous *opening* of the poem. The same feeling I had received from the crashing overture to the grand chapter of Daniel—"Belshazzar the king made a great feast to a thousand of his lords." But, above all, I felt this effect produced in the two opening lines of "Macbeth:"—

"WHEN—(but watch that an emphasis of thunder dwells upon that word 'when')—

> WHEN shall we three meet again—
> In thunder, lightning, or in rain?"

What an orchestral crash bursts upon the ear in that all-shattering question! And one syllable of apologetic preparation, so as to meet the suggestion of Horace, would have the effect of emasculating the whole tremendous alarum. The passage in Phaedrus differs thus far from that in "Macbeth," that the first line, simply stating a matter of fact, with no more of sentiment than belongs to the word *ingentem*, and to the antithesis between the two parties so enormously divided,—Aesop the slave and the Athenians,—must be read as an *appoggiatura*, or hurried note of introduction flying forward as if on wings to descend with the fury and weight of a thousand orchestras upon the immortal passion of the second line—"Servumque collocârunt ETERNA IN BASI." This passage from Phaedrus, which might be briefly designated *The Apotheosis of the Slave*, gave to me my first grand and jubilant sense of the moral sublime.

Two other experiences of mine of the same class had been earlier, and these I had shared with my sister Elizabeth. The first was derived from the "Arabian Nights." Mrs. Barbauld, a lady now very nearly forgotten,[47] then filled a large space in the public eye; in fact, as a writer for children, she occupied the place from about 1780 to 1805 which, from 1805 to 1835, was occupied by Miss Edgeworth. Only, as unhappily Miss Edgeworth is also now very nearly forgotten, this is to explain *ignotum per ingnotius*, or at least one *ignotum* by another *ignotum*. However, since it cannot be helped, this unknown and also most well-known woman, having occassion, in the days of her glory, to speak of the "Arabian Nights," insisted on Aladdin, and secondly, on Sinbad, as the two jewels of the collection. Now, on the contrary, my sister and myself pronounced Sinbad to be very bad, and Aladdin to be pretty nearly the worst, and upon grounds that still strike me as just. For, as to Sinbad, it is not a story at all, but a mere succession of adventures, having no unity of interest whatsoever; and in Aladdin, after the possession of the lamp has been once secured by a pure accident, the story ceases to move. All the rest is a mere record of upholstery: how this saloon was finished to-day, and that window on the next day, with no fresh incident whatever, except the single and transient misfortune arising out of the advantage given to the magician by the unpardonable stupidity of Aladdin in regard to the lamp. But, whilst my sister and I agreed in despising Aladdin so much as almost to be on the verge of despising the queen of all the bluestockings for so ill-directed a preference, one solitary section there was of that tale which was fixed and fascinated my gaze, in a degree that I never afterwards forgot, and did not at that time comprehend. The sublimity which it involved was mysterious and unfathomable as regarded any key which I possessed

---

[47] "*Very nearly forgotten.*"—Not quite however. It must be hard upon eighty or eighty-five years since she first commenced authorship—a period which allows time for a great deal of forgetting; and yet, in the very week when I am revising this passage, I observe advertised a new edition, attractively illustrated, of the "Evenings at Home"—a joint work of Mrs. Barbauld's and her brother's, (the elder Dr. Aikin.) Mrs. Barbauld was exceedingly clever. Her mimicry of Dr. Johnson's style was the best of all that exist. Her blank verse "Washing Day," descriptive of the discomforts attending a mistimed visit to a rustic friend, under the affliction of a family washing, is picturesquely circumstantiated. And her prose hymns for children have left upon my childish recollection a deep impression of solemn beauty and simplicity. Coleridge, who scattered his sneering compliments very liberally up and down the world, used to call the elder Dr. Aikin (allusively to Pope's well-known line—

"No craving void left aching in the breast")

an aching void; and the nephew, Dr. Arthur Aikin, by way of variety, *a void aching*; whilst Mrs. Barbault he designated as *that pleonasm of nakedness*; since, as if it were not enough to be *bare*, she was also *bald*.

for deciphering its law or origin. Made restless by the blind sense which I had of its grandeur, I could not for a moment succeed in finding out *why* it should be grand. Unable to explain my own impressions in "Aladdin," I did not the less obstinately persist in believing a sublimity which I could not understand. It was, in fact, one of those many important cases which elsewhere I have called *involutes* of human sensibility; combinations in which the materials of future thought or feeling are carried as imperceptibly into the mind as vegetable seeds are carried variously combined through the atmosphere, or by means of rivers, by birds, by winds, by waters, into remote countries. But the reader shall judge for himself. At the opening of the tale, a magician living in the central depths of Africa is introduced to us as one made aware by his secret art of an enchanted lamp endowed with supernatural powers available for the service of any man whatever who should get it into his keeping. But *there* lies the difficulty. The lamp is imprisoned in subterraneous chambers, and from these it can be released only by the hands of an innocent child. But this is not enough: the child must have a special horoscope written in the stars, or else a peculiar destiny written in his constitution, entitling him to take possession of the lamp. Where shall such a child be found? Where shall he be sought? The magician knows: he applies his ear to the earth; he listens to the innumerable sounds of footsteps that at the moment of his experiment are tormenting the surface of the globe; and amongst them all, at a distance of six thousand miles, playing in the streets of Bagdad, he distinguishes the peculiar steps of the child Aladdin. Through this mighty labyrinth of sounds, which Archimedes, aided by his *arenarius*, could not sum or disentangle, one solitary infant's feet are distinctly recognized on the banks of the Tigris, distant by four hundred and forty days' march of an army or a caravan. These feet, these steps, the sorcerer knows, and challenges in his heart as the feet, as the steps of that innocent boy, through whose hands only he could have a chance for reaching the lamp.

It follows, therefore, that the wicked magician exercises two demoniac gifts. First, he has the power to disarm Babel itself of its confusion. Secondly, after having laid aside as useless many billions of earthly sounds, and after having fastened his murderous[48] attention upon one insulated tread, he has the power, still more unsearchable, of reading in that hasty movement an alphabet of new and infinite symbols; for, in order that the sound of the child's feet should be significant and intelligible, that sound must open into a gamut of infinite compass. The pulses of the heart, the motions of the will, the phantoms of the brain must repeat themselves in secret hieroglyphics uttered by the flying footsteps. Even the inarticulate or brutal sounds of the globe must be all so many languages and ciphers that somewhere have their corresponding keys—have their own grammar and syntax; and thus the least things in the universe must be secret mirrors to the greatest. Palmistry has something of the same dark sublimity. All this, by rude efforts at explanation that mocked my feeble command of words, I communicated to my sister; and she, whose sympathy with my meaning was always so quick and true, often outrunning electrically my imperfect expressions, felt the passage in the same way as my-

---

[48] *"Murderous;"* for it was his intention to leave Aladdin immurred in the subterraneous chambers.

self,[49] but not, perhaps, in the same degree. She was much beyond me in velocity of apprehension and many other qualities of intellect. Here only, viz., on cases of the *dark* sublime, where it rested upon dim abstractions, and when no particular trait of *moral* grandeur came forward, we differed—differed, that is to say, as by more or by less. Else, even as to the sublime, and numbers of other intellectual questions which rose up to us from our immense reading, we drew together with a perfect fidelity of sympathy; and therefore I pass willingly from a case which exemplified one of our rare differences to another, not less interesting for itself, which illustrated (what occurred so continually) the intensity of our agreement.

No instance of noble revenge that ever I heard of seems so effective, if considered as applied to a noble-minded wrong doer, or in any case as so pathetic. From what quarter the story comes originally, was unknown to us at the time, and I have never met it since; so that possibly it may be new to the reader. We found it in a book written for the use of his own children by Dr. Percival, the physician who attended at Greenhay. Dr. P. was a literary man, of elegant tastes and philosophic habits. Some of his papers may be found in the "Manchester Philosophic Transactions;" and these I have heard mentioned with respect, though, for myself, I have no personal knowledge of them. Some presumption meantime arises in their favor from the fact that he had been a favored correspondent of the most eminent Frenchmen at that time who cultivated literature jointly with philosophy. Voltaire, Diderot, Maupertuis, Condorcet, and D'Alembert had all treated him with distinction; and I have heard my mother say that, in days before I or my sister could have known him, he attempted vainly to interest her in these French luminaries by reading extracts from their frequent letters; which, however, so far from reconciling her to the letters, or to the writers of the letters, had the unhappy effect of riveting her dislike (previously budding) to the doctor, as their reciever, and the *proneur* of their authors. The tone of the letters—hollow, insincere, and full of courtly civilities to Dr. P., as a known friend of *"the tolerance"* (meaning, of toleration)—certainly was not adapted to the English taste; and in this respect was specially offensive to my mother, as always assuming of the doctor, that, by mere necessity, as being a philosopher, he must be an infidel. Dr. P. left that question, I believe, *"in medio,"* neither assenting nor denying; and undoubtedly there was no particular call upon him to publish his confession of Faith before one who, in the midst of her rigourous politeness, suffered it to be too transparent that she did not like him. It is always a pity to see any thing lost and wasted, especially love; and, therefore, it was no subject for lamentation, that too probably the philosophic doctor did not enthusiastically like *her*. But, if really so, that made no difference in his feelings towards my sister and myself. Us he *did* like; and, as one proof of his regard, he presented us jointly with such of his works as could be supposed interesting to two young literati, whos combined ages made no more at this pe-

------

[49] The reader will not understand me as attributing to the Arabian originator of Aladdin all the sentiment of the case as I have endeavored to disentangle it. He spoke what he did not understand; for, as to sentiment of any kind, all Orientals are obtuse and impassive. There are other sublimities (some, at least) in the "Arabian Nights," which first become such—a gas that first kindles—when entering into combination with new elements in a Christian atmosphere.

riod than a baker's dozen. These presentation copies amount to two at the lest, both *octavoes*, and one of them entitled *The Father's*—something or other; what was it?—*Assistant*, perhaps. How much assistance the doctor might furnish to the fathers upon this wicked little planet, I cannot say. But fathers are a stubborn race; it is very little use trying to assist *them*. Better always to prescribe for the rising generation. And certainly the impression which he made upon us—my sister and myself—by the story in question was deep and memorable: my sister wept over it, and wept over the remembrance of it; and, not long after, carried its sweet aroma off with her to heaven; whilst I, for *my* part, have never forgotten it. Yet, perhaps, it is injudicious to have too much excited the reader's expectations; therefore, reader, understand what it is that you are invited to hear—not much of a story, but simply a noble sentiment, such as that of Louis XII, when he refused, as King of France, to avenge his own injuries as Duke of Orleans—such as that of Hadrian, when he said that a Roman imperator ought to die standing, meaning that Caesar, as the man who represented almighty Rome, should face the last enemy as the first in an attitude of unconquerable defiance. Here is Dr. Percival's story, which (again I warn you) will collapse into nothing at all, unless you yourself are able to dilate it by expansive sympathy with its sentiment.

A young officer (in what army, no matter) had so far forgotten himself, in a moment of irritation, as to strike a private soldier, full of personal dignity, (as sometimes happens in all ranks,) and distinguished for his courage. The inexorable laws of military discipline forbade to the injured soldier any practical redress—he could look for no retaliation by acts. Words only were at his command; and, in a tumult of indignation, as he turned away, the soldier said to his officer that he would "make him repent it." This, wearing the shape of a menace, naturally rekindled the officer's anger, and intercepted any disposition which might be rising within him towards a sentiment of remorse; and thus the irritation between the two young men grew hotter than before. Some weeks after this a partial action took place with the enemy. Suppose yourself a spectator, and looking down into a valley occupied by the two armies. They are facing each other, you see, in martial array. But it is no more than a skirmish which is going on; in the course of which, however, an occasion suddenly arises for a desperate service. A redoubt, which has fallen into the enemy's hands, must be recaptured at any price, and under circumstances of all but hopeless difficulty. A strong party has volunteered for the service; there is a cry for somebody to head them; you see a soldier step out from the ranks to assume this dangerous leadership; the party moves rapidly forward; in a few minutes it is swallowed up from your eyes in clouds of smoke; for one half hour, from behind these clouds, you receive hieroglyphic reports of bloody strife—fierce repeating signals, flashes from the guns, rolling musketry, and exulting hurrahs advancing or receding, slackening or redoubling. At length all is over; the redoubt has been recovered; that which was lost is found again; the jewel which had been made captive is ransomed with blood. Crimsoned with glorious gore, the wreck of the conquering party is relieved, and at liberty to return. From the river you see it ascending. The plume-crested officer in command rushes forward, with his left hand raising his hat in homage to the blackened fragments of what once was a flag, whilst, with his right hand, he seizes that of the leader, though no more than a private from the ranks. *That* perplexes you not; mystery you see none in *that*. For distinctions of order perish, ranks are confounded, "high and low" are words without a meaning, and to wreck goes every notion or feeling that divides the noble from the noble, or the brave man from the brave. But wherefore is it that now, when suddenly they wheel into mutual recognition, suddenly they pause? This soldier, this officer—who are they? O reader! once before they had stood face to face—the soldier it is that was struck; the officer it is that struck him. Once again they are meeting; and the gaze of armies is upon them. If for a moment a doubt divides them, in a moment the doubt has perished. One glance exchanged between them publishes the forgiveness that is sealed forever. As one who recovers a brother whom he had accounted dead, the officer sprang forward, threw his arms around the neck of the soldier, and kissed him, as if he were some martyr glorified by that shadow of death from which he was returning; whilst, on *his* part, the soldier, stepping back, and carrying his open hand through the beautiful motions of the military salute to a superior, makes this immortal answer—that answer which shut up forever the memory of the indignity offered to him, even whilst for the last time alluding to it: "Sir," he said, "I told you before that I would *make you repent it.*"

CHAPTER IV.

THE FEMALE INFIDEL.

At the time of my father's death, I was nearly seven years old. In the next four years, during which we continued to live at Greenhay, nothing memorable occurred, except, indeed, that troubled parenthesis in my life which connected me with my brother William,—this certainly was memorable to myself,—and, secondly, the visit of a most eccentric young woman, who, about nine years later, drew the eyes of all England upon herself by her unprincipled conduct in an affair affecting the life of two Oxonian undergraduates. She was the daughter of Lord Le Despencer, (known previously as Sir Francis Dashwood;) and at this time (meaning the time of her visit to Greenhay) she was about twenty-two years old, with a face and a figure classically beautiful, and with the reputation of extraordinary accomplishments; these accomplishments being not only eminent in their degree, but rare and interesting in their kind. In particular, she astonished every person by her *impromptu* performances on the organ, and by her powers of disputation. These last she applied entirely to attacks upon Christianity; for she openly professed infidelity in the most audacious form; and at my mother's table she certainly proved more than a match for all the clergymen of the neighboring towns, some of whom (as the most intellectual persons of that neighborhood) were daily invited to meet her. It was a mere accident which had introduced her to my mother's house. Happening to hear from my sister Mary's governess[50] that she and

---

[50] *"My sister Mary's governess."*—This governess was a Miss Wesley, niece to John Wesley, the founder of Methodism. And the mention of *her* recalls to me a fact, which was recently revived and misstated by the whole newspaper press of the island. It had been always known that some relationship existed between the Wellesleys and John Wesley. Their names had, in fact, been originally the same; and the Duke of Wellington himself, in the earlier part of his career, when sitting in the Irish House of Commons, was always known to the Irish journals as Captain Wesley. Upon this arose a natural belief that the aristocratic branch of the house had improved the name into Wellesley. But the true process of change had been precisely the other way. Not Wesley had been expanded into Wellesley, but, inversely, Wellesley had been contracted by household usage into Wesley. The name must have been *Wellesley* in its earliest stage, since it was founded upon a connection with Wells Cathedral, It had obeyed the same process as prevails in many hundreds of other names: St. Leger, for instance, is always pronounced as if written Sillinger; Cholmondeley as Chumleigh; Marjoribanks as Marchbanks; and the illustrious name of Cavendish was for centuries familiarly pronounced Candish; and Wordsworth has even introduced this name into verse so as to compel the reader, by a metrical coercion, into calling it Candish. Miss Wesley's family had great musical sensibility and skill. This led the family into giving musical parties, at which was constantly to be found Lord Mornington, the father of the Duke

her pupil were going on a visit to an old Catholic family in the county of Durham, (the family of Mr. Swinburne, who was known advantageously to the public by his "Travels in Spain and Sicily," &c.,) Mrs. Lee, whose education in a French convent, aided by her father's influence, had introduced her extensively to the knowledge of Catholic families in England land, and who had herself an invitation to the same house at the same time, wrote to offer the use of her carriage to convey all three — *i.e.*, herself, my sister, and her governess — to Mr. Swinburne's. This naturally drew forth from my mother an invitation to Greenhay; and to Greenhay she came. On the imperial of her carriage, and else-where, she described herself as the *Hon.* Antonina Dashwood Lee. But, in fact, being only the illegitimate daughter of Lord Le Despencer, she was not entitled to that designation. She had, however, received a bequest even more enviable from her father, viz., not less than forty-five thousand pounds. At a very early age, she had married a young Oxonian, distinguished for nothing but a very splendid person, which had procured him the distinguishing title of *Handsome Lee;* and from him she had speedily separated, on the agreement of dividing the fortune.

My mother little guessed what sort of person it was whom she had asked into her family. So much, however, she had understood from Miss Wesley — that Mrs. Lee was a bold thinker; and that, for a woman, she had an astonishing command of theological learning. This it was that suggested the clerical invitations, as in such a case likely to furnish the most appropriate society. But this led to a painful result. It might easily have happened that a very learned clergyman should not specially have qualified himself for the service of a theological tournament; and my mother's range of acquaintance was not very extensive amongst the clerical body. But of these the two leaders, as regarded public consideration, were Mr. H— —, my guardian, and Mr. Clowes, who for more than fifty years officiated as rector of St. John's Church in Manchester. In fact, the *golden*[51] jubilee of his pastoral connection with St. John's was celebrated many years after with much demonstrative expression of public sympathy on the part of universal Manchester — the most important city in the island next after London. No men could have been found who were less fitted to act as champions in a duel on behalf of Christianity. Mr. H— — <u>was dreadfully commonplace; dull, dreadfully dull; and, by the</u> necessity of his

of Wellington. For these parties it was, as Miss Wesley informed me, that the earl composed his most celebrated glee.

Here also it was, or in similar musical circles gathered about himself by the first Lord Mornington, that the Duke of Wellington had formed and cultivated his unaffected love for music of the highest class, *i.e.*, for the impassioned music of the serious opera. And it occurs to me as highly probable, that Mrs. Lee's connection with the Wesleys, through which it was that she became acquainted with my mother, must have rested upon the common interest which she and the Wesleys had in the organ and in the class of music suited to that instrument. Mrs. Lee herself was an improvisatrice of the first class upon the organ; and the two brothers of Miss Wesley, Samuel and Charles, ranked for very many years as the first organists in Europe.

[51] *"The golden jubilee."* —This, in Germany, is used popularly as a technical expression: a married couple, when celebrating the fiftieth anniversary of their marriage day, are said to keep their *golden* jubilee; but on the twenty-fifth anniversary they have credit only for a *silver* jubilee.

nature, incapable of being in deadly earnest, which his splendid antagonist at all times was. His encounter, therefore, with Mrs. Lee presented the distressing spectacle of an old, toothless, mumbling mastiff, fighting for the household to which he owed allegiance against a young leopardess fresh from the forests. Every touch from *her*, every velvety pat, drew blood. And something comic mingled with what my mother felt to be paramount tragedy. Far different was Mr. Clowes: holy, visionary, apostolic, he could not be treated disrespectfully. No man could deny him a qualified homage. But for any polemic service he wanted the taste, the training, and the particular sort of erudition required. Neither would such advantages, if he had happened to possess them, have at all availed him in a case like this. Horror, blank horror, seized him upon seeing a woman, a young woman, a woman of captivating beauty, whom God had adorned so eminently with gifts of person and of mind, breathing sentiments that to him seemed fresh from the mintage of hell. He could have apostrophized her (as long afterwards he himself told me) in the words of Shakspeare's Juliet—

"Beautiful tyrant! fiend angelical!"

for he was one of those who never think of Christianity as the subject of defence. Could sunshine, could light, could the glories of the dawn call for defence? Not as a thing to be defended, but as a thing to be interpreted, as a thing to be illuminated, did Christianity exist for *him*. He, therefore, was even more unserviceable as a champion against the deliberate impeacher of Christian evidences than my reverend guardian.

Thus it was that he himself explained his own position in after days, when I had reached my sixteenth year, and visited him upon terms of friendship as close as can ever have existed between a boy and a man already gray headed. Him and his noiseless parsonage, the pensive abode for sixty years of religious revery and anchoritish self-denial, I have described farther on. In some limited sense he belongs to our literature, for he was, in fact, the introducer of Swedenborg to this country; as being himself partially the translator of Swedenborg; and still more as organizing a patronage to other people's translations; and also, I believe, as republishing the original Latin works of Swedenborg. To say *that* of Mr. Clowes, was, until lately, but another way of describing him as a delirious dreamer. At present, (1853,) I presume the reader to be aware that Cambridge has, within the last few years, unsettled and even revolutionized our estimates of Swedenborg as a philosopher. That man, indeed, whom Emerson ranks as one amongst his inner consistory of intellectual potentates cannot be the absolute trifler that Kant, (who knew him only by the most trivial of his pretensions,) eighty years ago, supposed him. Assuredly, Mr. Clowes was no trifler, but lived habitually a life of power, though in a world of religious mysticism and of apocalyptic visions. To him, being such a man by nature and by habit, it was in effect the lofty Lady Geraldine from Coleridge's "Christabel" that stood before him in this infidel lady. A magnificent witch she was, like the Lady Geraldine; having the same superb beauty; the same power of throwing spells over the ordinary gazer; and yet at intervals unmasking to some solitary, unfascinated spectator the same dull blink of a snaky eye; and revealing, through the most fugitive of gleams, a traitress couchant beneath what

else to all others seemed the form of a lady, armed with incomparable pretensions—one that was

> "Beautiful exceedingly,
> Like a lady from a far countrie."

The scene, as I heard it sketched long years afterwards by more than one of
those who had witnessed it, was painful in excess. And the shock given to my
mother was memorable. For the first and the last time in her long and healthy life,
she suffered an alarming nervous attack. Partly this arose from the conflict between herself in the character of hostess, and herself as a loyal daughter of Christian faith; she shuddered, in a degree almost incontrollable and beyond her power
to dissemble, at the unfeminine intrepidity with which "the leopardess" conducted her assaults upon the sheepfolds of orthodoxy; and partly, also, this internal
conflict arose from concern on behalf of her own servants, who waited at dinner,
and were inevitably liable to impressions from what they heard. My mother, by
original choice, and by early training under a very aristocratic father, recoiled as
austerely from all direct communication with her servants as the Pythia at Delphi
from the attendants that swept out the temple. But not the less her conscience, in
all stages of her life, having or *not* having any special knowledge of religion, acknowledged a pathetic weight of obligation to remove from her household all confessedly corrupting influences. And here was one which she could not remove.
What chiefly she feared, on behalf of her servants, was either, 1st, the danger from
the simple *fact*, now suddenly made known to them, that it was possible for a person unusually gifted to deny Christianity; such a denial and haughty abjuration
could not but carry itself more profoundly into the reflective mind, even of servants, when the arrow came winged and made buoyant by the gay feathering of so
many splendid accomplishments. This general fact was appreciable by those who
would forget, and never could have understood, the particular arguments of the
infidel. Yet, even as regarded these particular arguments, 2dly, my mother feared
that some one—brief, telling, and rememberable—might be singled out from the
rest, might transplant itself to the servants' hall, and take root for life in some mind
sufficiently thoughtful to invest it with interest, and yet far removed from any
opportunities, through books or society, for disarming the argument of its sting.
Such a danger was quickened by the character and pretensions of Mrs. Lee's foot-
man, who was a daily witness, whilst standing behind his mistress's chair at dinner, to the confusion which she carried into the hostile camp, and might be supposed to renew such discussions in the servants' hall with singular advantages for
a favorable attention. For he was a showy and most audacious Londoner, and
what is *technically* known in the language of servants' hiring offices as "a man of
figure." He might, therefore, be considered as one dangerously armed for shaking
religious principles, especially amongst the female servants. Here, however, I believe that my mother was mistaken. Women of humble station, less than any other
class, have any tendency to sympathize with boldness that manifests itself in
throwing off the yoke of religion. Perhaps a natural instinct tells them that levity
of that nature will pretty surely extend itself contagiously to other modes of conscientious obligation; at any rate, my own experience would warrant me in doubt-

ing whether any instance were ever known of a woman, in the rank of servant, regarding infidelity or irreligion as something brilliant, or interesting, or in any way as favorably distinguishing a man. Meantime, this conscientious apprehension on account of the servants applied to contingencies that were remote. But the pity on account of the poor lady herself applied to a danger that seemed imminent and deadly. This beautiful and splendid young creature, as my mother knew, was floating, without anchor or knowledge of any anchoring grounds, upon the unfathomable ocean of a London world, which, for *her*, was wrapped in darkness as regarded its dangers, and thus for *her* the chances of shipwreck were seven times multiplied. It was notorious that Mrs. Lee had no protector or guide, natural or legal. Her marriage had, in fact, instead of imposing new restraints, released her from old ones. For the legal separation of Doctors' Commons—technically called a divorce simply *à mensâ et thoro*, (from bed and board,) and not *à vinculo matrimonii* (from the very tie and obligation of marriage)—had removed her by law from the control of her husband; whilst, at the same time, the matrimonial condition, of course, enlarged that liberty of action which else is unavoidably narrowed by the reserve and delicacy natural to a young woman, whilst yet unmarried. Here arose one peril more; and, 2dly, arose this most unusual aggravation of that peril—that Mrs Lee was deplorably ignorant of English life; indeed, of life universally. Strictly speaking, she was even yet a raw, untutored novice, turned suddenly loose from the twilight of a monastic seclusion. Under any circumstances, such a situation lay open to an amount of danger that was afflicting to contemplate. But one dreadful exasperation of these fatal auguries lay in the peculiar *temper* of Mrs. Lee, as connected with her infidel thinking. Her nature was too frank and bold to tolerate any disguise; and my mother's own experience had now taught her that Mrs. Lee would not be content, to leave to the random call of accident the avowal of her principles. No passive or latent spirit of freethinking was hers—headlong it was, uncompromising, almost fierce, and regarding no restraints of place or season. Like Shelley, some few years later, whose day she would have gloried to welcome, she looked upon her principles not only as conferring rights, but also as imposing duties of active proselytism. From this feature in her character it was that my mother foresaw an *instant* evil, which she urged Miss Wesley to press earnestly on her attention, viz., the inevitable alienation of all her female friends. In many parts of the continent (but too much we are all in the habit of calling by the wide name of "the continent," France, Germany, Switzerland, and Belgium) my mother was aware that the most flagrant proclamation of infidelity would not stand in the way of a woman's favorable reception into society. But in England, at that time, this was far otherwise. A display such as Mrs. Lee habitually forced upon people's attention would at once have the effect of banishing from her house all women of respectability. She would be thrown upon the society of *men*—bold and reckless, such as either agreed with herself, or, being careless on the whole subject of religion, pretended to do so. Her income, though diminished now by the partition with Mr. Lee, was still above a thousand per annum; which, though trivial for any purpose of display in a place so costly as London, was still important enough to gather round her unprincipled adventurers, some of whom might be noble enough to obey no attraction but that which lay in her marble beauty, in her Athenian grace and eloquence, and the wild, impassioned nature of her accomplishments. By her acting, her dancing, her conversation, her musical improvisations, she was qualified to attract the most intellectual men; but baser attractions would exist for baser men; and my mother urged Miss Wesley, as one whom Mrs. Lee admitted to her confidence, above all things to act upon her pride by forewarning her that such men, in the midst of lip homage to her charms, would be sure to betray its hollowness by declining to let their wives and daughters visit her. Plead what excuses they would, Mrs. Lee might rely upon it, that the true ground for this insulting absence of female visitors would be found to lie in her profession of infidelity. This alienation of female society would, it was clear, be precipitated enormously by Mrs. Lee's frankness. A result that might by a dissembling policy have been delayed indefinitely, would now be hurried forward to an immediate crisis. And in this result went to wreck the very best part of Mrs. Lee's securities against ruin.

It is scarcely necessary to say, that all the evil followed which had been predicted, and through the channels which had been predicted. Some time was required on so vast a stage as London to publish the facts of Mrs. Lee's free-thinking—that is, to publish it as a matter of systematic purpose. Many persons had at first made a liberal allowance for her, as tempted by some momentary impulse into opinions that she had not sufficiently considered, and might forget as hastily as she had adopted them. But no sooner was it made known as a settled fact, that she had deliberately dedicated her energies to the interests of an anti-Christian system, and that she hated Christianity, than the whole body of her friends within the pale of social respectability fell away from her, and forsook her house. To *them* succeeded a clique of male visitors, some of whom were doubtfully respectable, and others (like Mr. Frend, memorable for his expulsion from Cambridge on account of his public hostility to Trinitarianism) were distinguished by a tone of intemperate defiance to the spirit of English society. Thrown upon such a circle, and emancipated from all that temper of reserve which would have been impressed upon her by habitual anxiety for the good opinion of virtuous and high-principled women, the poor lady was tempted into an elopement with two dissolute brothers; for what ultimate purpose on either side, was never made clear to the public. Why a lady should elope from her own house, and the protection of her own servants, under whatever impulse, seemed generally unintelligible. But apparently it was precisely this protection from her own servants which presented itself to the brothers in the light of an obstacle to their objects. What these objects might ultimately be, I do not *entirely* know; and I do not feel myself authorized, by any thing which of my own knowledge I know, to load either of them with mercenary imputations. One of them (the younger) was, or fancied himself, in love with Mrs. Lee. It was impossible for him to marry her; and possibly he may have fancied that in some rustic retirement, where the parties were unknown, it would be easier than in London to appease the lady's scruples in respect to the sole mode of connection which the law left open to them. The frailty of the will in Mrs. Lee was as manifest in this stage of the case as subsequently, when she allowed herself to be over-clamored by Mr. Lee and his friends into a capital prosecution of the brothers. After she had once allowed herself to be put into a post chaise, she was persuaded to believe (and such was her ignorance of English society, that possibly she *did* believe) herself through the rest of the journey liable at any moment to summary coercion in the case of attempting any resistance. The brothers and herself left London in the evening. Consequently, it was long after midnight when the party halted at a town in Gloucestershire, two stages beyond Oxford. The younger gentleman then persuaded her, but (as she alleged) under the impression on her part that resistance was unavailing, and that the injury to her reputation was by this time irreparable, to allow of his coming to her bed room. This was perhaps not entirely a fraudulent representation in Mrs. Lee. The whole circumstances of the case made it clear, that, with any decided opening for deliverance, she would have caught at it; and probably would again, from wavering of mind, have dallied with the danger.

Perhaps at this point, having already in this last paragraph shot ahead by some nine years of the period when she visited Greenhay, allowing myself this license in order to connect my mother's warning through Miss Wesley with the practical sequel of the case, it may be as well for me to pursue the arrears of the story down to its final incident. In 1804, at the Lent Assizes for the county of Oxford, she appeared as principal witness against two brothers, L—t G—n, and L—n G—n, on a capital charge of having forcibly carried her off from her own house in London, and afterwards of having, at some place in Gloucestershire, by collusion with each other and by terror, enabled one of the brothers to offer the last violence to her person. The circumstantial accounts published at the time by the newspapers were of a nature to conciliate the public sympathy altogether to the prisoners; and the general belief accorded with what was, no doubt, the truth—that the lady had been driven into a false accusation by the overpowering remonstrances of her friends, joined, in this instance, by her husband, all of whom were willing to believe, or willing to have it believed by the public, that advantage had been taken of her little acquaintance with English usages. I was present at the trial. The court opened at eight o'clock in the morning; and such was the interest in the case, that a mob, composed chiefly of gownsmen, besieged the doors for some time before the moment of admission. On this occasion, by the way, I witnessed a remarkable illustration of the profound obedience which Englishmen under all circumstances pay to the law. The constables, for what reason I do not know, were very numerous and very violent. Such of us as happened to have gone in our academic dress had our caps smashed in two by the constables' staves; *why*, it might be difficult for the officers to say, as none of us were making any tumult, nor had any motive for doing so, unless by way of retaliation. Many of these constables were bargemen or petty tradesmen, who in their ex-official character had often been engaged in rows with undergraduates, and usually had had the worst of it. At present, in the service of the blindfold goddess, these equitable men were no doubt taking out their vengeance for past favors. But under all this wanton display of violence, the gownsmen practised the severest forbearance. The pressure from behind made it impossible to forbear pressing ahead; crushed, you were obliged to crush; but, beyond that, there was no movement or gesture on our part to give any colorable warrant to the brutality of the officers. For nearly a whole hour, I saw this expression of reverence to the law triumphant over all provocations. It may be presumed, that, to prompt so much crowding, there must have been some commensurate interest. There was so, but that interest was not at all in Mrs. Lee. She was entirely unknown; and even by reputation or rumor, from so vast a wilderness as London, neither her beauty nor her intellectual pretensions had travelled down to Oxford. Possibly, in each section of 300 men, there might be one individual whom accident had brought acquainted, as it had myself, with her extraordinary endowments. But the general and academic interest belonged exclusively to the accused. They were both Oxonians—one belonging to University College, and the other, perhaps, to Baliol; and, as they had severally taken the degree of A. B., which implies a residence of *at least* three years, they were pretty extensively known. But, known or not known personally, in virtue of the *esprit de corps*, the accused parties would have benefited in any case by a general brotherly interest. Over and above which, there was in this case the interest attached to an almost unintelligible accusation. A charge of personal violence, under the roof of a respectable English posting house, occupied always by a responsible master and mistress, and within call at every moment of numerous servants,—what could that mean? And, again, when it became understood that this violence was alleged to have realized itself under a delusion, under a preoccupation of the victim's mind, that resistance to it was hopeless, how, and under what profound ignorance of English society, had such a preoccupation been possible? To the accused, and to the incomprehensible accusation, therefore, belonged the whole weight of the interest; and it was a very secondary interest indeed, and purely as a reflex interest from the main one, which awaited the prosecutress. And yet, though so little curiosity "awaited" her, it happened of necessity that, within a few moments after her first coming forward in the witness box, she had created a separate one for herself—first, through her impressive appearance; secondly, through the appalling coolness of her answers. The trial began, I think, about nine o'clock in the morning; and, as some time was spent on the examination of Mrs. Lee's servants, of postilions, hostlers, &c., in pursuing the traces of the affair from London to a place seventy miles north of London, it was probably about eleven in the forenoon before the prosecutress was summoned. My heart throbbed a little as the court lulled suddenly into the deep stillness of expectation, when that summons was heard: "Rachael Frances Antonina Dashwood Lee" resounded through all the passages; and immediately in an adjoining anteroom, through which she was led by her attorney, for the purpose of evading the mob that surrounded the public approaches, we heard her advancing steps. Pitiable was the humiliation expressed by her carriage, as she entered the witness box. Pitiable was the change, the world of distance, between this faltering and dejected accuser, and that wild leopardess that had once worked her pleasure amongst the sheepfolds of Christianity, and had cuffed my poor guardian so unrelentingly, right and left, front and rear, when he attempted the feeblest of defences. However, she was not long exposed to the searching gaze of the court and the trying embarrassments of her situation. A single question brought the whole investigation to a close. Mrs. Lee had been sworn. After a few questions, she was suddenly asked by the counsel for the defence whether she believed in the Christian religion? Her answer was brief and peremptory, without distinction or circumlocution—*No.* Or, perhaps, not in God? Again she replied, *No;* and again her answer was prompt and *sans phrase.* Upon this the judge declared that he could not permit the trial to proceed. The jury had heard what the witness said:

she only could give evidence upon the capital part of the charge; and she had openly incapacitated herself before the whole court. The jury instantly acquitted the prisoners. In the course of the day I left my name at Mrs. Lee's lodgings; but her servant assured me that she was too much agitated to see any body till the evening. At the hour assigned I called again. It was dusk, and a mob had assembled. At the moment I came up to the door, a lady was issuing, muffled up, and in some measure disguised. It was Mrs. Lee. At the corner of an adjacent street a post chaise was drawn up. Towards this, under the protection of the attorney who had managed her case, she made her way as eagerly as possible. Before she could reach it, however, she was detected; a savage howl was raised, and a rush made to seize her. Fortunately, a body of gownsmen formed round her, so as to secure her from personal assault: they put her rapidly into the carriage; and then, joining the mob in their hootings, sent off the horses at a gallop. Such was the mode of her exit from Oxford.

Subsequently to this painful collision with Mrs. Lee at the Oxford Assizes, I heard nothing of her for many years, excepting only this—that she was residing in the family of an English clergyman distinguished for his learning and piety. This account gave great pleasure to my mother—not only as implying some chance that Mrs. Lee might be finally reclaimed from her unhappy opinions, but also as a proof that, in submitting to a rustication so mortifying to a woman of her brilliant qualifications, she must have fallen under some influences more promising for her respectability and happiness than those which had surrounded her in London. Finally, we saw by the public journals that she had written and published a book. The title I forget; but by its subject it was connected with political or social philosophy. And one eminent testimony to its merit I myself am able to allege, viz., Wordsworth's. Singular enough it seems, that he who read so very little of modern literature, in fact, next to nothing, should be the sole critic and reporter whom I have happened to meet upon Mrs. Lee's work. But so it was: accident had thrown the book in his way during one of his annual visits to London, and a second time at Lowther Castle. He paid to Mrs. Lee a compliment which certainly he paid to no other of her contemporaries, viz., that of reading her book very nearly to the end; and he spoke of it repeatedly as distinguished for vigor and originality of thought.

CHAPTER V.

I AM INTRODUCED TO THE WARFARE OF A PUBLIC SCHOOL.

Four years after my father's death, it began to be perceived that there was no purpose to be answered in any longer keeping up the costly establishment of Greenhay. A head gardener, besides laborers equal to at least two more, were required for the grounds and gardens. And no motive existed any longer for being near to a great trading town, so long after the commercial connection with it had ceased. Bath seemed, on all accounts, the natural station for a person in my mother's situation; and thither, accordingly, she went. I, who had been placed under the tuition of one of my guardians, remained some time longer under his care. I was then transferred to Bath. During this interval the sale of the house and grounds took place. It may illustrate the subject of *guardianship*, and the ordinary execution of its duties, to mention the result. The year was in itself a year of great depression, and every way unfavorable to such a transaction; and the particular night for which the sale had been fixed turned out remarkably wet; yet no attempt was made to postpone it, and it proceeded. Originally the house and grounds had cost about £6000. I have heard that only one offer was made, viz., of £2500. Be that as it may, for the sum of £2500 it was sold; and I have been often assured that, by waiting a few years, four to six times that sum might have been obtained with ease. This is not improbable, as the house was then out in the country; but since then the town of Manchester has gathered round it and enveloped it. Meantime, my guardians were all men of honor and integrity; but their hands were filled with their own affairs. One (my tutor) was a clergyman, rector of a church, and having his parish, his large family, and three pupils to attend. He was, besides, a very sedentary and indolent man—loving books, hating business. Another was a merchant. A third was a country magistrate, overladen with official business: him we rarely saw. Finally, the fourth was a banker in a distant county, having more knowledge of the world, more energy, and more practical wisdom than all the rest united, but too remote for interfering effectually.

Reflecting upon the evils which befell me, and the gross mismanagement, under my guardians, of my small fortune, and that of my brothers and sisters, it has often occurred to me that so important an office, which, from the time of Demosthenes, has been proverbially maladministered, ought to be put upon a new footing, plainly guarded by a few obvious provisions. As under the Roman laws, for a long period, the guardian should be made responsible in law, and should give security from the first for the due performance of his duties. But, to give him a motive for doing this, of course he must be paid. With the new obligations and liabilities will commence commensurate emoluments. If a child is made a ward in Chancery, its property is managed expensively, but always advantageously. Some great change is imperatively called for—no duty in the whole compass of human life being so scandalously treated as this.

In my twelfth year it was that first of all I entered upon the arena of a great public school, viz., the Grammar School[52] of Bath, over which at that time presided a most accomplished Etonian—Mr. (or was he as yet Doctor?) Morgan. If he was not, I am sure he ought to have been; and, with the reader's concurrence, will therefore create him a doctor on the spot. Every man has reason to rejoice who enjoys the advantage of a public training. I condemned, and *do* condemn, the practice of sending out into such stormy exposures those who are as yet too young, too dependent on female gentleness, and endowed with sensibilities originally too exquisite for such a warfare. But at nine or ten the masculine energies of the character are beginning to develop themselves; or, if not, no discipline will better aid in their development than the bracing intercourse of a great English classical school. Even the selfish are *there* forced into accommodating themselves to a public standard of generosity, and the effeminate in conforming to a rule of manliness. I was myself at two public schools, and I think with gratitude of the benefits which I reaped from both; as also I think with gratitude of that guardian in whose quiet household I learned Latin so effectually. But the small private schools, of which I had opportunities for gathering some brief experience,—schools containing thirty to forty boys,—were models of ignoble manners as regarded part of the juniors, and of favoritism as regarded the masters. Nowhere is the sublimity of public justice so broadly exemplified as in an English public school on the old Edward the Sixth or Elizabeth foundation. There is not in the universe such an Areopagus for

[52] *"Grammar School."*—By the way, as the grammar schools of England are amongst her most eminent distinctions, and, with submission to the innumerable wretches (gentlemen I should say) that hate England "worse than toad or asp," have never been rivalled by any corresponding institutions in other lands, I may as well take this opportunity of explaining the word *grammar*, which most people misapprehend. Men suppose a grammar school to mean a school where they teach grammar. But this is not the true meaning, and tends to calumniate such schools by ignoring their highest functions. Limiting by a false limitation the earliest object contemplated by such schools, they obtain a plausible pretext for representing all beyond grammar as something extraneous and casual that did not enter into the original or normal conception of the founders, and that may therefore have been due to alien suggestion. But now, when Suetonius writes a little book, bearing this title, "De Illustribus Grammaticis," what does he mean? What is it that he promises? A memoir upon the eminent *grammarians* of Rome? Not at all, but a memoir upon the distinguished literati of Rome. *Grammatica* does certainly mean sometimes grammar; but it is also the best Latin word for literature. A *grammaticus* is what the French express by the word *litterateur*. We unfortunately have no corresponding term in English: a *man of letters* is our awkward periphrasis in the singular, (too apt, as our jest books remind us, to suggest the postman;) whilst in the plural we resort to the Latin word *literati*. The school which professes to teach *grammatica*, professes, therefore, the culture of literature in the widest and most liberal extent, and is opposed *generically* to schools for teaching mechanic arts; and, within its own *sub-genus* of schools dedicated to liberal objects, is opposed to schools for teaching mathematics, or, more widely, to schools for teaching science.

fair play, and abhorrence of all crooked ways, as an English mob, or one of the time-honored English "foundation" schools. But my own first introduction to such an establishment was under peculiar and contradictory circumstances. When my "rating," or graduation in the school, was to be settled, naturally my altitude (to speak astronomically) was taken by my proficiency in Greek. But here I had no advantage over others of my age. My guardian was a feeble Grecian, and had not excited my ambition; so that I could barely construe books as easy as the Greek Testament and the Iliad. This was considered quite well enough for my age; but still it caused me to be placed under the care of Mr. Wilkins, the second master out of four, and not under Dr. Morgan himself. Within one month, however, my talent for Latin verses, which had by this time gathered strength and expansion, became known. Suddenly I was honored as never was man or boy since Mordecai the Jew. Without any colorable relation to the doctor's jurisdiction, I was now weekly paraded for distinction at the supreme tribunal of the school; out of which, at first, grew nothing but a sunshine of approbation delightful to my heart. Within six weeks all this had changed. The approbation indeed continued, and the public expression of it. Neither would there, in the ordinary course, have been any painful reaction from jealousy, or fretful resistance, to the soundness of my pretensions; since it was sufficiently known to such of my school-fellows as stood on my own level in the school, that I, who had no male relatives but military men, and those in India, could not have benefited by any clandestine aid. But, unhappily, Dr. Morgan was at that time dissatisfied with some points in the progress of his head class;[53] and, as it soon appeared, was continually throwing in their teeth the brilliancy of my verses at eleven or twelve, by comparison with theirs at seventeen, eighteen, and even nineteen. I had observed him sometimes pointing to myself, and was perplexed at seeing this gesture followed by gloomy looks, and what French reporters call "sensation," in these young men, whom naturally I viewed with awe as my leaders—boys that were called young men, men that were reading Sophocles, (a name that carried with it the sound of something seraphic to my ears,) and who had never vouchsafed to waste a word on such a child as myself. The day was come, however, when all that would be changed. One of these leaders strode up to me in the public playground, and, delivering a blow on my shoulder, which was not intended to hurt me, but as a mere formula of introduction, asked me "what the devil I meant by bolting out of the course, and annoying other people in that manner. Were 'other people' to have no rest for me and my verses, which, after all, were horribly bad?" There might have been some difficulty in returning an answer to this address, but none was required. I was briefly admonished to see that I wrote worse for the future, or else— —. At this *aposiopesis* I looked inquiringly at the speaker, and he filled up the chasm by saying that he would "annihilate" me. Could any person fail to be aghast at such a demand? I was to write worse than my own standard, which, by his account of my verses, must be difficult; and I was to write worse than himself, which might be impossible. My feelings revolted against so arrogant a demand, unless it had been far otherwise expressed; if death on the spot had awaited me, I could not have controlled myself;

---

[53] *"Class,"* or *"form."* —One knows not how to make one's self intelligible, so different are the terms locally.

and on the next occasion for sending up verses to the head master, so far from attending to the orders issued, I double-shotted my guns; double applause descended on myself; but I remarked with some awe, though not repenting of what I had done, that double confusion seemed to agitate the ranks of my enemies. Amongst them loomed out in the distance my "annihilating" friend, who shook his huge fist at me, but with something like a grim smile about his eyes. He took an early opportunity of paying his respects to me again, saying, "You little devil, do you call this writing your worst?" "No," I replied; "I call it writing my best." The annihilator, as it turned out, was really a good-natured young man; but he was on the wing for Cambridge; and with the rest, or some of them, I continued to wage war for more than a year. And yet, for a word spoken with kindness, how readily I would have resigned (had it been altogether at my own choice to do so) the peacock's feather in my cap as the merest of bawbles. Undoubtedly, praise sounded sweet in *my* ears also; but that was nothing by comparison with what stood on the other side. I detested distinctions that were connected with mortification to others; and, even if I could have got over *that*, the eternal feud fretted and tormented my nature. Love, that once in childhood had been so mere a necessity to me, *that* had long been a reflected ray from a departed sunset. But peace, and freedom from strife, if love were no longer possible, (as so rarely it is in this world,) was the clamorous necessity of my nature. To contend with somebody was still my fate; how to escape the contention I could not see; and yet, for itself, and for the deadly passions into which it forced me, I hated and loathed it more than death. It added to the distraction and internal feud of my mind, that I could not *altogether* condemn the upper boys. I was made a handle of humiliation to them. And, in the mean time, if I had an undeniable advantage in one solitary accomplishment, which is all a matter of accident, or sometimes of peculiar direction given to the taste, they, on the other hand, had a great advantage over me in the more elaborate difficulties of Greek and of choral Greek poetry. I could not altogether wonder at their hatred of myself. Yet still, as they had chosen to adopt this mode of conflict with me, I did not feel that I had any choice but to resist. The contest was terminated for me by my removal from the school, in consequence of a very threatening illness affecting my head; but it lasted more than a year, and it did not close before several among my public enemies had become my private friends. They were much older, but they invited me to the houses of their friends, and showed me a respect which affected me—this respect having more reference, apparently, to the firmness I had exhibited, than to any splendor in my verses. And, indeed, these had rather drooped from a natural accident; several persons of my own class had formed the practice of asking me to write verses for *them*. I could not refuse. But, as the subjects given out were the same for the entire class, it was not possible to take so many crops off the ground without starving the quality of all.

The most interesting public event which, during my stay at this school, at all connected itself with Bath, and indeed with the school itself, was the sudden escape of Sir Sidney Smith from the prison of the Temple in Paris. The mode of his escape was as striking as its time was critical. Having accidentally thrown a ball beyond the prison bounds in playing at tennis, or some such game, Sir Sidney was surprised to observe that the ball thrown back was not the same. Fortunately, he had the presence of mind to dissemble his sudden surprise. He retired, examined the ball, found it stuffed with letters; and, in the same way, he subsequently conducted a long correspondence, and arranged the whole circumstances of his escape; which, remarkably enough, was accomplished exactly eight days before the sailing of Napoleon with the Egyptian expedition; so that Sir Sidney was just in time to confront, and utterly to defeat, Napoleon in the breach of Acre. But for Sir Sidney, Bonaparte would have overrun Syria, *that* is certain. What would have followed from that event is a far more obscure problem.

Sir Sidney Smith, I must explain to readers of this generation, and Sir Edward Pellew, (afterwards Lord Exmouth,) figured as the two[54] Paladins of the first war with revolutionary France. Rarely were these two names mentioned but in connection with some splendid, prosperous, and unequal contest. Hence the whole nation was saddened by the account of Sir Sidney's capture; and this must be understood, in order to make the joy of his sudden return perfectly intelligible. Not even a rumor of Sir Sidney's escape had or could have run before him; for, at the moment of reaching the coast of England, he had started with post horses to Bath. It was about dusk when he arrived: the postilions were directed to the square in which his mother lived: in a few minutes he was in his mother's arms, and in fifty minutes more the news had flown to the remotest suburb of the city. The agitation of Bath on this occasion was indescribable. All the troops of the line then quartered in that city, and a whole regiment of volunteers, immediately got under arms, and marched to the quarter in which Sir Sidney lived. The small square overflowed with the soldiery; Sir Sidney went out, and was immediately lost to us, who were watching for him, in the closing ranks of the troops. Next morning, however, I, my younger brother, and a school-fellow of my own age, called formally upon the naval hero. *Why*, I know not, unless as *alumni* of the school at which Sir Sidney Smith had received his own education, we were admitted without question or demur; and I may record it as an amiable trait in Sir Sidney, that he received us then with great kindness, and took us down with him to the pump room. Considering, however, that we must have been most afflicting bores to Sir Sidney,—a fact which no self-esteem could even then disguise from us,—it puzzled me at first to understand the principle of his conduct. Having already done more than enough in courteous acknowledgment of our fraternal claims as fellow-students at the Bath Grammar School, why should he think it necessary to burden himself further with our worshipful society? I found out the secret, and will explain it. A very slight attention to Sir Sidney's deportment in public revealed to me that he was morbidly afflicted with nervous sensibility and with *mauvaise honte*. He that had faced so cheerfully crowds of hostile and threatening eyes, could not support without trepidation those gentle eyes, beaming with gracious admiration, of his fair young countrywomen. By accident, at that moment Sir Sidney had no acquaintances in

---

[54] To *them* in the next stage of the ward succeeded Sir Michael Seymour, and Lord Cochrane, (the present Earl of Dundonald,) and Lord Camelford. The two last were the regular fireeaters of the day. Sir Horatio Nelson being already an admiral, was no longer looked to for insulated exploits of brilliant adventure: his name was now connected with larger and combined attacks, less dashing and adventurous, because including heavier responsibilities.

Bath,[55] a fact which is not at all to be wondered at. Living so much abroad and at sea, an English sailor, of whatever rank, has few opportunities for making friends at home. And yet there was a necessity that Sir Sidney should gratify the public interest, so warmly expressed, by presenting himself somewhere or other to the public eye. But how trying a service to the most practised and otherwise most callous veteran on such an occasion, that he should step forward, saying in effect, "So you are wanting to see me: well, then, here I am: come and look at me!" Put it into what language you please, such a summons was written on all faces, and countersigned by his worship the mayor, who began to whisper insinuations of riots if Sir Sidney did not comply. Yet, if he *did*, inevitably his own act of obedience to the public pleasure took the shape of an ostentatious self-parading under the construction of those numerous persons who knew nothing of the public importunity, or of Sir Sidney's unaffected and even morbid reluctance to obtrude himself upon the public eye. The thing was unavoidable; and the sole palliation that it admitted was — to break the concentration of the public gaze, by associating Sir Sidney with some alien group, no matter of what cattle. Such a group would relieve both parties — gazer and gazee — from too distressing a consciousness of the little business on which they had met. We, the schoolboys, being three, intercepted and absorbed part of the enemy's fire, and, by furnishing Sir Sidney with real *bona fide* matter of conversation, we released him from the most distressing part of his sufferings, viz., the passive and silent acquiescence in his own apotheosis — holding a lighted candle, as it were, to the glorification of his own shrine. With our help, he weathered the storm of homage silently ascending. And we, in fact, whilst seeming to ourselves too undeniably a triad of bores, turned out the most serviceable allies that Sir Sidney ever had by land or sea, until several moons later, when he formed the invaluable acquaintance of the Syrian "butcher," viz., Djezzar, the Pacha of Acre. I record this little trait of Sir Sidney's constitutional temperament, and the little service through which I and my two comrades contributed materially to his relief, as an illustration of that infirmity which besieges the nervous system of our nation. It is a sensitiveness which sometimes amounts to lunacy, and sometimes even tempts to suicide. It is a mistake, however, to suppose this morbid affection unknown to Frenchmen, or unknown to men of the world. I have myself known it to exist in both, and particularly in a man that might be said to live in the street, such was the American publicity which circumstances threw around his life; and so far were his habits of life removed from reserve, or from any predisposition to gloom. And at this moment I recall a remarkable illustration of what I am saying, communicated by Wordsworth's accomplished friend, Sir George Beaumont. To *him* I had been sketching the distressing sensitiveness of Sir Sidney pretty much as I have sketched it to the reader; and how he, the man that on the breach at Acre valued not the eye of Jew, Christian, or Turk, shrank back — *me ipso teste* — from the gentle, though eager — from admiring, yet affectionate — glances of three very young ladies in Gay Street, Bath, the oldest (I should say) not more than seventeen. Upon which Sir George mentioned, as a parallel experience of his own, that Mr. Canning, being ceremoniously introduced to himself (Sir George) about the time

---

[55] Lord Camelford was, I believe, his first cousin; Sir Sidney's mother and Lady Camelford being sisters. But Lord Camelford was then absent from Bath.

when he had reached the meridian of his fame as an orator, and should therefore have become *blasé* to the extremity of being absolutely seared and case-hardened against all impressions whatever appealing to his vanity or egotism, did absolutely (*credite posteri!*) blush like any roseate girl of fifteen. And that this was no accident growing out of a momentary agitation, no sudden spasmodic pang, anomalous and transitory, appeared from other concurrent anecdotes of Canning, reported by gentlemen from Liverpool, who described to us most graphically and picturesque-ly the wayward fitfulness (not coquettish, or wilful, but nervously overmastering and most unaffectedly distressing) which besieged this great artist in oratory, and the time approached — was coming — was going, at which the private signal should have been shown for proposing his health. Mr. P. (who had been, I think, the may-or on the particular occasion indicated) described the restlessness of his manner; how he rose, and retired for half a minute into a little parlor behind the chairman's seat; then came back; then whispered, *Not yet I beseech you; I cannot face them yet;* then sipped a little water, then moved uneasily on his chair, saying, *One moment, if you please: stop, stop: don't hurry: one moment, and I shall be up to the mark:* in short, fighting with the necessity of taking the final plunge, like one who lingers on the scaffold.

Sir Sidney was at the time slender and thin; having an appearance of emaci-ation, as though he had suffered hardships and ill treatment, which, however, I do not remember to have heard. Meantime, his appearance, connected with his recent history, made him a very interesting person to women; and to this hour it remains a mystery with me, why and how it came about, that in every distribution of honors Sir Sidney Smith was overlooked. In the Mediterranean he made many enemies, especially amongst those of his own profession, who used to speak of him as far too fine a gentleman, and above his calling. Certain it is that he liked better to be doing business on shore, as at Acre, although he commanded a fine 80 gun ship, the Tiger. But however that may have been, his services, whether classed as military or naval, were memorably splendid. And, at that time, his connection, of whatsoever nature, with the late Queen Caroline had not occurred. So that alto-gether, to me, his case is inexplicable.

From the Bath Grammar School I was removed, in consequence of an accident, by which at first it was supposed that my skull had been fractured; and the sur-geon who attended me at one time talked of trepanning. This was an awful word; but at present I doubt whether in reality any thing very serious had happened. In fact, I was always under a nervous panic for my head, and certainly exaggerated my internal feelings without meaning to do so; and this misled the medical atten-dants. During a long illness which succeeded, my mother, amongst other books past all counting, read to me, in Hoole's translation, the whole of the "Orlando Furioso;" meaning by *the whole* the entire twenty-four books into which Hoole had condensed the original forty-six of Ariosto; and, from my own experience at that time, I am disposed to think that the homeliness of this version is an advan-tage, from not calling off the attention at all from the narration to the narrator. At this time also I first read the "Paradise Lost;" but, oddly enough, in the edition of Bentley, that great *paradiorthotaes*, (or pseudo-restorer of the text.) At the close of my illness, the head master called upon my mother, in company with his son-in-law, Mr. Wilkins, as did a certain Irish Colonel Bowes, who had sons at the school, requesting earnestly, in terms most flattering to myself, that I might be suffered to remain there. But it illustrates my mother's moral austerity, that she was shocked at my hearing compliments to my own merits, and was altogether disturbed at what doubtless these gentlemen expected to see received with maternal pride. She declined to let me continue at the Bath School; and I went to another, at Winkfield, in the county of Wilts, of which the chief recommendation lay in the religious character of the master.

CHAPTER VI.

I ENTER THE WORLD.

Yes, at this stage of my life, viz., in my fifteenth year, and from this sequestered school, ankle deep I first stepped into the world. At Winkfield I had staid about a year, or not much more, when I received a letter from a young friend of my own age, Lord Westport,[56] the son of Lord Altamont, inviting me to accompany him to Ireland for the ensuing summer and autumn. This invitation was repeated by his tutor; and my mother, after some consideration, allowed me to accept it.

In the spring of 1800, accordingly, I went up to Eton, for the purpose of joining my friend. Here I several times visited the gardens of the queen's villa at Frogmore; and, privileged by my young friend's introduction, I had opportunities of seeing and hearing the queen and all the princesses; which at that time was a novelty in my life, naturally a good deal prized. Lord Westport's mother had been, before her marriage, Lady Louisa Howe, daughter to the great admiral, Earl Howe, and intimately known to the royal family, who, on her account, took a continual and especial notice of her son.

On one of these occasions I had the honor of a brief interview with the king. Madame De Campan mentions, as an amusing incident in her early life, though terrific at the time, and overwhelming to her sense of shame, that not long after her establishment at Versailles, in the service of some one amongst the daughters of Louis XV., having as yet never seen the king, she was one day suddenly introduced to his particular notice, under the following circumstances: The time was morning; the young lady was not fifteen; her spirits were as the spirits of a fawn in May; her *tour* of duty for the day was either not come, or was gone; and, finding herself alone in a spacious room, what more reasonable thing could she do than amuse herself with *making cheeses?* that is, whirling round, according to a fashion practised by young ladies both in France and England, and pirouetting until the petticoat is inflated like a balloon, and then sinking into a courtesy. Mademoiselle was very solemnly rising from one of these courtesies, in the centre of her collapsing petticoats, when a slight noise alarmed her. Jealous of intruding eyes, yet not dreading more than a servant at worst, she turned, and, O Heavens! whom should she behold but his most Christian majesty advancing upon her, with a brilliant suite of gentlemen, young and old, equipped for the chase, who had been all silent

[56] My acquaintance with Lord Westport was of some years' standing. My father, whose commercial interests led him often to Ireland, had many friends there. One of these was a country gentleman connected with the west; and at his house I first met Lord Westport.

spectators of her performances? From the king to the last of the train, all bowed to her, and all laughed without restraint, as they passed the abashed amateur of cheese making. But she, to speak Homerically, wished in that hour that the earth might gape and cover her confusion. Lord Westport and I were about the age of mademoiselle, and not much more decorously engaged, when a turn brought us full in view of a royal party coming along one of the walks at Frogmore. We were, in fact, theorizing and practically commenting on the art of throwing stones. Boys have a peculiar contempt for female attempts in that way. For, besides that girls fling wide of the mark, with a certainty that might have won the applause of Galerius,[57] there is a peculiar sling and rotary motion of the arm in launching a stone, which no girl ever *can* attain. From ancient practice, I was somewhat of a proficient in this art, and was discussing the philosophy of female failures, illustrating my doctrines with pebbles, as the case happened to demand; whilst Lord Westport was practising on the peculiar whirl of the wrist with a shilling; when suddenly he turned the head of the coin towards me with a significant glance, and in a low voice he muttered some words, of which I caught *"Grace of God,"* *"France*[58] *and*

---

[57] "Sir," said the emperor to a soldier who had missed the target in succession I know not how many times, (suppose we say fifteen,) "allow me to offer my congratulations on the truly admirable skill you have shown in keeping clear of the mark. Not to have hit once in so many trials, argues the most splendid talents for missing."

[58] *France* was at that time among the royal titles, the act for altering the king's style and title not having then passed. As connected with this subject, I may here mention a project (reported to have been canvassed in council at the time when that alteration *did* take place) for changing the title from king to emperor. What then occurred strikingly illustrates the general character of the British policy as to all external demonstrations of pomp and national pretension, and its strong opposition to that of France under corresponding circumstances. The principle *of esse quam videri*, and the carelessness about names when the thing is unaffected, generally speaking, must command praise and respect. Yet, considering how often the reputation of power becomes, for international purposes, nothing less than power itself, and that words, in many relations of human life, are emphatically things, and sometimes are so to the exclusion of the most absolute things themselves, men of all qualities being often governed by names, the policy of France seems the wiser, viz., *se faire valoir*, even at the price of ostentation. But, at all events, no man is entitled to exercised that extrem candor, forbearance, and spirit of ready concession *in re aliena*, and, above all, *in re politica*, which, on its own account, might be altogether honorable. The council might give away their own honors, but not yours and mine. On a public (or at least on a foreign) interest, it is the duty of a good citizen to be lofty, exacting, almost insolent. And, on this principle, when the ancient style and title of the kingdom fell under revision, if—as I do not deny—it was advisable to retrench all obsolete pretensions as so many memorials of a greatness that in that particular manifestation was now extinct, and therefore, *pro tanto*, rather presumtions of weakness than of strength as being mementoes of our losses, yet, on the other hand, all countervailing claims which had since arisen, and had far more than equiponderated the declension in that one direction, should have been then adopted into the titular heraldry of the nation. It was neither wise nor just to insult foreign nations with assumptions which no longer stood upon any basis of reality. And on that ground *France* was, perhaps, rightly omitted. But why, when the crown was thus remoulded, and its jewelry unset, if this one pearl were to be surrendered as an ornament no longer ours, why, we may ask, were not the many and gorgeous jewels, achieved by the national wisdom and power in later times, adopted into the recomposed tiara? Upon what principle did the Romans, the wisest among

the children of this world, leave so many inscriptions, as records of their power or their triumphs, upon columns, arches, temples, *basilicae*, or medals? A national act, a solemn and deliberate act, delivered to history, is a more imperishable monument than any made by hands; and the title, as revised, which ought to have expressed a change in the dominion simply as to the mode and form of its expansion, now remains as a false, base, abject confession of absolute contraction: once we had A, B, and C; now we have dwindled into A and B: true, most unfaithful guardian of the national honors, we had lost C, and that you were careful to remember. But we happend to have gained D, E, F,—and so downwards to Z,—all of which duly you forgot.

On this argument, it was urged at the time, in high quarters, that the new re-cast of the crown and sceptre should come out of the furnace *equally* improved; as much for what they were authorized to claim as for what they were compelled to disclaim. And, as one mode of effecting this, it was proposed that the king should become an emperor. Some, indeed, alleged that an emperor, but its very idea, as received in the Chancery of Europe, presupposes a king paramount over vassal or tributary kings. But it is a sufficient answer to say that an emperor is a prince, united in his own person the *thrones* of several distinct kingdoms; and in effect we adopt that view of the case in giving the title of imperial to the parliament, or common assembly of the three kingdoms. However, the title of the prince was a matter trivial in comparison of the title of his *ditio*, or extent of jurisdiction. This point admits of a striking illustration: in the "Paradise Regained," Milton has given us, in close succession, three matchless pictures of civil grandeur, as exemplified in three different modes by three different states. Availing himself of the brief scriptural notice,—"The devil taketh him up into an exceeding high mountain, and showeth him all the kingdoms of the world, and the glory of them,"—he causes to pass, as in a solemn pageant before us, the two military empires then coexisting, of Parthia and Rome, and finally (under another idea of political greatness) the intellectual glories of Athens. From the picture of the Roman grandeur I extract, and beg the reader to weigh, the following lines:—

> "Thence to the gates cast round thine eye, and see—at
> What conflux issuing forth or entering in;
> Pretors, proconsuls, to their provinces
> Hasting, or on return in robes of state;
> Lictors and rods, the ensigns of their power;
> Legions or cohorts, turns of horse and wings;
> Or embassies from regions far remote,
> In various habits on the Appian road,
> Or on the Emilian; some from farthest south,
> Syene, and where the shadow both way falls,
> Meroë, Nilotic isle: and, more to west,
> The realm of Bocchus to the Blackmoor Sea;
> From India and the Golden Chersonese,
> And utmost Indian isle, Taprobane,
> —Dusk faces with white silken turbans wreathed;
> From Gallia, Gades, and the British, west,
> Germans, and Scythians, and Sarmatians, north,
> Beyond Danubius to the Tauric pool."

With this superb picture, or abstraction of the Roman pomps and power, when ascending to their utmost altitude, confront the following representative sketch of a great English levee on some high solemnity, suppose the king's birthday: "Amongst the presentations to his majesty, we noticed Lord O. S., the governor general of India, on his departure for Bengal; Mr. U. Z., with an address from the Upper and Lower Canadas; Sir L. V., on his

Ireland," "*Defender off the Faith, and so forth.*" This solemn recitation of the legend on the coin was meant as a fanciful way of apprising me that the king was approaching; for Lord W. had himself lost somewhat of the awe natural to a young person in a first situation of this nature, through his frequent admissions to the royal presence. For my own part, I was as yet a stranger even to the king's person. I had, indeed, seen most or all the princesses in the way I have mentioned above; and occasionally, in the streets of Windsor, the sudden disappearance of all hats from all heads had admonished me that some royal personage or other was then <u>traversing (or, if not traversing, was crossing) the street; but either</u> his majesty had appointment as commander of the forces in Nova Scotia; General Sir — —, on his return from the Burmese war, ["the Golden Chersonese,"] the commander-in-chief of the Mediterranean fleet; Mr. B. Z., on his appointment to the chief justiceship at Madras; Sir R. G., the late attorney general at the Cape of Good Hope; General Y. X., on taking leave for the governorship of Ceylon, ["the utmost Indian isle, Taprobane;"] Lord F. M., the bearer of the last despatches from head quarters in Spain; Col. P., on going out as captain general of the forces in New Holland; Commodore St. L., on his return from a voyage of discovery towards the north pole; the King of Owhyhee, attended by chieftains from the other islands of that cluster; Col. M'P., on his return from the war in Ashantee, upon which occasion the gallant colonel presented the treaty and tribute from that country; Admiral — —, on his appointment to the Baltic fleet; Captain O. N., with despatches from the Red Sea, advising the destruction of the piratical armament and settlements in that quarter, as also in the Persian Gulf; Sir T. O'N., the late resident in Nepaul, to present his report of the war in that territory, and in adjacent regions—names as yet unknown in Europe; the governor of the Leeward Islands, on departing for the West Indies; various deputations with petitions, addresses, &c., from islands in remote quarters of the globe, amongst which we distinguished those from Prince Edward Island, in the Gulf of St. Lawrence, from, the Mauritius, from Java, from the British settlement in Terra del Fuego, from the Christian churches in the Society, Friendly, and Sandwich Islands—as well as other groups less known in the South Seas; Admiral H. A., on assuming the command of the Channel fleet; Major Gen. X. L., on resigning the lieutenant governorship of Gibraltar; Hon. G. F., on going out as secretary to the governor of Malta," &c.

This sketch, too hastily made up, is founded upon a base of a very few years; *i.e.*, we have, in one or two instances, placed in juxtaposition, as coexistences, events separated by a few years. But if (like Milton's picture of the Roman grandeur) the abstraction had been made from a base of thirty years in extent, and had there been added to the picture (according to his precedent) the many and remote embassies to and from independent states, in all quarters of the earth, with how many more groups might the spectacle have been crowded, and especially of those who fall within that most picturesque delineation—

"Dusk faces with white silken turbans wreathed"!

As it is, I have noticed hardly any places but such as lie absolutely within our jurisdiction. And yet, even under that limitation, how vastly more comprehensive is the chart of British dominion than of the Roman! To this gorgeous empire, some corresponding style and title should have been adapted at the revision of the old title, and should yet be adapted.

Apropos of the proposed change in the king's title: Coleridge, on being assured that the new title of the king was to be Emperor of the British Islands and their dependencies, and on the coin *Imperator Britanniarum*, remarked, that, in this remanufactured form, the title might be said to be *japanned*; alluding to this fact, that amongst *insular* sovereigns, the only one known to Christian diplomacy by the title of emperor is the Sovereign of Japan.

never been of the party, or, from distance, I had failed to distinguish him. Now, for the first time, I was meeting him nearly face to face; for, though the walk we occupied was not that in which the royal party were moving, it ran so near it, and was connected by so many cross walks at short intervals, that it was a matter of necessity for us, as we were now observed, to go and present ourselves. What happened was pretty nearly as follows: The king, having first spoken with great kindness to my companion, inquiring circumstantially about his mother and grandmother, as persons particularly well known to himself, then turned his eye upon me. My name, it seems, had been communicated to him; he did not, therefore, inquire about that. Was I of Eton? This was his first question. I replied that I was not, but hoped I should be. Had I a father living? I had not: my father had been dead about eight years. "But you have a mother?" I had. "And she thinks of sending you to Eton?" I answered, that she had expressed such an intention in my hearing; but I was not sure whether that might not be in order to waive an argument with the person to whom she spoke, who happened to have been an Etonian. "O, but all people think highly of Eton; every body praises Eton. Your mother does right to inquire; there can be no harm in that; but the more she inquires, the more she will be satisfied — that I can answer for."

Next came a question which had been suggested by my name. Had my family come into England with the Huguenots at the revocation of the edict of Nantz? This was a tender point with me: of all things I could not endure to be supposed of French descent; yet it was a vexation I had constantly to face, as most people supposed that my name argued a French origin; whereas a Norman origin argued pretty certainly an origin *not* French. I replied, with some haste, "Please your majesty, the family has been in England since the conquest." It is probable that I colored, or showed some mark of discomposure, with which, however, the king was not displeased, for he smiled and said, "How do you know that?" Here I was at a loss for a moment how to answer; for I was sensible that it did not become me to occupy the king's attention with any long stories or traditions about a subject so unimportant as my own family; and yet it was necessary that I should say something, unless I would be thought to have denied my Huguenot descent upon no reason or authority. After a moment's hesitation, I said, in effect, that the family from which I traced my descent had certainly been a great and leading one at the era of the barons' wars, as also in one at least of the crusades; and that I had myself seen many notices of this family, not only in books of heraldry, &c., but in the very earliest of all English books. "And what book was that?" "Robert of Gloucester's 'Metrical Chronicle,' which I understood, from internal evidence, to have been written about 1280." The king smiled again, and said, "I know, I know." But what it was that he knew, long afterwards puzzled me to conjecture. I now imagine, however, that he meant to claim a knowledge of the book I referred to — a thing which at that time I thought improbable, supposing the king's acquaintance with literature not to be very extensive, nor likely to have comprehended any knowledge at all of the blackletter period. But in this belief I was greatly mistaken, as I was afterwards fully convinced by the best evidence from various quarters. That library of 120,000 volumes, which George IV. presented to the nation, and which has since gone to swell the collection at the British Museum, had been formed (as

I was often assured by persons to whom the whole history of the library, and its growth from small rudiments, was familiarly known) under the direct personal superintendence of George III. It was a favorite and pet creation; and his care extended even to the dressing of the books in appropriate bindings, and (as one man told me) to their *health*; explaining himself to mean, that in any case where a book was worm-eaten, or touched however slightly with the worm, the king was anxious to prevent the injury from extending, or from infecting others by close neighborhood; for it is supposed by many that such injuries spread rapidly in favorable situations. One of my informants was a German bookbinder of great respectability, settled in London, and for many years employed by the Admiralty as a confidential binder of records or journals containing secrets of office, &c. Through this connection he had been recommended to the service of his majesty, whom he used to see continually in the course of his attendance at Buckingham House, where the books were deposited. This artist had (originally in the way of his trade) become well acquainted with the money value of English books; and that knowledge cannot be acquired without some concurrent knowledge of their subject and their kind of merit. Accordingly, he was tolerably well qualified to estimate any man's attainments as a reading man; and from him I received such circumstantial accounts of many conversations he had held with the king, evidently reported with entire good faith and simplicity, that I cannot doubt the fact of his majesty's very general acquaintance with English literature. Not a day passed, whenever the king happened to be at Buckingham House, without his coming into the binding room, and minutely inspecting the progress of the binder and his allies— the gilders, toolers, &c. From the outside of the book the transition was natural to its value in the scale of bibliography; and in that way my informant had ascertained that the king was well acquainted, not only with Robert of Gloucester, but with all the other early chronicles, published by Hearne, and, in fact, possessed that entire series which rose at one period to so enormous a price. From this person I learned afterwards that the king prided himself especially upon his early folios of Shakspeare; that is to say, not merely upon the excellence of the individual copies in a bibliographical sense, as *"tall* copies" and having large margins, &c., but chiefly from their value in relation to the most authentic basis for the text of the poet. And thus it appears, that at least two of our kings, Charles I. and George III., have made it their pride to profess a reverential esteem for Shakspeare. This bookbinder added his attestation to the truth (or to the generally reputed truth) of a story which I had heard from other authority, viz., that the librarian, or, if not officially the librarian, at least the chief director in every thing relating to the books, was an illegitimate son of Frederic, Prince of Wales, (son to George II.,) and therefore half-brother of the king. His own taste and inclinations, it seemed, concurred with his brother's wishes in keeping him in a subordinate rank and an obscure station; in which, however, he enjoyed affluence without anxiety, or trouble, or courtly envy, and the luxury, which he most valued, of a superb library. He lived and died, I have heard, as plain Mr. Barnard. At one time I disbelieved the story, (which possibly may have been long known to the public,) on the ground that even George III. would not have differed so widely from princes in general as to leave a brother of his own, however unaspiring, wholly undistinguished by public honors. But having since ascertained that a naval officer, well known to my own family, and to a naval brother of my own in particular, by assistance rendered to him repeatedly when a midshipman in changing his ship, was undoubtedly an illegitimate son of George III., and yet that he never rose higher than the rank of post captain, though privately acknowledged by his father and other members of the royal family, I found the insufficiency of that objection. The fact is, and it does honor to the king's memory, he reverenced the moral feelings of his country, which are, in this and in all points of domestic morals, severe and high toned, (I say it in defiance of writers, such as Lord Byron, Mr. Hazlitt, &c., who hated alike the just and the unjust pretensions of England,) in a degree absolutely incomprehensible to *Southern* Europe. He had his frailties like other children of Adam; but he did not seek to fix the public attention upon them, after the fashion of Louis Quatorze, or our Charles II., and so many other continental princes. There were living witnesses (more than one) of *his* aberrations as of theirs; but he, with better feelings than they, did not choose, by placing these witnesses upon a pedestal of honor, surmounted by heraldic trophies, to emblazon his own transgressions to coming generations, and to force back the gaze of a remote posterity upon his own infirmities. It was his ambition to be the *father* of his people in a sense not quite so literal. These were things, however, of which at that time I had not heard.

During the whole dialogue, I did not even once remark that hesitation and iteration of words generally attributed to George III.; indeed, *so* generally, that it must often have existed; but in this case, I suppose that the brevity of his sentences operated to deliver him from any embarrassment of utterance, such as might have attended longer and more complex sentences, where some anxiety was natural to overtake the thoughts as they arose. When we observed that the king had paused in his stream of questions, which succeeded rapidly to each other, we understood it as a signal of dismissal; and making a profound obeisance, we retired backwards a few steps. His majesty smiled in a very gracious manner, waved his hand towards us, and said something (I did not know what) in a peculiarly kind accent; he then turned round, and the whole party along with him; which set us at liberty without impropriety to turn to the right about ourselves, and make our egress from the gardens.

This incident, to me at my age, was very naturally one of considerable interest. One reflection it suggested afterwards, which was this: Could it be likely that much truth of a general nature, bearing upon man and social interests, could ever reach the ear of a king, under the etiquette of a court, and under that one rule which seemed singly sufficient to foreclose all natural avenues to truth? — the rule, I mean, by which it is forbidden to address a question to the king. I was well aware, before I saw him, that in the royal presence, like the dead soldier in Lucan, whom the mighty necromancing witch tortures back into a momentary life, I must have no voice except for *answers*: —

> "Vox illi linguaque tantum
> *Responsura* datur."[59]

---

[59] For the sake of those who are no classical scholars, I explain: Voice and language are restored to him only to the extent of *replying*.

I was to originate nothing myself; and at my age, before so exalted a personage, the mere instincts of reverential demeanor would at any rate have dictated such a rule. But what becomes of that man's general condition of mind in relation to all the great objects moving on the field of human experience, where it is a law generally for almost all who approach him, that they shall confine themselves to replies, absolute responses, or, at most, to a prosecution or carrying forward of a proposition delivered by the *protagonist,* or supreme leader of the conversation? For it must be remembered that, generally speaking, the effect of putting no question is to transfer into the other party's hands the entire *originating* movement of the dialogue; and thus, in a musical metaphor, the great man is the sole modulator and determiner of the key in which the conversation proceeds. It is true, that sometimes, by travelling a little beyond the question in your answer, you may enlarge the basis, so as to bring up some new train of thought which you wish to introduce, and may suggest fresh matter as effectually as if you had the liberty of more openly guiding the conversation, whether by way of question or by direct origination of a topic; but this depends on skill to improve an opening, or vigilance to seize it at the instant, and, after all, much upon accident; to say nothing of the crime, (a sort of petty treason, perhaps, or, what is it?) if you should be detected in your "improvements" and "enlargements of basis." The king might say, "Friend, I must tell my attorney general to speak with you, for I detect a kind of treason in your replies. They go too far. They include something which tempts my majesty to a notice; which is, in fact, for the long and the short of it, that you have been circumventing me half unconsciously into answering a question which has silently been insinuated by *you.*" Freedom of communication, unfettered movement of thought, there can be none under such a ritual, which tends violently to a Byzantine, or even to a Chinese result of freezing, as it were, all natural and healthy play of the faculties under the petrific mace of absolute ceremonial and fixed precedent. For it will hardly be objected, that the privileged condition of a few official councillors and state ministers, whose hurry and oppression of thought from public care will rarely allow them to speak on any other subject than business, *can* be a remedy large enough for so large an evil. True it is, that a peculiarly frank or jovial temperament in a sovereign may do much for a season to thaw this punctilious reserve and ungenial constraint; but *that* is an accident, and personal to an individual. And, on the other hand, to balance even this, it may be remarked, that, in all noble and fashionable society, where there happens to be a pride in sustaining what is deemed a good *tone* in conversation, it is peculiarly aimed at, (and even artificially managed,) that no lingering or loitering upon one theme, no protracted discussion, shall be allowed. And, doubtless, as regards merely the treatment of convivial or purely *social* communication of ideas, (which also is a great art,) this practice is right. I admit willingly that an uncultured brute, who is detected at an elegant table in the atrocity of absolute discussion or disputation, ought to be summarily removed by a police officer; and possibly the law will warrant his being held to bail for one or two years, according to the enormity of his case. But men are not always enjoying, or seeking to enjoy, social pleasure; they seek also, and have need to seek continually, both through books and men, intellectual growth, fresh power, fresh strength, to keep themselves ahead or abreast of this moving, surging, billowing world of ours; especially in these modern times, when society revolves through so many new phases, and shifts its aspects with so much more velocity than in past ages. A king, especially of this country, needs, beyond most other men, to keep himself in a continual state of communication, as it were, by some vital and *organic* sympathy, with the most essential of these changes. And yet this punctilio of etiquette, like some vicious forms of law or technical fictions grown too narrow for the age, which will not allow of cases coming before the court in a shape desired alike by the plaintiff and the defendant, is so framed as to defeat equally the wishes of a prince disposed to gather knowledge wherever he can find it, and of those who may be best fitted to give it.

For a few minutes on three other occasions, before we finally quitted Eton, I again saw the king, and always with renewed interest. He was kind to every body—condescending and affable in a degree which I am bound to remember with personal gratitude; and one thing I *had* heard of him, which even then, and much more as my mind opened to a wider compass of deeper reflection, won my respect. I have always reverenced a man of whom it could be truly said that he had once, and once only, (for more than once implies another unsoundness in the quality of the passion,) been desperately in love; in love, that is to say, in a terrific excess, so as to dally, under suitable circumstances, with the thoughts of cutting his own throat, or even (as the case might be) the throat of her whom he loved above all this world. It will be understood that I am not justifying such enormities; on the contrary, they are wrong, exceedingly wrong; but it is evident that people in general feel pretty much as I do, from the extreme sympathy with which the public always pursue the fate of any criminal who has committed a murder of this class, even though tainted (as generally it is) with jealousy, which, in itself, wherever it argues habitual mistrust, is an ignoble passion.[60]

Great passions, (do not understand me, reader, as though I meant great appetites,) passions moving in a great orbit, and transcending little regards, are always arguments of some latent nobility. There are, indeed, but few men and few women capable of great passions, or (properly speaking) of passions at all. Hartley, in his mechanism of the human mind, propagates the sensations by means of vibrations, and by miniature vibrations, which, in a Roman form for such miniatures, he terms *vibratiuncles*. Now, of men and women generally, parodying that terminology, we ought to say—not that they are governed by passions, or at all capable of passions, but of *passiuncles*. And thence it is that few men go, or can go, beyond a little *love-liking*, as it is called; and hence also, that, in a world where so little conformity takes place between the ideal speculations of men and the gross realities of life, where marriages are governed in so vast a proportion by convenience, prudence, self-interest,—any thing, in short, rather than deep sympathy

[60] Accordingly, Coleridge has contended, and I think with truth, that the passion of Othello is *not* jealousy. So much I know by report, as the *result* of a lecture which he read at the Royal Institution. His arguments I did not hear. To me it is evident that Othello's state of feeling was not that of a degrading, suspicious rivalship, but the state of perfect misery, arising out of this dilemma, the most affecting, perhaps, to contemplate of any which *can* exist, viz., the dire necessity of loving without limit one whom the heart pronounces to be unworthy of that love.

between the parties,—and, consequently, where so many men must be crossed in their inclinations, we yet hear of so few tragic catastrophes on that account. The king, however, was certainly among the number of those who are susceptible of a deep passion, if every thing be true that is reported of him. All the world has heard that he was passionately devoted to the beautiful sister of the then Duke of Richmond. That was before his marriage; and I believe it is certain that he not only wished, but sincerely meditated, to have married her. So much is matter of notoriety. But other circumstances of the case have been sometimes reported, which imply great distraction of mind and a truly profound possession of his heart by that early passion; which, in a prince whose feelings are liable so much to the dispersing and dissipating power of endless interruption from new objects and fresh claims on the attention, coupled also with the fact that he never, but in this one case, professed any thing amounting to extravagant or frantic attachment, do seem to argue that the king was truly and passionately in love with Lady Sarah Lennox. He had a *demon* upon him, and was under a real *possession*. If so, what a lively expression of the mixed condition of human fortunes, and not less of another truth equally affecting, viz., the dread conflicts with the will, the mighty agitations which silently and in darkness are convulsing many a heart, where, to the external eye, all is tranquil,—that this king, at the very threshold of his public career, at the very moment when he was binding about his brows the golden circle of sovereignty, when Europe watched him with interest, and the kings of the earth with envy, not one of the vulgar titles to happiness being wanting,—youth, health, a throne the most splendid on this planet, general popularity amongst a nation of freemen, and the hope which belongs to powers as yet almost untried,—that, even under these most flattering auspices, he should be called upon to make a sacrifice the most bitter of all to which human life is liable! He made it; and he might then have said to his people, "For you, and to my public duties, I have made a sacrifice which none of you would have made for me." In years long ago, I have heard a woman of rank recurring to the circumstances of Lady Sarah's first appearance at court after the king's marriage. If I recollect rightly, it occurred after that lady's own marriage with Sir Charles Bunbury. Many eyes were upon both parties at that moment,—female eyes, especially,—and the speaker did not disguise the excessive interest with which she herself observed them. Lady Sarah was not agitated, but the king *was*. He seemed anxious, sensibly trembled, changed color, and *shivered*, as Lady S. B. drew near. But, to quote the one single eloquent sentiment, which I remember after a lapse of thirty years, in Monk Lewis's Romantic Tales, "In this world all things pass away; blessed be Heaven, and the bitter pangs by which sometimes it is pleased to recall its wanderers, even our passions pass away!" And thus it happened that this storm also was laid asleep and forgotten, together with so many others of its kind that have been, and that shall be again, so long as man is man, and woman woman. Meantime, in justification of a passion so profound, one would be glad to think highly of the lady that inspired it; and, therefore, I heartily hope that the insults offered to her memory in the scandalous "Memoirs of the Duc de Lauzun" are mere calumnies, and records rather of his presumptuous wishes than of any actual successes.[61]

[61] That book, I am aware, is generally treated as a forgery; but internal evidence,

However, to leave dissertation behind me, and to resume the thread of my narrative, an incident, which about this period impressed me even more profoundly than my introduction to a royal presence, was my first visit to London.

---

drawn from the tone and quality of the revelations there made, will not allow me to think it altogether such. There is an *abandon* and carelessness in parts which mark its sincerity. Its authenticity I cannot doubt. But *that* proves nothing for the truth of the particular stories which it contains. A book of scandalous and defamatory stories, especially where the writer has had the baseness to betray the confidence reposed in his honor by women, and to boast of favors alleged to have been granted him, it is always fair to consider as *ipso facto* a tissue of falsehoods: and on the following argument, that these are exposures which, even if true, none but the basest of men would have made. Being, therefore, on the hypothesis most favorable to his veracity, the basest of men, the author is self-denounced as vile enough to have forged the stories, and cannot complain if he should be roundly accused of doing that which he has taken pains to prove himself capable of doing. This way of arguing might be applied with fatal effect to the Duc de Lauzun's "Memoirs," supposing them written with a view to publication. But, by possibility, that was not the case. The Duc de L. terminated his profligate life, as is well known, on the scaffold, during the storms of the French revolution; and nothing in his whole career won him so much credit as the way in which he closed it; for he went to his death with a romantic carelessness, and even gayety of demeanor. His "Memoirs" were not published by himself: the publication was posthumous; and by whom authorized, or for what purpose, is not exactly known. Probably the manuscript fell into mercenary hands, and was published merely on a speculation of pecuniary gain. From some passages, however, I cannot but infer that the writer did not mean to bring it before the public, but wrote it rather as a series of private memoranda, to aid his own recollection of circumstances and dates. The Duc de Lauzun's account of his intrigue with Lady Sarah goes so far as to allege, that he rode down in disguise, from London to Sir Charles B.'s country seat, agreeably to a previous assignation, and that he was admitted, by that lady's confidential attendant, through a back staircase, at the time when Sir Charles (a fox hunter, but a man of the highest breeding and fashion) was himself at home, and occupied in the duties of hospitality.

CHAPTER VII.

THE NATION OF LONDON.

It was a most heavenly day in May of the year (1800) when I first beheld and first entered this mighty wilderness, the city—no, not the city, but the nation—of London. Often since then, at distances of two and three hundred miles or more from this colossal emporium of men, wealth, arts, and intellectual power, have I felt the sublime expression of her enormous magnitude in one simple form of ordinary occurrence, viz., in the vast droves of cattle, suppose upon the great north roads, all with their heads directed to London, and expounding the size of the attracting body, together with the force of its attractive power, by the never-ending succession of these droves, and the remoteness from the capital of the lines upon which they were moving. A suction so powerful, felt along radii so vast, and a consciousness, at the same time, that upon other radii still more vast, both by land and by sea, the same suction is operating, night and day, summer and winter, and hurrying forever into one centre the infinite means needed for her infinite purposes, and the endless tributes to the skill or to the luxury of her endless population, crowds the imagination with a pomp to which there is nothing corresponding upon this planet, either amongst the things that have been or the things that are. Or, if any exception there is, it must be sought in ancient Rome.[62] We, upon this

---

[62] *"Ancient Rome."*—Vast, however, as the London is of this day, I incline to think that it is below the Rome of Trajan. It has long been a settled opinion amongst scholars, that the computations of Lipsius, on this point, were prodigiously overcharged; and formerly I shared in that belief. But closer study of the question, and a laborious *collation* of the different data, (for any single record, independently considered, can here establish nothing,) have satisfied me that Lipsius was nearer the truth than his critics; and that the Roman population of every class— slaves, aliens, peoples of the suburbs, included—lay between four and six millions; in which case the London of 1833, which counts more than a million and a half, but less than two millions, [*Note.*—Our present London of 1853 counts two millions, plus as many thousands as there are days in the year,] may be taken, *chata platos* as lying between one fourth and one third of Rome. To discuss this question thoroughly would require a separate memoir, for which, after all, there are not sufficient materials: meantime I will make this remark: That the ordinary computations of a million, or a million and a quarter, derived from the surviving accounts of the different "regions," apply to Rome *within* the Pomaerium, and are, therefore, no more valid for the total Rome of Trajan's time, stretching so many miles beyond it, than the bills of mortality for what is technically "London within the walls" can serve at this day as a base for estimating the population of that total London which we mean and presume in our daily conversation. *Secondly*, even for the Rome within these limits the computations are not commensurate, by not allowing for the prodigious *height* of the houses in Rome, which much transcended that of modern cities. On this last

occasion, were in an open carriage, and, chiefly (as I imagine) to avoid the dust, we approached London by rural lanes, where any such could be found, or, at least, along by-roads, quiet and shady, collateral to the main roads. In that mode of approach we missed some features of the sublimity belonging to any of the common approaches upon a main road; we missed the whirl and the uproar, the tumult and the agitation, which continually thicken and thicken throughout the last dozen miles before you reach the suburbs. Already at three stages' distance, (say 40 miles from London,) upon some of the greatest roads, the dim presentment of some vast capital reaches you obscurely and like a misgiving. This blind sympathy with a mighty but unseen object, some vast magnetic range of Alps, in your

point I will translate a remarkable sentence from the Greek rhetorician Aristides, [*Note.*— Aelius Aristides, Greek by his birth, who flourished in the time of the Antonines;] to some readers it will be new and interesting: "And, as oftentimes we see that a man who greatly excels others in bulk and strength is not content with any display, however ostentatious, of his powers, short of that where he is exhibited surmounting himself with a pyramid of other men, one set standing upon the shoulders of another, so also this city, stretching forth her foundations over areas so vast, is yet not satisfied with those superficial dimensions; *that* contents her not; but upon one city rearing another of corresponding proportions, and upon that another, pile resting upon pile, houses overlaying houses, in aerial succession: so, and by similar steps, she achieves a character of architecture justifying, as it were, the very promise of her name; and with reference to that name, and its Grecian meaning, we may say, that here nothing meets our eyes in any direction but mere *Rome! Rome!*" [Note.— This word *Romae*, (Romé,) on which the rhetorician plays, is the common Greek term for *strength*.] "And hence," says Aristides, "I derive the following conclusion: that if any one, decomposing this series of strata, were disposed to unshell, as it were, this existing Rome from its present crowded and towering coacervations, and, thus degrading these aerial Romes, were to plant them on the ground, side by side, in orderly succession, according to all appearance, the whole vacant area of Italy would be filled with these dismantled stories of Rome, and we should be presented with the spectacle of one continuous city, stretching its labyrinthine pomp to the shores of the Adriatic." This is so far from being meant as a piece of rhetoric, that, on the very contrary, the whole purpose is to substitute for a vague and rhetorical expression of the Roman grandeur one of a more definite character—viz., by presenting its dimensions in a new form, and supposing the city to be uncrested, as it were; its upper tiers to be what the sailors call *unshipped*; and the dethroned stories to be all drawn up in rank and file upon the ground; according to which assumption he implies that the city would stretch from the *mare Superum* to the *mare Inferum, i.e.,* from the sea of Tuscany to the Adriatic.

The fact is, as Casaubon remarked, upon occasion of a ridiculous blunder in estimating the largesses of a Roman emperor, that the error on most questions of Roman policy or institutions tends not, as is usual, in the direction of excess, but of defect. All things were colossal there; and the probable, as estimated upon our modern scale, is not unfrequently the impossible, as regarded Roman habits. Lipsius certainly erred extravagantly at times, and was a rash speculator on many subjects; witness his books on the Roman amphitheatres; but not on the magnitude of Rome, or the amount of its population. I will add, upon this subject, that the whole political economy of the ancients, if we except Boeckh's accurate investigation, (*Die Staatshaushaltung der Athener,*) which, properly speaking, cannot be called political economy, is a mine into which scarce a single shaft has yet been sunk. But I must also add, that every thing will depend upon *collation* of facts, and the bringing of indirect notices into immediate juxtaposition, so as to throw light on each other. *Direct* and positive information there is little on these topics; and that has been gleaned.

neighborhood, continues to increase you know not now. Arrived at the last station for changing horses, Barnet, suppose, on one of the north roads, or Hounslow on the western, you no longer think (as in all other places) of naming the next stage; nobody says, on pulling up, "Horses on to London"—that would sound ludicrous; one mighty idea broods over all minds, making it impossible to suppose any other destination. Launched upon this final stage, you soon begin to feel yourself entering the stream as it were of a Norwegian *maelstrom*; and the stream at length becomes the rush of a cataract. What is meant by the Latin word *trepidatio*? Not any thing peculiarly connected with panic; it belongs as much to the hurrying to and fro of a coming battle as of a coming flight; to a marriage festival as much as to a massacre; *agitation* is the nearest English word. This *trepidation* increases both audibly and visibly at every half mile, pretty much as one may suppose the roar of Niagara and the thrilling of the ground to grow upon the senses in the last ten miles of approach, with the wind in its favor, until at length it would absorb and extinguish all other sounds whatsoever. Finally, for miles before you reach a suburb of London such as Islington, for instance, a last great sign and augury of the immensity which belongs to the coming metropolis forces itself upon the dullest observer, in the growing sense of his own utter insignificance. Every where else in England, you yourself, horses, carriage, attendants, (if you travel with any,) are regarded with attention, perhaps even curiosity; at all events, you are seen. But after passing the final posthouse on every avenue to London, for the latter ten or twelve miles, you become aware that you are no longer noticed: nobody sees you; nobody hears you; nobody regards you; you do not even regard yourself. In fact, how should you, at the moment of first ascertaining your own total unimportance in the sum of things?—a poor shivering unit in the aggregate of human life. Now, for the first time, whatever manner of man you were, or seemed to be, at starting, squire or "squireen," lord or lordling, and however related to that city, hamlet, or solitary house from which yesterday or to-day you slipped your cable, beyond disguise you find yourself but one wave in a total Atlantic, one plant (and a parasitical plant besides, needing alien props) in a forest of America.

These are feelings which do not belong by preference to thoughtful people—far less to people merely sentimental. No man ever was left to himself for the first time in the streets, as yet unknown, of London, but he must have been saddened and mortified, perhaps terrified, by the sense of desertion and utter loneliness which belong to his situation. No loneliness can be like that which weighs upon the heart in the centre of faces never ending, without voice or utterance for him; eyes innumerable, that have "no speculation" in their orbs which *he* can understand; and hurrying figures of men and women weaving to and fro, with no apparent purposes intelligible to a stranger, seeming like a mask of maniacs, or, oftentimes, like a pageant of phantoms. The great length of the streets in many quarters of London; the continual opening of transient glimpses into other vistas equally far stretching, going off at right angles to the one which you are traversing; and the murky atmosphere which, settling upon the remoter end of every long avenue, wraps its termination in gloom and uncertainty,—all these are circumstances aiding that sense of vastness and illimitable proportions which forever brood over the aspect of London in its interior. Much of the feeling which belongs to the outside of London, in its approaches for the last few miles, I had lost, in consequence of the stealthy route of by-roads, lying near Uxbridge and Watford, through which we crept into the suburbs. But for that reason, the more abrupt and startling had been the effect of emerging somewhere into the Edgeware Road, and soon afterwards into the very streets of London itself; through *what* streets, or even what quarter of London, is now totally obliterated from my mind, having perhaps never been comprehended. All that I remember is one monotonous awe and blind sense of mysterious grandeur and Babylonian confusion, which seemed to pursue and to invest the whole equipage of human life, as we moved for nearly two[63] hours through streets; sometimes brought to anchor for ten minutes or more by what is technically called a "lock," that is, a line of carriages of every description inextricably massed, and obstructing each other, far as the eye could stretch; and then, as if under an enchanter's rod, the "lock" seemed to thaw; motion spread with the fluent race of light or sound through the whole ice-bound mass, until the subtile influence reached *us* also, who were again absorbed into the great rush of flying carriages; or, at times, we turned off into some less tumultuous street, but of the same mile-long character; and, finally, drawing up about noon, we alighted at some place, which is as little within my distinct remembrance as the route by which we reached it.

For what had we come? To see London. And what were the limits within which we proposed to crowd that little feat? At five o'clock we were to dine at Porters — —, a seat of Lord Westport's grandfather; and, from the distance, it was necessary that we should leave London at half past three; so that a little more than three hours were all we had for London. Our charioteer, my friend's tutor, was summoned away from us on business until that hour; and we were left, therefore, entirely to ourselves and to our own skill in turning the time to the best account, for contriving (if such a thing were possible) to do something or other which, by any fiction of courtesy, or constructively, so as to satisfy a lawyer, or in a sense sufficient to win a wager, might be taken and received for having "seen London."

What could be done? We sat down, I remember, in a mood of despondency, to consider. The spectacles were too many by thousands; *inopes nos copia fecit*; our very wealth made us poor; and the choice was distracted. But which of them all could be thought general or representative enough to stand for the universe of London? We could not traverse the whole circumference of this mighty orb; that was clear; and, therefore, the next best thing was to place ourselves as much as possible in some relation to the spectacles of London, which might answer to the centre. Yet how? That sounded well and metaphysical; but what did it mean if acted upon? What was the centre of London for any purpose whatever, latitudinarian or longitudinarian, literary, social, or mercantile, geographical, astronomical, or (as Mrs. Malaprop kindly suggests) diabolical? Apparently that we should stay at our inn; for in that way we seemed best to distribute our presence equally amongst all, viz., by going to none in particular.

---

[63] *"Two hours."* — This slow progress must, however, in part be ascribed to Mr. Gr—
—'s non-acquaintance with the roads, both town and rural, along the whole line of our progress from Uxbridge.

Three times in my life I have had my taste—that is, my sense of proportions—memorably outraged. Once was by a painting of Cape Horn, which seemed almost treasonably below its rank and office in this world, as the terminal abutment of our mightiest continent, and also the hinge, as it were, of our greatest circumnavigations—of all, in fact, which can be called *classical* circumnavigations. To have "doubled Cape Horn"—at one time, what a sound it had! yet how ashamed we should be if that cape were ever to be seen from the moon! A party of Englishmen, I have heard, went up Mount Aetna, during the night, to be ready for sunrise—a common practice with tourists both in Switzerland, Wales, Cumberland, &c.; but, as all must see who take the trouble to reflect, not likely to repay the trouble; seeing that every thing which offers a *picture,* when viewed from a station nearly horizontal, becomes a mere *map* to an eye placed at an elevation of 3000 feet above it; and so thought, in the sequel, the Aetna party. The sun, indeed, rose visibly, and not more apparelled in clouds than was desirable; yet so disappointed were they, and so disgusted with the sun in particular, that they unanimously *hissed* him; though, of course, it was useless to cry "Off! off!" Here, however, the fault was in their own erroneous expectations, and not in the sun, who, doubtless, did his best. For, generally, a sunrise and a sunset ought to be seen from the valley, or at most horizontally.[64] But as to Cape Horn, *that* (by comparison with its position and its functions) was really a disgrace to the planet; it is not the spectator that is in fault *here,* but the object itself, the Birmingham cape. For, consider, it is not only the "specular mount," keeping watch and ward over a sort of trinity of oceans, and, by all tradition, the circumnavigator's gate of entrance to the Pacific, but also it is the temple of the god Terminus for all the Americas. So that, in relation to such dignities, it seemed to me, in the drawing, a makeshift, put up by a carpenter, until the true Cape Horn should be ready; or, perhaps, a drop scene from the opera house. This was one case of disproportion: the others were—the final and ceremonial valediction of Garrick, on retiring from his profession; and the Pall Mall inauguration of George IV. on the day of his accession[65] to the throne. The utter *ir*

---

[64] Hence it may be said, that nature regulates our position for such spectacles, without any intermeddling of ours. When, indeed, a mountain stands, like Snowdon or Great Gavel in Cumberland, at the centre of a mountainous region, it is not denied that, at some seasons, when the early beams strike through great vistas in the hills, splendid effects of light and shade are produced; strange, however, rather than beautiful. But from an insulated mountain, or one upon the outer ring of the hilly tract, such as Skiddaw, in Cumberland, the first effect is to translate the landscape from a *picture* into a *map*; and the total result, as a celebrated author once said, is the *infinity of littleness.*

[65] Accession was it, or his proclamation? The case was this: About the middle of the day, the king came out into the portico of Carlton House; and addressing himself (addressing his gestures, I mean) to the assemblage of people in Pall Mall, he bowed repeatedly to the right and to the left, and then retired. I mean no disrespect to that prince in recalling those circumstances; no doubt, he acted upon the suggestion of others, and perhaps, also, under a sincere emotion on witnessing the enthusiasm of those outside; but *that* could not cure the original absurdity of recognizing as a representative audience, clothed with the national functions of recognizing *himself,* a chance gathering of passengers through a single street, between whom and any mob from his own stables and kitchens there could be no essential difference which logic, or law, or constitutional principle could recognize.

relation, in both cases, of the audience to the scene, (*audience* I say, as say we must, for the sum of the spectators in the second instance, as well as of the auditors in the first,) threw upon each a ridicule not to be effaced. It is in any case impossible for an actor to say words of farewell to those for whom he really designs his farewell. He cannot bring his true object before himself. To whom is it that he would offer his last adieus? We are told by one—who, if he loved Garrick, certainly did not love Garrick's profession, nor would even, through *him*, have paid it any undue compliment—that the retirement of this great artist had "eclipsed the gayety of nations." To nations, then, to his own generation, it was that he owed his farewell; but, of a generation, what organ is there which can sue or be sued, that can thank or be thanked? Neither by fiction nor by delegation can you bring their bodies into court. A king's audience, on the other hand, *might* be had as an authorized representative body. But, when we consider the composition of a casual and chance auditory, whether in a street or a theatre,—secondly, the small size of a modern audience, even in Drury Lane, (4500 at the most,) not by one eightieth part the *complement* of the Circus Maximus,—most of all, when we consider the want of symmetry or commensurateness, to any extended duration of time, in the *acts* of such an audience, which acts lie in the vanishing expressions of its vanishing emotions,—acts so essentially fugitive, even when organized into an art and a tactical system of *imbrices* and *bombi*, (as they were at Alexandria, and afterwards at the Neapolitan and Roman theatres,) that they could not protect themselves from dying in the very moment of their birth,—laying together all these considerations, we see the incongruity of any audience, so constituted, to any purpose less evanescent than their own tenure of existence.

Just such in disproportion as these cases had severally been, was our present problem in relation to our time or other means for accomplishing it. In debating the matter, we lost half an hour; but at length we reduced the question to a choice between Westminster Abbey and St. Paul's Cathedral. I know not that we could have chosen better. The rival edifices, as we understood from the waiter, were about equidistant from our own station; but, being too remote from each other to allow of our seeing both, "we tossed up," to settle the question between the elder lady and the younger. "Heads" came up, which stood for the abbey. But, as neither of us was quite satisfied with this decision, we agreed to make another appeal to the wisdom of chance, second thoughts being best. This time the cathedral turned up; and so it came to pass that, with us, the having *seen London* meant having seen St. Paul's.

The first view of St. Paul's, it may be supposed, overwhelmed us with awe; and I did not at that time imagine that the sense of magnitude could be more deeply impressed. One thing interrupted our pleasure. The superb objects of curiosity within the cathedral were shown for separate fees. There were seven, I think; and any one could be seen independently of the rest for a few pence. The whole amount was a trifle; fourteen pence, I think; but we were followed by a sort of persecution—"Would we not see the bell?" "Would we not see the model?" "Surely we would not go away without visiting the whispering gallery?"—solicitations which troubled the silence and sanctity of the place, and must tease others as it then teased us, who wished to contemplate in quiet this great monument of the national grandeur, which was at that very time[66] beginning to take a station also in the land, as a depository for the dust of her heroes. What struck us most in the whole *interior* of the pile was the view taken from the spot immediately under the dome, being, in fact, the very same which, five years afterwards, received the remains of Lord Nelson. In one of the aisles going off from this centre, we saw the flags of France, Spain, and Holland, the whole trophies of the war, swinging pompously, and expanding their massy draperies, slowly and heavily, in the upper gloom, as they were swept at intervals by currents of air. At this moment we were provoked by the showman at our elbow renewing his vile iteration of "Twopence, gentlemen; no more than twopence for each;" and so on, until we left the place. The same complaint has been often made as to Westminster Abbey. Where the wrong lies, or where it commences, I know not. Certainly I nor any man can have a right to expect that the poor men who attended us should give up their time for nothing, or even to be angry with them for a sort of persecution, on the degree of which possibly might depend the comfort of their own families. Thoughts of famishing children at home leave little room for nice regards of delicacy abroad. The individuals, therefore, might or might not be blamable. But in any case, the system is palpably wrong. The nation is entitled to a free enjoyment of its own public monuments; not free only in the sense of being gratuitous, but free also from the molestation of *showmen*, with their imperfect knowledge and their vulgar sentiment.

Yet, after all, what is this system of restriction and annoyance, compared with that which operates on the use of the national libraries? or *that* again, to the system of exclusion from some of these, where an absolute interdict lies upon any use at all of that which is confessedly national property? Books and manuscripts, which were originally collected and formally bequeathed to the public, under the generous and noble idea of giving to future generations advantages which the collector had himself not enjoyed, and liberating them from obstacles in the pursuit of knowledge which experience had bitterly imprinted upon his own mind, are at this day locked up as absolutely against me, you, or any body, as collections confessedly private. Nay, far more so; for most private collectors of eminence, as the late Mr. Heber, for instance, have been distinguished for liberality in lending the rarest of their books to those who knew how to use them with effect. But, in the cases I now contemplate, the whole funds for supporting the proper offices attached to a library, such as librarians, sub-librarians, &c., which of themselves (and without the express verbal evidence of the founder's will) presume a *public* in the daily use of the books, else they are superfluous, have been applied to the creation of lazy sinecures, in behalf of persons expressly charged with the care of shutting out the public. Therefore, it is true, they are *not* sinecures; for that one care, vigilantly to keep out the public,[67] they do take upon themselves; and why?

[66] Already monuments had been voted by the House of Commons in this cathedral, and I am not sure but they were nearly completed, to two captains who had fallen at the Nile.

[67] This place suggests the mention of another crying abuse connected with this subject. In the year 1811 or 1810 came under parliamentary notice and revision the law of

copyright. In some excellent pamphlets drawn forth by the occasion, from Mr. Duppa, for instance, and several others, the whole subject was well probed, and many aspects, little noticed by the public, were exposed of that extreme injustice attached to the law as it then stood. The several monopolies connected with books were noticed a *little*; and *not* a little notice was taken of the oppressive privilege with which certain public libraries (at that time, I think, eleven) were invested, of exacting, severally, a copy of each new book published. This downright robbery was palliated by some members of the House in that day, under the notion of its being a sort of exchange, or *quid pro quo* in return for the relief obtained by the statute of Queen Anne—the first which recognized literary property. "For," argued they, "previously to that statute, supposing your book pirated, at common law you could obtain redress only for each copy *proved* to have been sold by the pirate; and that might not be a thousandth part of the actual loss. Now, the statute of Queen Anne granting you a general redress, upon proof that a piracy had been committed, you, the party relieved, were bound to express your sense of this relief by a return made to the public; and the public is here represented by the great endowed libraries of the seven universities, the British Museum," &c., &c. But *prima facie*, this was that *selling of justice* which is expressly renounced in Magna Charta; and why were proprietors of copyright, more than other proprietors, to make an "acknowledgment" for their rights? But supposing *that* just, why, especially, to the given public bodies? Now, for my part, I think that this admits of an explanation: nine tenths of the authors in former days lay amongst the class who had received a college education; and most of these, in their academic life, had benefited largely by old endowments. Giving up, therefore, a small tribute from their copyright, there was some color of justice in supposing that they were making a slight acknowledgment for past benefits received, and exactly for those benefits which enabled them to appear with any advantage as authors. So, I am convinced, the "*servitude*" first arose, and under this construction; which, even for those days, was often a fiction, but now is generally such. However, be the origin what it may, the ground upon which the public mind in 1811 (that small part of it, at least, which the question attracted) reconciled itself to the abuse was this—for a trivial wrong, they alleged (but it was then shown that the wrong was not always trivial) one great good is achieved, viz., that all over the kingdom are dispersed eleven great depositories, in which all persons interested may, at all times, be sure of finding one copy of every book published. That *did* seem a great advantage, and a balance in point of utility (if none in point of justice) to the wrong upon which it grew. But now mark the degree in which this balancing advantage is made available. 1. The eleven bodies are not equally careful to exact their copies; that can only be done by retaining an agent in London; and this agent is careless about books of slight money value. 2. Were it otherwise, of what final avail would a perfect set of the year's productions prove to a public not admitted freely to the eleven libraries? 3. But, finally, if they were admitted, to what purpose (as regards this particular advantage) under the following custom, which, in some of these eleven libraries, (possibly in all,) *was*, I well knew, established: annually the principal librarian *weeded* the annual crop of all such books as displeased himself; upon which two questions arise: 1. Upon what principle? 2. With what result? I answer as to the first, that in this *lustration* he went upon no principle at all, but his own caprice, or what he called his own discretion; and accordingly it is a fact known to many as well as myself, that a book, which some people (and certainly not the least meditative of this age) have pronounced the most original work of modern times, was actually amongst the books thus degraded; it was one of those, as the phrase is, tossed "into the basket;" and universally this fate is more likely to befall a work of *original* merit, which disturbs the previous way of thinking and feeling, than one of timid compliance with ordinary models. Secondly, with what result? For the present, the degraded books, having been consigned to the basket, were forthwith consigned to a damp cellar. There, at any rate, they were in no condition to be consulted by the public, being piled up in close bales, and in a

A man loving books, like myself, might suppose that their motive was the ungenerous one of keeping the books to themselves. Far from it. In several instances, they will as little use the books as suffer them to be used. And thus the whole plans and cares of the good (weighing his motives, I will say of the *pious*) founder have terminated in locking up and sequestering a large collection of books, some being great rarities, in situations where they are not accessible. Had he bequeathed them to the catacombs of Paris or of Naples, he could not have better provided for their virtual extinction. I ask, Does no action at common law lie against the promoters of such enormous abuses? O thou fervent reformer,—whose fatal tread he that puts his ear to the ground may hear at a distance coming onwards upon *every* road,— if too surely thou wilt work for me and others irreparable wrong and suffering, work also for us a little good; this way turn the great hurricanes and levanters of thy wrath; winnow me this chaff; and let us enter at last the garners of pure wheat laid up in elder days for our benefit, and which for two centuries have been closed against our use!

London we left in haste, to keep an engagement of some standing at the Earl Howe's, my friend's grandfather. This great admiral, who had filled so large a station in the public eye, being the earliest among the naval heroes of England in the first war of the revolution, and the only one of noble birth, I should have been delighted to see; St. Paul's, and its naval monuments to Captain Riou and Captain — —, together with its floating pageantries of conquered flags, having awakened within me, in a form of peculiar solemnity, those patriotic remembrances of past glories, which all boys feel so much more vividly than men can do, in whom the sensibility to such impressions is blunted. Lord Howe, however, I was not destined to see; he had died about a year before. Another death there had been, and very recently, in the family, and under circumstances peculiarly startling; and the spirits of the whole house were painfully depressed by that event at the time of our visit. One of the daughters, a younger sister of my friend's mother, had been engaged for some time to a Scottish nobleman, the Earl of Morton, much esteemed by the royal family. The day was at length fixed for the marriage; and about a fortnight before that day arrived, some particular dress or ornament was brought to Porters, in which it was designed that the bride should appear at the altar. The fashion as to this point has often varied; but at that time, I believe the custom was for bridal parties to be in full dress. The lady, when the dress arrived, was, to all appearance, in good health; but, by one of those unaccountable misgivings which

place not publicly accessible. But there can be no doubt that, sooner or later, their mouldering condition would be made an argument for selling them. And such, when we trace the operation of this law to its final stage, is the ultimate result of an infringement upon private rights almost unexampled in any other part of our civil economy. That sole beneficial result, for the sake of which some legislators were willing to sanction a wrong otherwise admitted to be indefensible, is so little protected and secured to the public, that it is first of all placed at the mercy of an agent in London, whose negligence or indifference may defeat the provision altogether, (I know a publisher of a splendid botanical work, who told me that, by forbearing to attract notice to it within the statutable time, he saved his eleven copies;) and placed at the mercy of a librarian, who (or any one of his successors) may, upon a motive of malice to the author or an impulse of false taste, after all proscribe any part of the books thus dishonorably acquired.

are on record in so many well-attested cases, (as that, for example, of Andrew Marveil's father,) she said, after gazing for a minute or two at the beautiful dress, firmly and pointedly, "So, then, *that* is my wedding dress; and it is expected that I shall wear it on the 17th; but I shall *not*; I shall never wear it. On Thursday, the 17th, I shall be dressed in a shroud!" All present were shocked at such a declaration, which the solemnity of the lady's manner made it impossible to receive as a jest. The countess, her mother, even reproved her with some severity for the words, as an expression of distrust in the goodness of God. The bride elect made no answer but by sighing heavily. Within a fortnight, all happened, to the letter, as she had predicted. She was taken suddenly ill; she died about three days before the marriage day, and was finally dressed in her shroud, according to the natural course of the funeral arrangements, on the morning that was to have been the wedding festival.

Lord Morton, the nobleman thus suddenly and remarkably bereaved of his bride, was the only gentleman who appeared at the dinner table. He took a particular interest in literature; and it was, in fact, through *his* kindness that, for the first time in my life, I found myself somewhat in the situation of a *"lion."* The occasion of Lord Morton's flattering notice was a particular copy of verses which had gained for me a public distinction; not, however, I must own, a very brilliant one; the prize awarded to me being not the first, nor even the second,—what on the continent is called the *accessit,*—it was simply the third; and that fact, stated nakedly, might have left it doubtful whether I were to be considered in the light of one honored or of one stigmatized. However, the judges in this case, with more honesty, or more self-distrust, than belongs to most adjudications of the kind, had printed the first three of the successful essays. Consequently, it was left open to each of the less successful candidates to benefit by any difference of taste amongst their several friends; and *my* friends in particular, with the single and singular exception of my mother, who always thought her own children inferior to other people's, had generally assigned the palm to myself. Lord Morton protested loudly that the case admitted of no doubt; that gross injustice had been done me; and, as the ladies of the family were much influenced by his opinion, I thus came, not only to wear the laurel in their estimation, but also with the advantageous addition of having suffered some injustice. I was not only a victor, but a victor in misfortune.

At this moment, looking back from a distance of fifty years upon those trifles, it may well be supposed that I do not attach so much importance to the subject of my fugitive honors as to have any very decided opinion one way or the other upon my own proportion of merit. I do not even recollect the major part of the verses: that which I *do* recollect, inclines me to think that, in the structure of the metre and in the choice of the expressions, I had some advantage over my competitors, though otherwise, perhaps, my verses were less finished; Lord Morton might, therefore, in a partial sense, have been just, as well as kind. But, little as that may seem likely, even then, and at the moment of reaping some advantage from my honors, which gave me a consideration with the family I was amongst such as I could not else have had, most unaffectedly I doubted in my own mind whether I were really entitled to the praises which I received. My own verses had not at all satisfied myself; and though I felt elated by the notice they had gained me, and gratified by the generosity of the earl in taking my part so warmly, I was so more in a spirit of sympathy with the kindness thus manifested in my behalf, and with the consequent kindness which it procured me from others, than from any incitement or support which it gave to my intellectual pride. In fact, whatever estimate I might make of those intellectual gifts which I believed or which I knew myself to possess, I was inclined, even in those days, to doubt whether my natural vocation lay towards poetry. Well, indeed, I knew, and I know that, had I chosen to enlist amongst the *soi disant* poets of the day,—amongst those, I mean, who, by mere force of *talent* and mimetic skill, contrive to sustain the part of poet in a scenical sense and with a scenical effect,—I also could have won such laurels as are won by such merit; I also could have taken and sustained a place *taliter qualiter* amongst the poets of the time. Why *not* then? Simply because I knew that me, as them, would await the certain destiny in reversion of resigning that place in the next generation to some younger candidate having equal or greater skill in appropriating the vague sentiments and old traditionary language of passion spread through books, but having also the advantage of novelty, and of a closer adaptation to the prevailing taste of the day. Even at that early age, I was keenly alive, if not so keenly as at this moment, to the fact, that by far the larger proportion of what is received in every age for poetry, and for a season usurps that consecrated name, is *not* the spontaneous overflow of real unaffected passion, deep, and at the same time original, and also forced into public manifestation of itself from the necessity which cleaves to all passion alike of seeking external sympathy: this it is *not*; but a counterfeit assumption of such passion, according to the more or less accurate skill of the writer in distinguishing the key of passion suited to the particular age; and a concurrent assumption of the language of passion, according to his more or less skill in separating the spurious from the native and legitimate diction of genuine emotion. Rarely, indeed, are the reputed poets of any age men who groan, like prophets, under the burden of a message which they have to deliver, and *must* deliver, of a mission which they *must* discharge. Generally, nay, with much fewer exceptions, perhaps, than would be readily believed, they are merely simulators of the part they sustain; speaking not out of the abundance of their own hearts, but by skill and artifice assuming or personating emotions at second hand; and the whole is a business of talent, (sometimes even of great talent,) but not of original power, of genius,[68] or authentic inspiration.

---

[68] The words *genius* and *talent* are frequently distinguished from each other by those who evidently misconstrue the true distinction entirely, and sometimes so grossly as to use them by way of expressions for a mere difference in *degree*. Thus, "a man of great talent, absolutely a *genius*" occurs in a very well-written tale at this moment before me; as if being a man of genius implied only a greater than ordinary degree of talent.

Talent and *genius* are in not one point allied to each other, except generically—that both express modes of intellectual power. But the kinds of power are not merely different; they are in polar opposition to each other. *Talent* is intellectual power of every kind, which acts and manifests itself by and through the *will* and the *active* forces.

Genius, as the verbal origin implies, is that much rarer species of intellectual power which is derived from the *genial* nature,—from the spirit of suffering and enjoying,—from

From Porters, after a few days' visit, we returned to Eton. Her majesty about this time gave some splendid *fêtes* at Frogmore, to one or two of which she had directed that we should be invited. The invitation was, of course, on my friend's account; but her majesty had condescended to direct that I, as his visitor, should be specially included. Lord Westport, young as he was, had become tolerably indifferent about such things; but to me such a scene was a novelty; and, on that account, it was settled we should go as early as was permissible. We *did* go; and I was not sorry to have had the gratification of witnessing (if it were but for once or twice) the splendors of a royal party. But, after the first edge of expectation was taken off,—after the vague uncertainties of rustic ignorance had given place to absolute realities, and the eye had become a little familiar with the flashing of the jewelry,—I began to suffer under the constraints incident to a young person in such a situation—the situation, namely, of sedentary passiveness, where one is acted upon, but does not act. The music, in fact, was all that continued to delight me; and, but for *that*, I believe I should have had some difficulty in avoiding so monstrous an indecorum as yawning. I revise this faulty expression, however, on the spot; not the music only it was, but the music combined with the dancing, that so deeply impressed me. The ball room—a temporary erection, with something of the character of a pavilion about it—wore an elegant and festal air; the part

---

the spirit of pleasure and pain, as organized more or less perfectly; and this is independent of the will. It is a function of the *passive* nature. Talent is conversant with the adaptation of means to ends. But genius is conversant only with ends. Talent has no sort of connection, not the most remote or shadowy, with the *moral* nature or temperament; genius is steeped and saturated with this moral nature.

This was written twenty years ago. Now, (1853,) when revising it, I am tempted to add three brief annotations:—

1st. It scandalizes me that, in the occasional comments upon this distinction which have reached my eye, no attention should have been paid to the profound suggestions as to the radix of what is meant by *genius* latent in the word *genial*. For instance, in an extract made by "The Leader," a distinguished literary journal, from a recent work entitled "Poetics," by Mr. Dallas, there is not the slightest notice taken of this subtile indication and leading towards the truth. Yet surely *that* is hardly philosophic. For could Mr. Dallas suppose that the idea involved in the word *genial* had no connection, or none but an accidental one, with the idea involved in the word *genius*? It is clear that from the Roman conception (whencesoever emanating) of the natal genius, as the secret and central representative of what is most characteristic and individual in the nature of every human being, are derived alike the notion of the *genial* and our modern notion of *genius* as contradistinguished from *talent*.

2d. As another broad character of distinction between *genius* and *talent*, I would observe, that *genius* differentiates a man from all other men; whereas *talent* is the same in one man as in another; that is, where it exists at all, it is the mere echo and reflex of the same talent, as seen in thousands of other men, differing only by more and less, but not at all in quality. In genius, on the contrary, no two men were ever duplicates of each other.

3d. All talent, in whatsoever class, reveals itself as an effort—as a counteraction to an opposing difficulty or hinderance; whereas genius universally moves in headlong sympathy and concurrence with spontaneous power. Talent works universally by intense resistance to an antagonist force; whereas genius works under a rapture of necessity and spontaneity.

allotted to the dancers being fenced off by a gilded lattice work, and ornamented beautifully from the upper part with drooping festoons of flowers. But all the luxury that spoke to the eye merely faded at once by the side of impassioned dancing, sustained by impassioned music. Of all the scenes which this world offers, none is to me so profoundly interesting, none (I say it deliberately) so affecting, as the spectacle of men and women floating through the mazes of a dance; under these conditions, however, that the music shall be rich, resonant, and festal, the execution of the dancers perfect, and the dance itself of a character to admit of free, fluent, and *continuous* motion. But this last condition will be sought vainly in the quadrilles, &c., which have for so many years banished the truly beautiful *country dances* native to England. Those whose taste and sensibility were so defective as to substitute for the *beautiful* in dancing the merely *difficult*, were sure, in the end, to transfer the depravations of this art from the opera house to the floors of private ball rooms. The tendencies even then were in that direction; but as yet they had not attained their final stage; and the English country dance[69] was still in estimation at the courts of princes. Now, of all dances, this is the only one, as a class, of which you can truly describe the motion to be *continuous,* that is, not interrupted or fitful, but unfolding its fine mazes with the equability of light in its diffusion through free space. And wherever the music happens to be not of a light, trivial character, but charged with the spirit of festal pleasure, and the performers in the dance so far skilful as to betray no awkwardness verging on the ludicrous, I believe that many people feel as I feel in such circumstances, viz., derive from the spectacle the very grandest form of passionate sadness which can belong to any spectacle whatsoever. *Sadness* is not the exact word; nor is there any word in any language (because none in the finest languages) which exactly expresses the state; since it is not a depressing, but a most elevating state to which I allude. And, certainly, it is

----

[69] This word, I am well aware, grew out of the French word *contre danse*; indicating the regular contraposition of male and female partners in the first arrangement of the dancers. The word *country dance* was therefore originally a corruption; but, having once arisen and taken root in the language, it is far better to retain it in its colloquial form; better, I mean, on the general, principle concerned in such cases. For it is, in fact, by such corruptions, by offsets upon an old stock, arising through ignorance or mispronunciation originally, that every language is frequently enriched; and new modifications of thought, unfolding themselves in the progress of society, generate for themselves concurrently appropriate expressions. Many words in the Latin can be pointed out as having passed through this process. It must not be allowed to weigh against the validity of a word once fairly naturalized by use, that originally it crept in upon an abuse or a corruption. *Prescription* is as strong a ground of legitimation in a case of this nature as it is in law. And the old axiom is applicable—*Fieri non debuit, factum valet*. Were it otherwise, languages would be robbed of much of their wealth. And, universally, the class of *purists*, in matters of language, are liable to grievous suspicion, as almost constantly proceeding on *half* knowledge and on insufficient principles. For example, if I have read one, I have read twenty letters, addressed to newspapers, denouncing the name of a great quarter in London, *Mary-le-bone*, as ludicrously ungrammatical. The writers had learned (or were learning) French; and they had thus become aware, that neither the article nor the adjective was right. True, not right for the current age, but perfectly right for the age in which the name arose; but, for want of elder French, they did not know that in our Chaucer's time both were right. *Le* was then the article feminine as well as masculine, and *bone* was then the true form for the adjective.

easy to understand, that many states of pleasure, and in particular the highest, are the most of all removed from merriment. The day on which a Roman triumphed was the most gladsome day of his existence; it was the crown and consummation of his prosperity; yet assuredly it was also to him the most solemn of his days. Festal music, of a rich and passionate character, is the most remote of any from vulgar hilarity. Its very gladness and pomp is impregnated with sadness, but sadness of a grand and aspiring order. Let, for instance, (since without individual illustrations there is the greatest risk of being misunderstood,) any person of musical sensibility listen to the exquisite music composed by Beethoven, as an opening for Burger's "Lenore," the running idea of which is the triumphal return of a crusading host, decorated with laurels and with palms, within the gates of their native city; and then say whether the presiding feeling, in the midst of this tumultuous festivity, be not, by infinite degrees, transcendent to any thing so vulgar as hilarity. In fact, laughter itself is of all things the most equivocal; as the organ of the ludicrous, laughter is allied to the trivial and the mean; as the organ of joy, it is allied to the passionate and the noble. From all which the reader may comprehend, if he should not happen experimentally to have felt, that a spectacle of young men and women, *flowing* through the mazes of an intricate dance under a full volume of music, taken with all the circumstantial adjuncts of such a scene in rich men's halls; the blaze of lights and jewels, the life, the motion, the sea-like undulation of heads, the interweaving of the figures, the *anachuchlosis* or self-revolving, both of the dance and the music, "never ending, still beginning," and the continual regeneration of order from a system of motions which forever touch the very brink of confusion; that such a spectacle, with such circumstances, may happen to be capable of exciting and sustaining the very grandest emotions of philosophic melancholy to which the human spirit is open. The reason is, in part, that such a scene presents a sort of mask of human life, with its whole equipage of pomps and glories, its luxury of sight and sound, its hours of golden youth, and the interminable revolution of ages hurrying after ages, and one generation treading upon the flying footsteps of another; whilst all the while the overruling music attempers the mind to the spectacle, the subject to the object, the beholder to the vision. And, although this is known to be but one phasis of life,—of life culminating and in ascent,—yet the other (and repulsive) phasis is concealed upon the hidden or averted side of the golden arras, known but not felt; or is seen but dimly in the rear, crowding into indistinct proportions. The effect of the music is, to place the mind in a state of elective attraction for every thing in harmony with its own prevailing key.

This pleasure, as always on similar occasions, I had at present; but naturally in a degree corresponding to the circumstances of *royal* splendor through which the scene revolved; and, if I have spent rather more words than should reasonably have been requisite in describing any obvious state of emotion, it is not because, in itself, it is either vague or doubtful, but because it is difficult, without calling upon a reader for a little reflection, to convince him that there is not something paradoxical in the assertion, that joy and festal pleasure, of the highest kind, are liable to a *natural* combination with solemnity, or even with melancholy the most profound. Yet, to speak in the mere simplicity of truth, so mysterious is human nature, and so little to be read by him who runs, that almost every weighty aspect of truth upon that theme will be found at first sight to be startling, or sometimes paradoxical. And so little need is there for chasing or courting paradox, that, on the contrary, he who is faithful to his own experiences will find all his efforts little enough to keep down the paradoxical air besieging much of what he *knows* to be the truth. No man needs to *search* for paradox in this world of ours. Let him simply confine himself to the truth, and he will find paradox growing every where under his hands as rank as weeds. For new truths of importance are rarely agreeable to any preconceived theories; that is, cannot be explained by these theories; which are insufficient, therefore, even where they are true. And universally, it must be borne in mind, that not that is paradox which, seeming to be true, is upon examination false, but that which, seeming to be false, may upon examination be found true.[70]

The pleasure of which I have been speaking belongs to all such scenes; but on this particular occasion there was also something more. To see persons in "the body" of whom you have been reading in newspapers from the very earliest of your reading days,—those, who have hitherto been great *ideas* in your childish thoughts, to see and to hear moving and talking as carnal existences amongst other human beings,—had, for the first half hour or so, a singular and strange effect. But this naturally waned rapidly after it had once begun to wane. And when these first startling impressions of novelty had worn off, it must be confessed that the peculiar circumstances attaching to a royal ball were not favorable to its joyousness or genial spirit of enjoyment. I am not going to repay her majesty's condescension so ill, or so much to abuse the privileges of a guest, as to draw upon my recollections of what passed for the materials of a cynical critique. Every thing was done, I doubt not, which court etiquette permitted, to thaw those ungenial restraints which gave to the whole too much of a ceremonial and official character, and to each actor in the scene gave too much of the air belonging to one who is discharging a duty, and to the youngest even among the principal personages concerned gave an apparent anxiety and jealousy of manner—jealousy, I mean, not of others, but a prudential jealousy of his own possible oversights or trespasses. In fact, a great personage bearing a state character cannot be regarded, nor regard himself, with the perfect freedom which belongs to social intercourse; no, nor ought to be. It is not rank alone which is here concerned; that, as being his own, he might lay aside for an hour or two; but he bears a representative character also. He has not his own rank only, but the rank of others, to protect; he (supposing him the sovereign or a prince near to the succession) embodies and impersonates the majesty of a great people; and this character, were you ever so much encouraged to do so, you, the *idiotaes*, the *lay* spectator or "assister," neither could nor ought to dismiss from your thoughts. Besides all which, it must be acknowledged, that to see brothers dancing with sisters—as too often occurred in those dances to which the princesses were parties—disturbed the appropriate interest of the scene, being

---

[70] And therefore it was with strict propriety that Boyle, anxious to fix public attention upon some truths of hydrostatics, published them avowedly as *paradoxes*. According to the false popular notion of what it is that constitutes a paradox, Boyle should be taken to mean that these hydrostatic theorems were fallacies. But far from it. Boyle solicits attention to these propositions—not as seeming to be true and turning out false, but, reversely, as wearing an air of falsehood and turning out true.

irreconcilable with the allusive meaning of dancing in general, and laid a weight upon its gayety which no condescensions from the highest quarter could remove. This infelicitous arrangement forced the thoughts of all present upon the exalted rank of the parties which could dictate and exact so unusual an assortment. And that rank, again, it presented to us under one of its least happy aspects; as insulating a blooming young woman amidst the choir of her coevals, and surrounding her with dreadful solitude amidst a vast crowd of the young, the brave, the beautiful, and the accomplished.

Meantime, as respected myself individually, I had reason to be grateful: every kindness and attention were shown to me. My invitation I was sensible that I owed entirely to my noble friend. But, *having* been invited, I felt assured, from what passed, that it was meant and provided that I should not, by any possibility, be suffered to think myself overlooked. Lord Westport and I communicated our thoughts occasionally by means of a language which we, in those days, found useful enough at times, and which bore the name of *Ziph*. The language and the name were both derived (that is, were *immediately* so derived, for *remotely* the Ziph language may ascend to Nineveh) from Winchester. Dr. Mapleton, a physician in Bath, who attended me in concert with Mr. Grant, an eminent surgeon, during the nondescript malady of the head, happened to have had three sons at Winchester; and his reason for removing them is worth mentioning, as it illustrates the well-known system of *fagging*. One or more of them showed to the quick medical eye of Dr. Mapleton symptoms of declining health; and, upon cross questioning, he found that, being (as juniors) *fags* (that is, bondsmen by old prescription) to appointed seniors, they were under the necessity of going out nightly into the town for the purpose of executing commissions; but this was not easy, as all the regular outlets were closed at an early hour. In such a dilemma, any route, that was barely practicable at whatever risk, must be traversed by the loyal fag; and it so happened that none of any kind remained open or accessible, except one; and this one communication happened to have escaped suspicion, simply because it lay through a succession of temples and sewers sacred to the goddesses Cloacina and Scavengerina. That of itself was not so extraordinary a fact: the wonder lay in the number, viz., seventeen. Such were the actual amount of sacred edifices which, through all their dust, and garbage, and mephitic morasses, these miserable vassals had to thread all *but* every night of the week. Dr. Mapleton, when he had made this discovery, ceased to wonder at the medical symptoms; and, as *faggery* was an abuse too venerable and sacred to be touched by profane hands, he lodged no idle complaints, but simply removed his sons to a school where the Serbonian bogs of the subterraneous goddess might not intersect the nocturnal line of march so *very* often. One day, during the worst of my illness, when the kind-hearted doctor was attempting to amuse me with this anecdote, and asking me whether I thought Hannibal would have attempted his march over the Little St. Bernard,—supposing that he and the elephant which he rode had been summoned to explore a route through seventeen similar nuisances,—he went on to mention the one sole accomplishment which his sons had imported from Winchester. This was the *Ziph* language, communicated at Winchester to any aspirant for a fixed fee of one half guinea, but which the doctor then communicated to me—as I do now to the reader—*gratis*. I make a present of this language without fee, or price, or entrance money, to my honored reader; and let him understand that it is undoubtedly a bequest of elder times. Perhaps it may be coeval with the pyramids. For in the famous "Essay on a Philosophical Character," (I forget whether *that* is the exact title,) a large folio written by the ingenious Dr. Wilkins, Bishop of Chester,[71] and published early in the reign of Charles II., a folio which I, in youthful days, not only read but studied, this language is recorded and accurately described amongst many other modes of cryptical communication, oral and visual, spoken, written, or symbolic. And, as the bishop does not speak of it as at all a *recent* invention, it may probably at that time have been regarded as an antique device for conducting a conversation in secrecy amongst bystanders; and this advantage it has, that it is applicable to all languages alike; nor can it possibly be penetrated by one not initiated in the mystery. The secret is this—(and the grandeur of simplicity at any rate it has)—repeat the vowel or diphthong of every syllable, prefixing to the vowel so repeated the letter G. Thus, for example: Shall we go away in an hour? Three hours we have already staid. This in Ziph becomes: *Shagall wege gogo agawagay igin agan hougour? Threegee hougours wege hagave agalreageadygy stagaid.*[72] It must not be supposed that Ziph proceeds slowly. A very little practice gives the greatest fluency; so that even now, though certainly I cannot have practised it for fifty years, my power of speaking the Ziph remains unimpaired. I forget whether in the Bishop of Chester's account of this cryptical language the consonant intercalated be G or not. Evidently any consonant will answer the purpose. F or L would be softer, and so far better.

In this learned tongue it was that my friend and I communicated our feelings; and, having staid nearly four hours, a time quite sufficient to express a proper sense of the honor, we departed; and, on emerging into the open high road, we threw up our hats and huzzaed, meaning no sort of disrespect, but from uncontrollable pleasure in recovered liberty.

Soon after this we left Eton for Ireland. Our first destination being Dublin, of course we went by Holyhead. The route at that time, from Southern England to Dublin, did not (as in elder and in later days) go round by Chester. A few miles after leaving Shrewsbury, somewhere about Oswestry, it entered North Wales; a stage farther brought us to the celebrated vale of Llangollen; and, on reaching the approach to this about sunset on a beautiful evening of June, I first found myself amongst the mountains—a feature in natural scenery for which, from my earliest days, it was not extravagant to say that I had hungered and thirsted. In no one expectation of my life have I been less disappointed; and I may add, that no one enjoyment has less decayed or palled upon my continued experience. A mountainous region, with a slender population, and *that* of a simple pastoral character; <u>behold my chief</u> conditions of a pleasant permanent dwelling-place! But, thus far

[71] This Dr. Wilkins was related to marriage to Cromwell, and is better known to the world, perhaps, by his Essay on the possibility of a passage (or, as the famous author of the "Pursuits of Literature" said, by way of an episcopal metaphor, the possibility of a *translation*) to the moon.

[72] One omission occurs to me on reviewing this account of the Ziph, which is—that I should have directed the accent to be placed on the intercalated syllable: thus *ship* becomes *shigip*, with the emphasis on *gip; run* becomes *rugún*, &c.

I have altered, that *now* I should greatly prefer forest scenery— such as the New Forest, or the Forest of Dean in Gloucestershire. The mountains of Wales range at about the same elevation as those of Northern England; three thousand and four to six hundred feet being the extreme limit which they reach. Generally speaking, their forms are less picturesque individually, and they are less happily grouped than their English brethren. I have since also been made sensible by Wordsworth of one grievous defect in the structure of the Welsh valleys; too generally they take the *basin* shape—the level area at their foot does not detach itself with sufficient precision from the declivities that surround them. Of this, however, I was not aware at the time of first seeing Wales; although the striking effect from the *opposite* form of the Cumberland and Westmoreland valleys, which almost universally present a flat area at the base of the surrounding hills, level, to use Wordsworth's expression, *"as the floor of a temple,"* would, at any rate, have arrested my eye, as a circumstance of impressive beauty, even though the want of such a feature might not, in any case, have affected me as a fault. As something that had a positive value, this characteristic of the Cambrian valleys had fixed my attention, but not as any telling point of contrast against the Cambrian valleys. No faults, however, at that early age disturbed my pleasure, except that, after one whole day's travelling, (for so long it cost us between Llangollen and Holyhead,) the want of water struck me upon review as painfully remarkable. From Conway to Bangor (seventeen miles) we were often in sight of the sea; but fresh water we had seen hardly any; no lake, no stream much beyond a brook. This is certainly a conspicuous defect in North Wales, considered as a region of fine scenery. The few lakes I have since become acquainted with, as that near Bala, near Beddkelert, and beyond Machynleth, are not attractive either in their forms or in their accompaniments; the Bala Lake being meagre and insipid, the others as it were unfinished, and unaccompanied with their furniture of wood.

At the *Head* (to call it by its common colloquial name) we were detained a few days in those unsteaming times by foul winds. Our time, however, thanks to the hospitality of a certain Captain Skinner on that station, did not hang heavy on our hands, though we were imprisoned, as it were, on a dull rock; for Holyhead itself is a little island of rock, an insulated dependency of Anglesea; which, again, is a little insulated dependency of North Wales. The packets on this station were at that time lucrative commands; and they were given (perhaps *are*[73] given?) to post captains in the navy. Captain Skinner was celebrated for his convivial talents; he did the honors of the place in a hospitable style; daily asked us to dine with him, and seemed as inexhaustible in his wit as in his hospitality.

This answered one purpose, at least, of special convenience to our party at that moment: it kept us from all necessity of meeting each other during the day, except under circumstances where we escaped the necessity of any familiar communication. Why that should have become desirable, arose upon the following mysterious change of relations between ourselves and the Rev. Mr. Gr——, Lord Westport's tutor. On the last day of our journey, Mr. G., who had accompanied us thus far, but now at Holyhead was to leave us, suddenly took offence (or, at

---

[73] Written twenty years ago.

least, then first *showed* his offence) at something we had said, done, or omitted, and never spoke one syllable to either of us again. Being both of us amiably disposed, and incapable of having seriously meditated either word or deed likely to wound any person's feelings, we were much hurt at the time, and often retraced the little incidents upon the road, to discover, if possible, what it was that had laid us open to misconstruction. But it remained to both of us a lasting mystery. This tutor was an Irishman, of Trinity College, Dublin, and, I believe, of considerable pretensions as a scholar; but, being reserved and haughty, or else presuming in us a knowledge of our offence, which we really had not, he gave us no opening for any explanation. To the last moment, however, he manifested a punctilious regard to the duties of his charge. He accompanied us in our boat, on a dark and gusty night, to the packet, which lay a little out at sea. He saw us on board; and then, standing up for one moment, he said, "Is all right on deck?" "All right, sir," sang out the ship's steward. "Have you, Lord Westport, got your boat cloak with you?" "Yes, sir." "Then, pull away, boatmen." We listened for a time to the measured beat of his retreating oars, marvelling more and more at the atrocious nature of our crime which could thus avail to intercept even his last adieus. I, for my part, never saw him again; nor, as I have reason to think, did Lord Westport. Neither did we ever unravel the mystery.

As if to irritate our curiosity still more, Lord Westport showed me a torn fragment of paper in his tutor's hand—writing, which, together with others, had been thrown (as he believed) purposely in his way. If he was right in that belief, it appeared that he had missed the particular fragment which was designed to raise the veil upon our guilt; for the one he produced contained exactly these words: "With respect to your ladyship's anxiety to know how far the acquaintance with Mr. De Q. is likely to be of service to your son, I think I may now venture to say that"—There the sibylline fragment ended; nor could we torture it into any further revelation. However, both of us saw the propriety of not ourselves practising any mystery, nor giving any advantage to Mr. G. by imperfect communications; and accordingly, on the day after we reached Dublin, we addressed a circumstantial account of our journey and our little mystery to Lady Altamont in England; for to her it was clear that the tutor had confided his mysterious wrongs. Her ladyship answered with kindness; but did not throw any light on the problem which exercised at once our memories, our skill in conjectural interpretation, and our sincere regrets. Lord Westport and I regretted much that there had not been a wider margin attached to the fragment of Mr. G.'s letter to Lady Altamont; in which case, as I could readily have mimicked his style of writing, it would have been easy for me to fill up thus: "With respect to your ladyship's anxiety, &c., I think I may now venture to say that, if the solar system were searched, there could not be found a companion more serviceable to your son than Mr. De Q. He speaks the Ziph most beautifully. He writes it, I am told, classically. And if there were a Ziph nation as well as a Ziph language, I am satisfied that he would very soon be at the head of it; as he already is, beyond all competition, at the head of the Ziph literature." Lady Altamont, on receiving this, would infallibly have supposed him mad; she would have written so to all her Irish friends, and would have commended the poor gentleman to the care of his nearest kinsmen; and thus we should have had some little indemnification for the annoyance he had caused us. I mention this tri-fle, simply because, trifle as it is, it involved a mystery, and furnishes an occasion for glancing at that topic. Mysteries as deep, with results a little more important and foundations a little sounder, have many times crossed me in life; one, for in-stance, I recollect at this moment, known pretty extensively to the neighborhood in which it occurred. It was in the county of S——. A lady married, and married well, as was thought. About twelve months afterwards, she returned alone in a post chaise to her father's house; paid, and herself dismissed, the postilion at the gate; entered the house; ascended to the room in which she had passed her youth, and known in the family by her name; took possession of it again; intimated by signs, and by one short letter at her first arrival, what she would require; lived for nearly twenty years in this state of *La Trappe* seclusion and silence; nor ever, to the hour of her death, explained what circumstances had dissolved the supposed happy connection she had formed, or what had become of her husband. Her looks and gestures were of a nature to repress all questions in the spirit of mere curios-ity; and the spirit of affection naturally respected a secret which was guarded so severely. This might be supposed a Spanish tale; yet it happened in England, and in a pretty populous neighborhood. The romances which occur in real life are too often connected with circumstances of criminality in some one among the parties concerned; on that account, more than any other, they are often suppressed; else, judging by the number which have fallen within my own knowledge, they must be of more frequent occurrence than is usually supposed. Among such romances, those cases, perhaps, form an unusual proportion in which young, innocent, and high-minded persons have made a sudden discovery of some great profligacy or deep unworthiness in the person to whom they had surrendered their entire af-fections. That shock, more than any other, is capable of blighting, in one hour, the whole after existence, and sometimes of at once overthrowing the balance of life or of reason. Instances I have known of both; and such afflictions are the less open to any alleviation, that sometimes they are of a nature so delicate as to preclude all confidential communication of them to another; and sometimes it would be even dangerous, in a legal sense, to communicate them.

A sort of adventure occurred, and not of a kind pleasant to recall, even on this short voyage. The passage to Dublin from the Head is about sixty miles, I believe; yet, from baffling winds, it cost us upwards of thirty hours. On the second day, going upon deck, we found that our only fellow-passenger of note was a woman of rank, celebrated for her beauty; and not undeservedly, for a lovely creature she was. The body of her travelling coach had been, as usual, unslung from the "carriage," (by which is technically meant the wheels and the perch,) and placed upon deck. This she used as a place of retreat from the sun during the day, and as a resting-place at night. For want of more interesting companions, she invited us, during the day, into her coach; and we taxed our abilities to make ourselves as entertaining as we could, for we were greatly fascinated by the lady's beauty. The second night proved very sultry; and Lord Westport and myself, suffering from the oppression of the cabin, left our berths, and lay, wrapped up in cloaks, upon deck. Having talked for some hours, we were both on the point of falling asleep, when a stealthy tread near our heads awoke us. It was starlight; and we traced between ourselves and the sky the outline of a man's figure. Lying upon a mass of tarpaulings, we were ourselves undistinguishable, and the figure moved in the direction of the coach. Our first thought was to raise an alarm, scarcely doubting that the purpose of the man was to rob the unprotected lady of her watch or purse. But, to our astonishment, we saw the coach door silently swing open under a touch from *within*. All was as silent as a dream; the figure entered, the door closed, and we were left to interpret the case as we might. Strange it was that this lady could permit herself to calculate upon absolute concealment in such circumstances. We recollected afterwards to have heard some indistinct rumor buzzed about the packet on the day preceding, that a gentleman, and some even spoke of him by name as a Colonel — —, for some unknown purpose, was concealed in the steerage of the packet. And other appearances indicated that the affair was not entirely a secret even amongst the lady's servants. To both of *us* the story proclaimed a moral already sufficiently current, viz., that women of the highest and the very lowest rank are alike thrown too much into situations of danger and temptation.[74] I might mention some additional circumstances of criminal aggravation in this lady's case; but, as they would tend to point out the real person to those acquainted with her history, I shall forbear. She has since made a noise in the world, and has maintained, I believe, a tolerably fair reputation. Soon after sunrise the next morning, a heavenly morning of June, we dropped our anchor in the famous Bay of Dublin. There was a dead calm; the sea was like a lake; and, as we were some miles from the Pigeon House, a boat was manned to put us on shore. The lovely lady, unaware that we were parties to her guilty secret, went with us, accompanied by her numerous attendants, and looking as beautiful, and hardly less innocent, than an angel. Long afterwards, Lord Westport and I met her, hanging upon the arm of her husband, a manly and good-natured man, of polished manners, to whom she introduced us; for she voluntarily challenged us as her fellow- voyagers, and, I suppose, had no suspicion which pointed in our direction. She even joined her husband in cordially pressing us to visit them at their magnificent *chateau*. Upon us, meantime, whatever might be *her* levity, the secret of which accident had put us in possession pressed with a weight of awe; we shuddered at our own discovery; and we both agreed to drop no hint of it in any direction.[75]

---

[74] But see the note on this point at the end of the volume.

[75] Lord Westport's age at that time was the same as my own; that is, we both wanted a few months of being fifteen. But I had the advantage, perhaps, in thoughtfulness and observation of life. Being thoroughly free, however, from opinionativeness, Lord Westport readily came over to any views of mine for which I could show sufficient grounds. And on this occasion I found no difficulty in convincing him that honor and fidelity did not form sufficient guaranties for the custody of secrets. Presence of mind so as to revive one's obligations in time, tenacity of recollection, and vigilance over one's own momentary slips of tongue, so as to keep watch over indirect disclosures, are also requisite. And at that time I had an instance within my own remembrance where a secret had been betrayed, by a person of undoubted honor, but most inadvertently betrayed, and in pure oblivion of his engagement to silence. Indeed, unless where the secret is of a nature to affect some person's life, I do not believe that most people would remember beyond a period of two years the most solemn obligations to secrecy. After a lapse of time, varying of course with the person, the substance of the secret will remain upon the mind; but how he came by the secret, or

Landing about three miles from Dublin, (according to my present remembrance at Dunleary,) we were not long in reaching Sackville Street.

---

under what circumstances, he will very probably have forgotten. It is unsafe to rely upon the most religious or sacramental obligation to secrecy, unless, together with the secret, you could transfer also a magic ring that should, by a growing pressure or puncture, *sting* a man into timely alarm and warning.

CHAPTER VIII.

DUBLIN.

In Sackville Street stood the town house of Lord Altamont; and here, in the breakfast room, we found the earl seated. Long and intimately as I had known Lord Westport, it so happened that I had never seen his father, who had, indeed, of late almost pledged himself to a continued residence in Ireland by his own patriotic earnestness as an agricultural improver; whilst for his son, under the difficulties and delays at that time of all travelling, any residence whatever in England seemed preferable, but especially a residence with his mother amongst the relatives of his distinguished English grandfather, and in such close neighborhood to Eton. Lord Altamont once told me, that the journey outward and inward between Eton and Westport, taking into account all the unavoidable deviations from the direct route, in compliance with the claims of kinship, &c., (a case which in Ireland forced a traveller often into a perpetual zigzag,) counted up to something more than a thousand miles. That is, in effect, when valued in loss of time, and allowance being made for the want of *continuity* in those parts of the travelling system that did not accurately dovetail into each other, not less than one entire fortnight must be annually sunk upon a labor that yielded no commensurate fruit. Hence the long three-years' interval which had separated father and son; and hence my own nervous apprehension, as we were racing through the suburbs of Dublin, that I should unavoidably lay a freezing restraint upon that reunion to which, after such a separation, both father and son must have looked forward with anticipation so anxious. Such cases of unintentional intrusion are at times inevitable; but, even to the least sensitive, they are always distressing; most of all they are so to the intruder, who in fact feels himself in the odd position of a criminal without a crime. He is in the situation of one who might have happened to be chased by a Bengal tiger (or, say that the tiger were a sheriff's officer) into the very centre of the Eleusinian mysteries. Do not tease me, my reader, by alleging that there were no sheriffs' officers at Athens or Eleusis. Not many, I admit; but perhaps quite as many as there were of Bengal tigers. In such a case, under whatever compulsion, the man has violated a holy seclusion. He has seen that which he ought *not* to have seen; and he is viewed with horror by the privileged spectators. Should he plead that this was his misfortune, and not his fault, the answer would be, "True; it was your misfortune; we know it; and it is *our* misfortune to be under the necessity of hating you for it." But there was no cause for similar fears at present; so uniformly considerate in his kindness was Lord Altamont. It is true, that Lord Westport, as an only child, and a child to be proud of,—for he was at that time rather handsome, and conciliated general good will by his engaging manners,—was viewed by his father with an anxiety of love that sometimes became almost painful to witness. But this natural self-surrender to a first involuntary emotion Lord Altamont did not suffer to usurp any such lengthened expression as might too painfully have reminded me of being "one too many." One solitary half minute being paid down as a tribute to the sanctities of the case, his next care was to withdraw me, the stranger, from any oppressive feeling of strangership. And accordingly, so far from realizing the sense of being an intruder, in one minute under his courteous welcome I had come to feel that, as the companion of his one darling upon earth, me also he comprehended within his paternal regards.

It must have been nine o'clock precisely when we entered the breakfast room. So much I know by an *a priori* argument, and could wish, therefore, that it had been scientifically important to know it—as important, for instance, as to know the occultation of a star, or the transit of Venus to a second. For the urn was at that moment placed on the table; and though Ireland, as a whole, is privileged to be irregular, yet such was our Sackville Street regularity, that not so much nine o'clock announced this periodic event, as inversely this event announced nine o'clock. And I used to affirm, however shocking it might sound to poor threadbare metaphysicians incapable of transcendental truths, that not nine o'clock was the cause of revealing the breakfast urn, but, on the contrary, that the revelation of the breakfast urn was the true and secret cause of nine o'clock—a phenomenon which otherwise no candid reader will pretend that he can satisfactorily account for, often as he has known it to come round. The urn was already throwing up its column of fuming mist; and the breakfast table was covered with June flowers sent by a lady on the chance of Lord Westport's arrival. It was clear, therefore, that we were expected; but so we had been for three or four days previously; and it illustrates the enormous uncertainties of travelling at this closing era of the eighteenth century, that for three or four days more we should have been expected without the least anxiety in case any thing had occurred to detain us on the road. In fact, the possibility of a Holyhead packet being lost had no place in the catalogue of adverse contingencies—not even when calculated by mothers. To come by way of Liverpool or Parkgate, was not without grounds of reasonable fear; I myself had lost acquaintances (schoolboys) on each of those lines of transit. Neither Bristol nor Milford Haven was entirely cloudless in reputation. But from Holyhead only one packet had ever been lost; and that was in the days of Queen Anne, when I have good reason to think that a villain was on board, who hated the Duke of Marlborough; so that this one exceptional case, far from being looked upon as a public calamity, would, of course, be received thankfully as cleansing the nation from a scamp.

* * * * *

Ireland was still smoking with the embers of rebellion; and Lord Cornwallis, who had been sent expressly to extinguish it, and had won the reputation of having fulfilled this mission with energy and success, was then the lord lieutenant; and at that moment he was regarded with more interest than any other public man. Accordingly I was not sorry when, two mornings after our arrival, Lord Altamont said to us at breakfast, "Now, if you wish to see what I call a great man, go with me this morning, and you shall see Lord Cornwallis; for that man who has given peace both to the east and to the west—taming a tiger in the Mysore that hated England as much as Hannibal hated Rome, and in Ireland pulling up by the roots a French invasion, combined with an Irish insurrection—will always for me rank as a great man." We willingly accompanied the earl to the Phoenix Park, where the lord lieutenant was then residing, and were privately presented to him. I had seen an engraving (celebrated, I believe, in its day) of Lord Cornwallis receiving the young Mysore princes as hostages at Seringapatam; and I knew the outline of his public services. This gave me an additional interest in seeing him; but I was disappointed to find no traces in his manner of the energy and activity I presumed him to possess; he seemed, on the contrary, slow or even heavy, but benevolent and considerate in a degree which won the confidence at once. Him we saw often; for Lord Altamont took us with him wherever and whenever we wished; and me in particular (to whom the Irish leaders of society were as yet entirely unknown by sight) it gratified highly to see persons of historical names—names, I mean, historically connected with the great events of Elizabeth's or Cromwell's era—attending at the Phoenix Park. But the persons whom I remember most distinctly of all whom I was then in the habit of seeing, were Lord Clare, the chancellor, the late Lord Londonderry, (then Castlereagh,) at that time the Irish chancellor of the exchequer, and the speaker of the House of Commons, (Mr. Foster, since, I believe, created Lord Oriel.) With the speaker, indeed, Lord Altamont had more intimate grounds of connection than with any other public man; both being devoted to the encouragement and personal superintendence of great agricultural improvements. Both were bent on introducing through models diffused extensively on their own estates, English husbandry, English improved breeds of cattle, and, where *that* was possible, English capital and skill, into the rural economy of Ireland.

Amongst the splendid spectacles which I witnessed, as the *most* splendid I may mention an installation of the Knights of St. Patrick. There were six knights installed on this occasion, one of the six being Lord Altamont. He had no doubt received his ribbon as a reward for his parliamentary votes, and especially in the matter of the union; yet, from all his conversation upon that question, and from the general conscientiousness of his private life, I am convinced that he acted all along upon patriotic motives, and in obedience to his real views (whether right or wrong) of the Irish interests. One chief reason, indeed, which detained us in Dublin, was the necessity of staying for this particular installation. At one time, Lord Altamont had designed to take his son and myself for the two esquires who attend the new-made knight, according to the ritual of this ceremony; but that plan was laid aside, on learning that the other five knights were to be attended by adults; and thus, from being partakers as actors, my friend and I became simple spectators of this splendid scene, which took place in the Cathedral of St. Patrick. So easily does mere external pomp slip out of the memory, as to all its circumstantial items, leaving behind nothing beyond the general impression, that at this moment I remember no one incident of the whole ceremonial, except that some foolish person laughed aloud as the knights went up with their offerings to the altar; the object of this unfeeling laughter being apparently Lord Altamont, who happened to be lame—a singular instance of levity to exhibit within the walls of such a building, and at the most solemn part of such a ceremony, which to my mind had a three-fold grandeur: 1st, as *symbolic* and shadowy; 2d, as representing the interlacings of chivalry with religion in the highest aspirations of both; 3d, as *national*; placing the heraldries and military pomps of a people, so memorably faithful to St. Peter's chair, at the foot of the altar. Lord Westport and I sat with Lord and Lady Castlereagh. They were both young at this time, and both wore an impressive appearance of youthful happiness; neither, happily for their peace of mind, able to pierce that cloud of years, not much more than twenty, which divided them from the day destined in one hour to wreck the happiness of both. We had met both on other occasions; and their conversation, through the course of that day's pomps, was the most interesting circumstance to me, and the one which I remember with most distinctness of all that belonged to the installation. By the way, one morning, on occasion of some conversation arising about Irish bulls, I made an agreement with Lord Altamont to note down in a memorandum book every thing throughout my stay in Ireland, which, to my feeling as an Englishman, should seem to be, or should approach to, a bull. And this day, at dinner, I report-ed from Lady Castlereagh's conversation what struck me as such. Lord Altamont laughed, and said, "My dear child, I am sorry that it should so happen, for it is bad to stumble at the beginning; your bull is certainly a bull;[76] but as certainly Lady Castlereagh is your countrywoman, and not an Irishwoman at all." Lady Castlereagh, it seems, was a daughter of Lord Buckinghamshire; and her maiden name was Lady Emily Hobart.

One other public scene there was, about this time, in Dublin, to the eye less captivating, but far more so in a moral sense; more significant practically, more burdened with hope and with fear. This was the final ratification of the bill which united Ireland to Great Britain. I do not know that any one public act, or celebra-tion, or solemnity, in my time, did, or could, so much engage my profoundest sympathies. Wordsworth's fine sonnet on the extinction of the Venetian republic had not then been published, else the last two lines would have expressed my feel-ings. After admitting that changes had taken place in Venice, which in a manner challenged and presumed this last and mortal change, the poet goes on to say, that all this long preparation for the event could not break the shock of it. Venice, it is true, had become a shade; but, after all,—

"Men are we, and must grieve when even the shade

---

[76] The idea of a *bull* is even yet undefined; which is most extraordinary, considering that Miss Edgeworth has applied all her tact and illustrative power to furnish the *matter* for such a definition, and Coleridge all his philosophic subtlety (but in this instance, I think, with a most infelicitous result) to furnish its *form*. But both have been too fastidious in their admission of bulls. Thus, for example, Miss Edgeworth rejects, as no true bull, the common Joe Miller story, that, upon two Irishmen reaching Barnet, and being told that it was still twelve miles to London, one of them remarked, "Ah! just six miles apace." This, says Miss E., is no bull, but a sentimental remark on the maxim, that friendship divides our pains. Nothing of the kind: Miss Edgeworth cannot have understood it. The bull is a true repre-sentative and exemplary specimen of the *genus*.

Of that which once was great has passed away."

But here the previous circumstances were far different from those of Venice. *There* we saw a superannuated and paralytic state, sinking at any rate into the grave, and yielding, to the touch of military violence, that only which a brief lapse of years must otherwise have yielded to internal decay. *Here,* on the contrary, we saw a young eagle, rising into power, and robbed prematurely of her natural honors, only because she did not comprehend their value, or because at this great crisis she had no champion. Ireland, in a political sense, was surely then in her youth, considering the prodigious developments she has since experienced in population and in resources of all kinds.

This great day of UNION had been long looked forward to by me; with some mixed feelings also by my young friend, for he had an Irish heart, and was jealous of whatever appeared to touch the banner of Ireland. But it was not for him to say any thing which should seem to impeach his father's patriotism in voting for the union, and promoting it through his borough influence. Yet oftentimes it seemed to me, when I introduced the subject, and sought to learn from Lord Altamont the main grounds which had reconciled him and other men, anxious for the welfare of Ireland, to a measure which at least robbed her of some splendor, and, above all, robbed her of a name and place amongst the independent states of Europe, that neither father nor son was likely to be displeased, should some great popular violence put force upon the recorded will of Parliament, and compel the two Houses to perpetuate themselves. Dolorous they must of course have looked, in mere consistency; but I fancied that internally they would have laughed. Lord Altamont, I am certain, believed (as multitudes believed) that Ireland would be bettered by the commercial advantages conceded to her as an integral province of the empire, and would have benefits which, as an independent kingdom, she had not. It is notorious that this expectation was partially realized. But let us ask, Could not a large part of these benefits have been secured to Ireland remaining as she was? Were they, in any sense, dependent on the sacrifice of her separate parliament? For my part, I believe that Mr. Pitt's motive for insisting on a legislative union was, in a small proportion, perhaps, the somewhat elevated desire to connect his own name with the historical changes of the empire; to have it stamped, not on events so fugitive as those of war and peace, liable to oblivion or eclipse, but on the permanent relations of its integral parts. In a still larger proportion I believe his motive to have been one of pure convenience, the wish to exonerate himself from the intolerable vexation of a double parliament. In a government such as ours, so care-laden at any rate, it is certainly most harassing to have the task of soliciting a measure by management and influence twice over—two trials to organize, two storms of anxiety to face, and two refractory gangs to discipline, instead of one. It must also be conceded that no treasury influence could *always* avail to prevent injurious collisions between acts of the Irish and the British Parliaments. In Dublin, as in London, the government must lay its account with being occasionally outvoted; this would be likely to happen peculiarly upon Irish questions. And acts of favor or protection would at times pass on behalf of Irish interests, not only clashing with more general ones of the central government, but indirectly also (through the virtual consolidation of the two islands since the era of steam) opening endless means for evading British acts, even within their own separate sphere of operation. On these considerations, even an Irishman must grant that public convenience called for the absorption of all local or provincial supremacies into the central supremacy. And there were two brief arguments which gave weight to those considerations: First, that the evils likely to arise (and which in France *have* arisen) from what is termed, in modern politics, the principle of *centralization*, have been for us either evaded or neutralized. The provinces, to the very farthest nook of these "nook-shotten" islands, react upon London as powerfully as London acts upon *them*; so that no counterpoise is required with us, as in France it is, to any inordinate influence at the centre. Secondly, the very pride and jealousy which could avail to dictate the retention of an independent parliament would effectually preclude any modern "Poyning's Act," having for its object to prevent the collision of the local with the central government. Each would be supreme within its own sphere, and those spheres could not but clash. The separate Irish Parliament was originally no badge of honor or independence: it began in motives of convenience, or perhaps necessity, at a period when the communication was difficult, slow, and interrupted. Any parliament, which arose on that footing, it was possible to guard by a Poyning's Act, making, in effect, all laws null which should happen to contradict the supreme or central will. But what law, in a corresponding temper, could avail to limit the jurisdiction of a parliament which confessedly had been retained on a principle of national honor? Upon every consideration, therefore, of convenience, and were it only for the necessities of public business, the absorption of the local into the central parliament had now come to speak a language that perhaps could no longer be evaded; and *that* Irishman only could consistently oppose the measure who should take his stand upon principles transcending convenience; looking, in fact, singly to the honor and dignity of a country which it was annually becoming less absurd to suppose capable of an independent existence.

Meantime, in those days, Ireland had no adequate champion; the Hoods and the Grattans were not up to the mark. Refractory as they were, they moved within the paling of order and decorum; they were not the Titans for a war against the heavens. When the public feeling beckoned and loudly supported them, they could follow a lead which they appeared to head; but they could not create such a body of public feeling, nor, when created, could they throw it into a suitable organization. What they could do, was simply as ministerial agents and rhetoricians to prosecute any general movement, when the national arm had cloven a channel and opened the road before them. Consequently, that great opening for a turbulent son of thunder passed unimproved; and the great day drew near without symptoms of tempest. At last it arrived; and I remember nothing which indicated as much ill temper in the public mind as I have seen on many hundreds of occasions, trivial by comparison, in London. Lord Westport and I were determined to lose no part of the scene, and we went down with Lord Altamont to the house. It was about the middle of the day, and a great mob filled the whole space about the two houses. As Lord Altamont's coach drew up to the steps of that splendid edifice, we heard a prodigious hissing and hooting; and I was really agitated to think that Lord Altamont, whom I loved and respected, would probably have to make his way through a tempest of public wrath—a situation more terrific to him than to others, from his embarrassed walking. I found, however, that I might have spared my anxiety; the subject of commotion was, simply, that Major Sirr, or Major Swan, I forget which, (both being celebrated in those days for their energy, as leaders of the police,) had detected a person in the act of mistaking some other man's pocket handkerchief for his own—a most natural mistake, I should fancy, where people stood crowded together so thickly. No storm of any kind awaited us, and yet at that moment there was no other arrival to divide the public attention; for, in order that we might see every thing from first to last, we were amongst the very earliest parties. Neither did our party escape under any mistake of the crowd: silence had succeeded to the uproar caused by the tender meeting between the thief and the major; and a man, who stood in a conspicuous situation, proclaimed aloud to those below him, the name or title of members as they drove up. "That," said he, "is the Earl of Altamont; the lame gentleman, I mean." Perhaps, however, his knowledge did not extend so far as to the politics of a nobleman who had taken no violent or factious part in public affairs. At. least, the dreaded insults did not follow, or only in the very feeblest manifestations. We entered; and, by way of seeing every thing, we went even to the robing room. The man who presented his robes to Lord Altamont seemed to me, of all whom I saw on that day, the one who wore the face of deepest depression. But whether this indicated the loss of a lucrative situation, or was really disinterested sorrow, growing out of a patriotic trouble, at the knowledge that he was now officiating for the last time, I could not guess. The House of Lords, decorated (if I remember) with hangings, representing the battle of the Boyne, was nearly empty when we entered—an accident which furnished to Lord Altamont the opportunity required for explaining to us the whole course and ceremonial of public business on ordinary occasions.

Gradually the house filled; beautiful women sat intermingled amongst the peers; and, in one party of these, surrounded by a bevy of admirers, we saw our fair but frail enchantress of the packet. She, on her part, saw and recognized us by an affable nod; no stain upon her cheek, indicating that she suspected to what extent she was indebted to our discretion; for it is a proof of the unaffected sorrow and the solemn awe which oppressed us both, that we had not mentioned even to Lord Altamont, nor ever *did* mention, the scene which chance had revealed to us. Next came a stir within the house, and an uproar resounding from without, which announced the arrival of his excellency. Entering the house, he also, like the other peers, wheeled round to the throne, and made to that mysterious seat a profound homage. Then commenced the public business, in which, if I recollect, the chancellor played the most conspicuous part—that chancellor (Lord Clare) of whom it was affirmed in those days, by a political opponent, that he might swim in the innocent blood which he had caused to be shed. But nautical men, I suspect, would have demurred to that estimate. Then were summoned to the bar—summoned for the last time—the gentlemen of the House of Commons; in the van of whom, and drawing all eyes upon himself, stood Lord Castlereagh. Then came the recitation of many acts passed during the session, and the sounding ratification, the Jovian

"Annuit, et nutu totum tremefecit Olympum,"

contained in the *Soit fait comme il est desiré*, or the more peremptory *Le roi le veut*. At which point in the order of succession came the royal assent to the union bill, I cannot distinctly recollect. But one thing I *do* recollect—that no audible expression, no buzz, nor murmur, nor *susurrus* even, testified the feelings which, doubtless, lay rankling in many bosoms. Setting apart all public or patriotic considerations, even then I said to myself, as I surveyed the whole assemblage of ermined peers, "How is it, and by what unaccountable magic, that William Pitt can have prevailed on all these hereditary legislators and heads of patrician houses to renounce so easily, with nothing worth the name of a struggle, and no reward worth the name of an indemnification, the very brightest jewel in their coronets? This morning they all rose from their couches peers of Parliament, individual pillars of the realm, indispensable parties to every law that could pass. Tomorrow they will be nobody—men of straw—*terrae filii*. What madness has persuaded them to part with their birthright, and to cashier themselves and their children forever into mere titular lords? As to the commoners at the bar, *their* case was different: they had no life estate at all events in their honors; and they might have the same chance for entering the imperial Parliament amongst the hundred Irish members as for reentering a native parliament. Neither, again, amongst the peers was the case always equal. Several of the higher had English titles, which would, at any rate, open the central Parliament to their ambition. That privilege, in particular, attached to Lord Altamont.[77] And he, in any case, from his large property, was tolerably sure of finding his way thither (as in fact for the rest of his life he *did*) amongst the twenty-eight representative peers. The wonder was in the case of petty and obscure lords, who had no weight personally, and none in right of their estates. Of these men, as they were notoriously not enriched by Mr. Pitt, as the distribution of honors was not very large, and as no honor could countervail the one they lost, I could not, and cannot, fathom the policy. Thus much I am sure of—that, had such a measure been proposed by a political speculator previously to Queen Anne's reign, he would have been scouted as a dreamer and a visionary, who calculated upon men being generally somewhat worse than Esau, viz., giving up their birthrights, and *without* the mess of pottage." However, on this memorable day, thus it was the union was ratified; the bill received the royal assent without a muttering, or a whispering, or the protesting echo of a sigh. Perhaps there might be a little pause—a silence like that which follows an earthquake; but there was no plain-spoken Lord Belhaven, as on the corresponding occasion in Edinburgh, to fill up the silence with "So, there's an end of an auld sang!" All was, or looked courtly, and free from vulgar emotion. One person only I remarked whose features were suddenly illuminated by a smile, a sarcastic smile, as I read it; which, however, might be all a fancy. It was Lord Castlereagh, who, at the moment when the irrevocable words were pronounced, looked with a penetrating glance amongst a party of ladies. His own wife was one of that party; but I did not discover the particular object on whom his smile had settled. After this I had no leisure to be interested in any thing which followed. "You are all," thought I to myself, "a pack of vagabonds henceforward, and interlopers, with actually no more right to be here than myself. I am an intruder; so are you." Apparently they thought so themselves; for,

[77] According to my remembrance, he was Baron Monteagle in the English peerage.

soon after this solemn *fiat* of Jove had gone forth, their lordships, having no further title to their robes, (for which I could not help wishing that a party of Jewish old clothes men would at this moment have appeared, and made a loud bidding,) made what haste they could to lay them aside forever. The house dispersed much more rapidly than it had assembled. Major Sirr was found outside, just where we left him, laying down the law (as before) about pocket handkerchiefs to old and young practitioners; and all parties adjourned to find what consolation they might in the great evening event of dinner.

Thus we were set at liberty from Dublin. Parliaments, and installations, and masked balls, with all other secondary splendors in celebration of primary splendors, reflex glories that reverberated original glories, at length had ceased to shine upon the Irish metropolis. The "season," as it is called in great cities, was over; unfortunately the last season that was ever destined to illuminate the society or to stimulate the domestic trade of Dublin. It began to be thought scandalous to be found in town; *nobody*, in fact, remained, except some two hundred thousand people, who never did, nor ever would, wear ermine; and in all Ireland there remained nothing at all to attract, except that which no king, and no two houses, can by any conspiracy abolish, viz., the beauty of her most verdant scenery. I speak of that part which chiefly it is that I know, — the scenery of the west, — Connaught beyond other provinces, and in Connaught, Mayo beyond other counties. There it was, and in the county next adjoining, that Lord Altamont's large estates were situated, the family mansion and beautiful park being in Mayo. Thither, as nothing else now remained to divert us from what, in fact, we had thirsted for throughout the heats of summer, and throughout the magnificences of the capital, at length we set off by movements as slow and circuitous as those of any royal *progress* in the reign of Elizabeth. Making but short journeys on each day, and resting always at the house of some private friend, I thus obtained an opportunity of seeing the old Irish nobility and gentry more extensively, and on a more intimate footing, than I had hoped for. No experience of this kind, throughout my whole life, so much interested me. In a little work, not much known, of Suetonius, the most interesting record which survives of the early Roman literature, it comes out incidentally that many books, many idioms, and verbal peculiarities belonging to the primitive ages of Roman culture were to be found still lingering in the old Roman settlements, both Gaulish and Spanish, long after they had become obsolete (and sometimes unintelligible) in Rome. From the tardiness and the difficulty of communication, the want of newspapers, &c., it followed, naturally enough, that the distant provincial towns, though not without their own separate literature and their own literary professors, were always two or three generations in the rear of the metropolis; and thus it happened, that, about the time of Augustus, there were some grammatici in Rome, answering to our black-letter critics, who sought the material of their researches in Boulogne, (*Gessoriacum,*) in Arles, (*Arelata,*) or in Marseilles, (*Massilia.*) Now, the old Irish nobility — that part, I mean, which might be called the rural nobility — stood in the same relation to English manners and customs. Here might be found old rambling houses in the style of antique English manorial chateaus, ill planned, perhaps, as regarded convenience and economy, with long rambling galleries, and windows innumerable, that evidently had never looked for that severe audit to which they were afterwards summoned by William Pitt; but displaying, in the dwelling rooms, a comfort and "cosiness," combined with magnificence, not always so effectually attained in modern times. Here were old libraries, old butlers, and old customs, that seemed all alike to belong to the era of Cromwell, or even an earlier era than his; whilst the ancient names, to one who had some acquaintance with the great events of Irish history, often strengthened the illusion. Not that I could pretend to be familiar with Irish history *as* Irish; but as a conspicuous chapter in the difficult policy of Queen Elizabeth, of Charles I., and of Cromwell, nobody who had read the English history could be a stranger to the O'Neils, the O'Donnells, the Ormonds, (*i. e.*, the Butlers,) the Inchiquins, or the De Burghs, and many scores beside. I soon found, in fact, that the aristocracy of Ireland might be divided into two great sections: the native Irish—territorial fixtures, so powerfully described by Maturin; and those, on the other hand, who spent so much of their time and revenues at Bath, Cheltenham, Weymouth, London, &c., as to have become almost entirely English. It was the former whom we chiefly visited; and I remarked that, in the midst of hospitality the most unbounded, and the amplest comfort, some of these were conspicuously in the rear of the English commercial gentry, as to modern refinements of luxury. There was at the same time an apparent strength of character, as if formed amidst turbulent scenes, and a raciness of manner, which were fitted to interest a stranger profoundly, and to impress themselves on his recollection.

CHAPTER IX.

FIRST REBELLION.

In our road to Mayo, we were often upon ground rendered memorable, not only by historical events, but more recently by the disastrous scenes of the rebellion, by its horrors or its calamities. On reaching Westport House, we found ourselves in situations and a neighborhood which had become the very centre of the final military operations, those which succeeded to the main rebellion; and which, to the people of England, and still more to the people of the continent, had offered a character of interest wanting to the inartificial movements of Father Roche and Bagenal Harvey.

In the year 1798, there were two great popular insurrections in Ireland. It is usual to talk of the Irish rebellion, as though there had been one rebellion and no more; but it must satisfy the reader of the inaccuracy pervading the common reports of this period, when he hears that there were two separate rebellions, separate in time, separate in space, separate by the character of their events, and separate even as regarded their proximate causes. The first of these arose in the vernal part of summer, and wasted its fury upon the county of Wexford, in the *centre* of the kingdom. The second arose in the autumn, and was confined entirely to the *western* province of Connaught. Each, resting (it is true) upon causes ultimately the same, had yet its own separate occasions and excitements; for the first arose upon a premature explosion from a secret society of most subtle organization; and the second upon the encouragement of a French invasion. And each of these insurrections had its own separate leaders and its own local agents. The first, though precipitated into action by fortunate discoveries on the part of the government, had been anxiously preconcerted for three years. The second was an unpremeditated effort, called forth by a most ill-timed, and also ill-concerted, foreign invasion. The general predisposing causes to rebellion were doubtless the same in both cases; but the exciting causes of the moment were different in each. And, finally, they were divided by a complete interval of two months.

One very remarkable feature there was, however, in which these two separate rebellions of 1798 coincided; and *that* was, the narrow range, as to time, within which each ran its course. Neither of them outran the limits of one *lunar* month. It is a fact, however startling, that each, though a perfect civil war in all its proportions, frequent in warlike incident, and the former rich in tragedy, passed through all the stages of growth, maturity, and final extinction within one single revolution of the moon. For all the rebel movements, subsequent to the morning of Vinegar Hill, are to be viewed not at all in the light of manoeuvres made in the spirit of military hope, but in the light of final struggles for self-preservation made in the spirit of absolute despair, as regarded the original purposes of the war, or, indeed, as regarded any purposes whatever beyond that of instant safety. The solitary object contemplated was, to reach some district lonely enough, and with elbow room enough, for quiet, unmolested dispersion.

A few pages will recapitulate these two civil wars. I begin with the first. The war of American separation touched and quickened the dry bones that lay waiting as it were for life through the west of Christendom. The year 1782 brought that war to its winding up; and the same year it was that called forth Grattan and the Irish volunteers. These *volunteers* came forward as allies of England against French and Spanish invasion; but once embattled, what should hinder them from detecting a flaw in their commission, and reading it as valid against England herself? In that sense they *did* read it. That Ireland had seen her own case dimly reflected in that of America, and that such a reference was stirring through the national mind, appears from a remarkable fact in the history of the year which followed. In 1783, a haughty petition was addressed to the throne, on behalf of the Roman Catholics, by an association that arrogated to itself the style and title of a *congress*. No man could suppose that a designation so ominously significant had been chosen by accident; and by the English government it was received, as it was meant, for an insult and a menace. What came next? The French revolution. All flesh moved under that inspiration. Fast and rank now began to germinate the seed sown for the ten years preceding in Ireland; too fast and too rankly for the policy that suited her situation. Concealment or delay, compromise or temporizing, would not have been brooked, at this moment, by the fiery temperament of Ireland, had it not been through the extraordinary composition of that secret society into which the management of her affairs now began to devolve. In the year 1792, as we are told, commenced, and in 1795 was finished, the famous association of *United Irishmen*. By these terms, *commenced* and *finished*, we are to understand, not the purposes or the arrangements of their conspiracy against the existing government, but that network of organization, delicate as lace for ladies, and strong as the harness of artillery horses, which now enmeshed almost every province of Ireland, knitting the strength of her peasantry into unity and disposable divisions. This, it seems, was completed in 1795. In a complete history of these times, no one chapter would deserve so ample an investigation as this subtile web of association, rising upon a large base, expanding in proportion to the extent of the particular county, and by intermediate links ascending to some unknown apex; all so graduated, and in such nice interdependency, as to secure the instantaneous propagation upwards and downwards, laterally or obliquely, of any impulse whatever; and yet so effectually shrouded, that nobody knew more than the two or three individual agents in immediate juxtaposition with himself, by whom he communicated with those above his head or below his feet. This organization, in fact, of the United Irishmen, combined the best features, as to skill, of the two most elaborate and most successful of all secret societies recorded in history; one of which went before the Irish Society by centuries, and one followed it after an interval of five-and-twenty years. These two are the *Fehm-Gericht,* or court of ban and extermination, which, having taken its rise in Westphalia, is usually called the secret Tribunal of Westphalia, and which reached its full development in the fourteenth century. The other is the Hellenistic Hetaeria, (*Aetairia*)—a society which, passing for one of pure literacy *dilettanti*, under the secret countenance of the late Capo d'Istria, (then a confidential minister of the czar,) did actually succeed so far in hoaxing the cabinets of Europe, that one third of European kings put down their names, and gave their aid, as conspirators against the Sultan of Turkey, whilst credulously supposing themselves honorary correspondents of a learned body for reviving the arts and literature of Athens. These two I call the most successful of all secret societies, because both were arrayed against the existing administrations throughout the entire lands upon which they sought to operate. The German society disowned the legal authorities as too weak for the ends of justice, and succeeded in bringing the cognizance of crimes within its own secret yet consecrated usurpation. The Grecian society made the existing powers the final object of its hostility; lived unarmed amongst the very oppressors whose throats it had dedicated to the sabre; and, in a very few years, saw its purpose accomplished.

The society of United Irishmen combined the best parts in the organization of both these secret fraternities, and obtained *their* advantages. The society prospered in defiance of the government; nor would the government, though armed with all the powers of the Dublin police and of state thunder, have succeeded in mastering this society, but, on the contrary, the society would assuredly have surprised and mastered the government, had it not been undermined by the perfidy of a confidential brother. One instrument for dispersing knowledge, employed by the United Irishmen, is worth mentioning, as it is applicable to any cause, and may be used with much greater effect in an age when every body is taught to read. They printed newspapers on a single side of the sheet, which were thus fitted for being placarded against the walls. This expedient had probably been suggested by Paris, where such newspapers were often placarded, and generally for the bloodiest purposes. But Louvet, in his "Memoirs," mentions one conducted by himself on better principles: it was printed at the public expense; and sometimes more than twenty thousand copies of a single number were attached to the corners of streets. This was called the "Centinel;" and those who are acquainted with the "Memoirs of Madame Roland" will remember that she cites Louvet's paper as a model for all of its class. The "Union Star" was the paper which the United Irishmen published upon this plan; previous papers, on the ordinary plan, viz., the "Northern Star" and the "Press," having been violently put down by the government. The "Union Star," however, it must be acknowledged, did not seek much to elevate the people by addressing them through their understandings; it was merely a violent appeal to their passions, and directed against all who had incurred the displeasure of the society. Newspapers, meantime, of every kind, it was easy for the government to suppress. But the secret society annoyed and crippled the government in other modes, which it was not easy to parry; and all blows dealt in return were dealt in the dark, and aimed at a shadow. The society called upon Irishmen to abstain generally from ardent spirits, as a means of destroying the excise; and it is certain that the society was obeyed, in a degree which astonished neutral observers, all over Ireland. The same society, by a printed proclamation, called upon the people not to purchase the quitrents of the crown, which were then on sale; and not to receive bank notes in payment, because (as the proclamation told them) a "burst" was coming, when such paper, and the securities for such purchases, would fall to a ruinous discount. In this ease, after much distress to the public service, government obtained a partial triumph by the law which cancelled the debt on a refusal to receive the state paper, and which quartered soldiers upon all tradesmen who demurred to such a tender. But, upon the whole, it was becoming pain fully evident, that in Ireland there were two coordinate governments coming into collision at every step, and that the one which more generally had the upper hand in the struggle was the secret society of United Irishmen; whose members individually, and whose local head quarters, were alike screened from the attacks of its rival, viz., the state government at the Castle, by a cloud of impenetrable darkness.

That cloud was at last pierced. A treacherous or weak brother, high in the ranks of the society, and deep in their confidence, happened, when travelling up to Dublin in company with a royalist, to speak half mysteriously, half ostentatiously, upon the delicate position which he held in the councils of his dangerous party. This weak man, Thomas Reynolds, a Roman Catholic gentleman, of Kilkea Castle, in Kildare, colonel of a regiment of United Irish, treasurer for Kildare, and in other offices of trust for the secret society, was prevailed on by Mr. William Cope, a rich merchant of Dublin, who alarmed his mind by pictures of the horrors attending a revolution under the circumstances of Ireland, to betray all he knew to the government. His treachery was first meditated in the last week of February, 1798; and, in consequence of his depositions, on March 12, at the house of Oliver Bond, in Dublin, the government succeeded in arresting a large body of the leading conspirators. The whole committee of Leinster, amounting to thirteen members, was captured on this occasion; but a still more valuable prize was made in the persons of those who presided over the Irish Directory, viz., Emmet, M'Niven, Arthur O'Connor, and Oliver Bond. As far as names went, their places were immediately filled up; and a hand-bill was issued, on the same day, with the purpose of intercepting the effects of despondency amongst the great body of the conspirators. But Emmet and O'Connor were not men to be effectually replaced: government had struck a fatal blow, without being fully aware at first of their own good luck. On the 19th of May following, in consequence of a proclamation (May 11) offering a thousand pounds for his capture, Lord Edward Fitzgerald was apprehended at the house of Mr. Nicholas Murphy, a merchant in Dublin, but after a very desperate resistance. The leader of the arresting party, Major Swan, a Dublin magistrate, distinguished for his energy, was wounded by Lord Edward; and Ryan, one of the officers, so desperately, that he died within a fortnight. Lord Edward himself languished for some time, and died in great agony on the 3d of June, from a pistol shot which took effect on his shoulder. Lord Edward Fitzgerald might be regarded as an injured man. From the exuberant generosity of his temper, he had powerfully sympathized with the French republicans at an early stage of their revolution; and having, with great indiscretion, but an indiscretion that admitted of some palliation in so young a man and of so ardent a temperament, publicly avowed his sympathy, he was ignominiously dismissed from the army. That act made an enemy of one who, on several grounds, was not a man to be despised; for, though weak as respected his powers of self-control, Lord Edward was well qualified to make himself beloved; he had considerable talents; his very name, as a sone of the only[78] ducal house in Ireland, was a spell and a rallying word for a day of battle to the Irish peasantry; and, finally, by his marriage with a natural daughter of the then Duke of Orleans, he had founded some important connections and openings to secret influence in France. The young lady whom he had married was generally known by the name of *Pamela;* and it has been usually supposed that she is the person described by Miss Edgeworth, under the name of Virginia, in the latter part of her "Belinda." How that may be, I cannot pretend to say: Pamela was certainly led into some indiscretions; in particular, she was said to have gone to a ball without shoes or stockings, which seems to argue the same sort of ignorance, and the same docility to any chance impressions, which characterize the Virginia of Miss Edgeworth. She was a reputed daughter (as I have said) of Philippe Egalité; and her putative mother was Madame de Genlis, who had been settled in that prince's family, as governess to his children, more especially to the sister of the present[79] French king. Lord Edward's whole course had been marked by generosity and noble feeling. Far better to have pardoned[80] such a man, and (if that were possible) to have conciliated his support; but, says a contemporary Irishman, "those were not times of conciliation."

Some days after this event were arrested the two brothers named Shearer, men of talent, who eventually suffered for treason. These discoveries were due to treachery of a peculiar sort; not to the treachery of an apostate brother breaking his faith, but of a counterfeit brother simulating the character of conspirator, and by that fraud obtaining a key to the fatal secrets of the United Irishmen. His perfidy, therefore, consisted, not in any betrayal of secrets, but in the fraud by which he obtained them. Government, without having yet penetrated to the very heart of the mystery, had now discovered enough to guide them in their most energetic precautions; and the result was, that the conspirators, whose policy had hitherto been to wait for the cooperation of a French army, now suddenly began to distrust that policy: their fear was, that the ground would be cut from beneath their feet if

[78] *"The only ducal house."* —That is, the only one not royal. There are four provinces in Ireland—*Ulster, Connaught, Munster,* which three give old traditional titles to three personages of the blood royal. Remains only *Leinster,* which gives the title of duke to the Fitzgeralds.

[79] *"Present French king."* —Viz., in the year 1833.

[80] *"To have pardoned,"* &c.—This was written under circumstances of great hurry; and, were it not for that palliation, would be inexcusably thoughtless. For, in a double sense, it is doubtful how far the government *could* have pardoned Lord Edward. First, in a prudential sense, was it possible (except in the spirit of a German sentimentalizing drama) to pardon a conspicuous, and within certain limits a very influential, officer for publicly avowing opinions tending to treason, and at war with the constitutional system of the land which fed him and which claimed his allegiance? Was it possible, in point of prudence or in point of dignity, to overlook such anti-national sentiments, whilst neither disavowed nor ever likely to be disavowed? Was this possible, regard being had to the inevitable effect of such *unearned* forgiveness upon the army at large? But secondly, in a merely logical sense of practical self-consistency, would it have been rational or even intelligible to pardon a man who probably *would* not be pardoned; that is, who must (consenting or not consenting) benefit by the concessions of the pardon, whilst disowning all reciprocal obligations?

they waited any longer. More was evidently risked by delay than by dispensing altogether with foreign aid. To forego this aid was perilous; to wait for it was ruin. It was resolved, therefore, to commence the insurrection on the 23d of May; and, in order to distract the government, to commence it by simultaneous assaults upon all the military posts in the neighborhood of Dublin. This plan was discovered, but scarcely in time to prevent the effects of a surprise. On the 21st, late in the evening, the conspiracy had been announced by the lord lieutenant's secretary to the lord mayor; and, on the following day, by a message from his excellency to both Houses of Parliament.

The insurrection, however, in spite of this official warning, began at the appointed hour. The skirmishes were many, and in many places; but, generally speaking, they were not favorable in their results to the insurgents. The mail coaches, agreeably to the preconcerted plan, had all been intercepted; their non-arrival being every where understood by the conspirators as a silent signal that the war had commenced. Yet this summons to the more distant provinces, though truly interpreted, had not been truly answered. The communication between the capital and the interior, almost completely interrupted at first, had been at length fully restored; and a few days saw the main strength (as it was supposed) of the insurrection suppressed without much bloodshed. But hush! what is *that* in the rear?

Just at this moment, when all the world was disposed to think the whole affair quietly composed, the flame burst out with tenfold fury in a part of the country from which government, with some reason, had turned away their anxieties and their preparations. This was the county of Wexford, which the Earl of Mountnorris had described to the government as so entirely well affected to the loyal cause, that he had personally pledged himself for its good conduct. On the night before Whitsunday, however, May 27, the standard of revolt was *there* raised by John Murphy, a Catholic priest, well know henceforwards under the title of Father Murphy.

The campaign opened inauspiciously for the royalists. The rebels had posted themselves on two eminences—Kilthomas, about ten miles to the westward of Gorey; and the Hill of Oulart, half way (*i.e.*, about a dozen miles) between Gorey and Wexford. They were attacked at each point on Whitsunday. From the first point they were driven easily, and with considerable loss; but at Oulart the issue was very different. Father Murphy commanded here in person; and, finding that his men gave way in great confusion before a picked body of the North Cork militia, under the command of Colonel Foote, he contrived to persuade them that their flight was leading them right upon a body of royal cavalry posted to intercept their retreat. This fear effectually halted them. The insurgents, through a prejudice natural to inexperience, had an unreasonable dread of cavalry. A second time, therefore, facing about to retreat from this imaginary body of horse, they came of necessity, and without design, full upon their pursuers, whom unhappily the intoxication of victory had by this time brought into the most careless disarray. These, almost to a man, the rebels annihilated: universal consternation followed amongst the royalists; Father Murphy led them to Ferns, and thence to the attack of Enniscorthy.

Has the reader witnessed, or has he heard described, the sudden burst—the explosion, one might say—by which a Swedish winter passes into spring, and spring simultaneously into summer? The icy sceptre of winter does not there thaw and melt away by just gradations; it is broken, it is shattered, in a day, in an hour, and with a violence brought home to *every* sense. No second type of resurrection, so mighty or so affecting, is manifested by nature in southern climates. Such is the headlong tumult, such "the torrent rapture," by which life is let loose amongst the air, the earth, and the waters under the earth. Exactly what this vernal resurrection is in manifestations of power and life, by comparison with climates that have no winter, such, and marked with features as distinct, was this Irish insurrection, when suddenly surrendered to the whole contagion of politico-religious fanaticism, by comparison with vulgar *martinet* strategics and the pedantry of technical warfare. What a picture must Enniscorthy have presented on the 27th of May! Fugitives, crowding in from Ferns, announced the rapid advance of the rebels, now, at least, 7000 strong, drunk with victory, and maddened with vindictive fury. Not long after midday, their advanced guard, well armed with muskets, (pillaged, be H observed, from royal magazines hastily deserted,) commenced a tumultuous assault. Less than 300 militia and yeomanry formed the garrison of the place, which had no sort of defences except the natural one of the River Slaney. This, however, was fordable, and *that* the assailants knew. The slaughter amongst the rebels, meantime, from the little caution they exhibited, and their total defect of military skill, was murderous. Spite of their immense numerical advantages, it is probable they would have been defeated. But in Enniscorthy, (as where not?) treason from within was emboldened to raise its crest at the very crisis of suspense; incendiaries were at work; and flames began to issue from many houses at once. Retreat itself became suddenly doubtful, depending, as it did, altogether upon the state of the wind. At the right hand of every royalist stood a traitor; in his own house oftentimes lurked other traitors, waiting for the signal to begin; in the front was the enemy; in the rear was a line of blazing streets. Three hours the battle had raged; it was now four, P. M., and at this moment the garrison hastily gave way, and fled to Wexford.

Now came a scene, which swallowed up all distinct or separate features in its frantic confluence of horrors. All the loyalists of Enniscorthy, all the gentry for miles around, who had congregated in that town, as a centre of security, were summoned at that moment, not to an orderly retreat, but to instant flight. At one end of the street were seen the rebel pikes, and bayonets, and fierce faces, already gleaming through the smoke; at the other end, volumes of fire, surging and billowing from the thatched roofs and blazing rafters, beginning to block up the avenues of escape. Then began the agony and uttermost conflict of what is worst and what is best in human nature. Then was to be seen the very delirium of fear, and the very delirium of vindictive malice; private and ignoble hatred, of ancient origin, shrouding itself in the mask of patriotic wrath; the tiger glare of just vengeance, fresh from intolerable wrongs and the never-to-be-forgotten ignominy of stripes and personal degradation; panic, self-palsied by its own excess; flight, eager or stealthy, according to the temper and the means; volleying pursuit; the very frenzy of agitation, under every mode of excitement; and here and there, towering aloft, the desperation of maternal love, victorious and supreme above all lower passions. I recapitulate and gather under general abstractions many an individual anecdote, reported by those who were on that day present in Enniscorthy; for at Ferns, not far off, and deeply interested in all those transactions, I had private friends, intimate participators in the trials of that fierce hurricane, and joint sufferers with those who suffered most. Ladies were then seen in crowds, hurrying on foot to Wexford, the nearest asylum, though fourteen miles distant, many in slippers, bareheaded, and without any supporting arm; for the flight of their defenders, having been determined by a sudden angular movement of the assailants, coinciding with the failure of their own ammunition, had left no time for warning; and fortunate it was for the unhappy fugitives, that the confusion of burning streets, concurring with the seductions of pillage, drew aside so many of the victors as to break the unity of a pursuit else hellishly unrelenting.

Wexford, meantime, was in no condition to promise more than a momentary shelter. Orders had been already issued to extinguish all domestic fires throughout the town, and to unroof all the thatched houses; so great was the jealousy of internal treason. From without, also, the alarm was every hour increasing. On Tuesday, the 29th of May, the rebel army advanced from Enniscorthy to a post called Three Rocks, not much above two miles from Wexford. Their strength was now increased to at least 15,000 men. Never was there a case requiring more energy in the disposers of the royal forces; never one which met with less, even in the most responsible quarters. The nearest military station was the fort at Duncannon, twenty-three miles distant. Thither, on the 29th, an express had been despatched by the mayor of Wexford, reporting their situation, and calling immediate aid. General Fawcet replied, that he would himself march that same evening with the 13th regiment, part of the Meath militia, and sufficient artillery. Relying upon these assurances, the small parties of militia and yeomanry then in Wexford gallantly threw themselves upon the most trying services in advance. Some companies of the Donegal militia, not mustering above 200 men, marched immediately to a position between the rebel camp and Wexford; whilst others of the North Cork militia and the local yeomanry, with equal cheerfulness, undertook the defence of that town. Meantime, General Fawcet had consulted his personal comfort by *halting for the night*, though aware of the dreadful emergency, at a station sixteen miles short of Wexford. A small detachment, however, with part of his artillery, he sent forward; these were the next morning intercepted by the rebels at Three Rocks, and massacred almost to a man. Two officers, who escaped the slaughter, carried the intelligence to the advanced post of the Donegals; but they, so far from being disheartened, marched immediately against the rebel army, enormous as was the disproportion, with the purpose of recapturing the artillery. A singular contrast this to the conduct of General Fawcet, who retreated hastily to Duncannon upon the first intelligence of this disaster. Such a regressive movement was so little anticipated by the gallant Donegals, that they continued to advance against the enemy, until the precision with which the captured artillery was served against themselves, and the non-appearance of the promised aid, warned them to retire. At Wexford, they found all in confusion and the hurry of retreat. The flight, as it may be called, of General Fawcet was now confirmed; and, as the local position of Wexford made it indefensible against artillery, the whole body of loyalists, except those whom insufficient warning had thrown into the rear, now fled from the wrath of the rebels to Duncannon. It is a shocking illustration (*if truly reported*) of the thoughtless ferocity which characterized too many of the Orange troops, that, along the whole line of this retreat, they continued to burn the cabins of Roman Catholics, and often to massacre, in cold blood, the unoffending inhabitants; totally forgetful of the many hostages whom the insurgents now held in their power, and careless of the dreadful provocations which they were thus throwing out to the bloodiest reprisals.

Thus it was, and through mismanagement thus mischievously alert, or through torpor thus unaccountably base, that actually, on the 30th of May, not having raised their standard before the 26th, the rebels had already been permitted to possess themselves of the county of Wexford in its whole southern division—Ross and Duncannon only excepted; of which the latter was not liable to capture by *coup de main*, and the other was saved by the procrastination of the rebels. The northern division of the county was overrun pretty much in the same hasty style, and through the same desperate neglect in previous concert of plans. Upon first turning their views to the north, the rebels had taken up a position on the Hill of Corrigrua, as a station from which they could march with advantage upon the town of Gorey, lying seven miles to the northward. On the 1st of June, a truly brilliant affair had taken place between a mere handful of militia and yeomanry from this town of Gorey and a strong detachment from the rebel camp. Many persons at the time regarded this as the best fought action in the whole war. The two parties had met about two miles from Gorey; and it is pretty certain that, if the yeoman cavalry could have been prevailed on to charge at the critical moment, the defeat would have been a most murderous one to the rebels. As it was, they escaped, though with considerable loss of honor. Yet even this they were allowed to retrieve within a few days, in a remarkable way, and with circumstances of still greater scandal to the military discretion in high quarters than had attended the movements of General Fawcet in the south.

On the 4th of June, a little army of 1500 men, under the command of Major General Loftus, had assembled at Gorey. The plan was, to march by two different roads upon the rebel encampment at Corrigrua; and this plan was adopted. Meantime, on that same night, the rebel army had put themselves in motion for Gorey; and of this counter movement full and timely information had been given by a farmer at the royal headquarters; but such was the obstinate infatuation, that no officer of rank would condescent to give him a hearing. The consequences may be imagined. Colonel Walpole, an Englishman, full of courage, but presumptuously disdainful of the enemy, led a division upon one of the two roads, having no scouts, nor taking any sort of precaution. Suddenly he found his line of march crossed by the enemy in great strength: he refused to halt or to retire; was shot through the head; and a great part of the advanced detachment was slaughtered on the spot, and his artillery captured. General Loftus, advancing on the parallel road, heard the firing, and detached the grenadier company of the Antrim militia to the aid of Walpole. These, to the amount of seventy men, were cut off almost to a man; and when the general, who could not cross over to the other road, through the enclosures, from the encumbrance of his artillery, had at length reached the scene of action by a long circuit, he found himself in the following truly ludicrous position: The rebels had pursued Colonel Walpole's division to Gorey, and possessed themselves of that place; the general had thus lost his head quarters, without having seen the army whom he had suffered to slip past him in the dark. He marched back disconsolately to Gorey, took a look at the rebel posts which now occupied the town in strength, was saluted with a few rounds from his own cannon, and finally retreated out of the county.

This movement of General Loftus, and the previous one of General Fawcet, circumstantially illustrate the puerile imbecility with which the royal cause was then conducted. Both movements foundered in an hour, through surprises, against which each had been amply forewarned. Fortunately for the government, the affairs of the rebels were managed even worse. Two sole enterprises were undertaken by them after this, previously to the closing battle of Vinegar Hill; both being of the very utmost importance to their interests, and both sure of success if they had been pushed forward in time. The first was the attack upon Ross, undertaken on the 29th of May, the day after the capture of Enniscorthy. Had that attack been pressed forward without delay, there never were two opinions as to the certainty of its success; and, *having* succeeded, it would have laid open to the rebels the important counties of Waterford and Kilkenny. Being delayed until the 5th of June, the assault was repulsed with prodigious slaughter, The other was the attack upon Arklow, in the north. On the capture of Gorey, on the night of June 4, as the immediate consequence of Colonel Walpole's defeat, had the rebels advanced upon Arklow, they would have found it for some days totally undefended; the whole garrison having retreated in panic, early on June 5, to Wicklow. The capture of this important place would have laid open the whole road to the capital; would probably have caused a rising in that great city; and, in any event, would have indefinitely prolonged the war, and multiplied the distractions of government. Merely from sloth and the spirit of procrastination, however, the rebel army halted at Gorey until the 9th, and then advanced with what seemed the overpowering force of 27,000 men. It is a striking lesson upon the subject of procrastination, that, precisely on that morning of June 9, the attempt had first become hopeless. Until then, the place had been positively emptied of all inhabitants whatsoever. Exactly on the 9th, the old garrison had been ordered back from Wicklow, and reënforced by a crack English regiment, (the Durham Fencibles,) on whom chiefly at this critical hour had devolved the defence, which was peculiarly trying, from the vast numbers of the assailants, but brilliant, masterly, and perfectly successful.

This obstinate and fiercely-contested battle of Arklow was indeed, by general consent, the hinge on which the rebellion turned. Nearly 30,000 men, armed every man of them with pikes, and 5000 with muskets, supported also by some artillery, sufficiently well served to do considerable execution at a most important point in the line of defence, could not be defeated without a very trying struggle. And here, again, it is worthy of record, that General Needham, who commanded on this day, would have followed the example of Generals Fawcet and Loftus, and have ordered a retreat, had he not been determinately opposed by Colonel Skerret, of the Durham regiment. Such was the imbecility, and the want of moral courage, on the part of the military leaders; for it would be unjust to impute any defect in animal courage to the feeblest of these leaders. General Needham, for example, exposed his person, without reserve, throughout the whole of this difficult day. Any amount of cannon shot he could face cheerfully, but not a trying responsibility.

From the defeat of Arklow, the rebels gradually retired, between the 9th and the 20th of June, to their main military position of Vinegar Hill, which lies immediately above the town of Enniscorthy, and had fallen into their hands, concurrently with that place, on the 28th of May. Here their whole forces, with the exception of perhaps 6000, who attacked General Moore (ten and a half years later, the Moore of Corunna) when marching on the 26th towards Wexford, had been concentrated; and to this point, therefore, as a focus, had the royal army, 13,000 strong, with a respectable artillery, under the supreme command of General Lake, converged in four separate divisions, about the 19th and 20th of June. The great blow was to be struck on the 21st; and the plan was, that the royal forces, moving to the assault of the rebel position upon four lines at right angles to each other, (as if, for instance, from the four cardinal points to the same centre,) should surround their encampment, and shut up every avenue to escape. On this plan, the field of battle would have been one vast slaughter house; for quarter was not granted on either side.[81] But the quadrille, if it were ever seriously concerted, was entirely defeated by the failure of General Needham, who did not present himself with *his* division until nine o'clock, a full half hour after the battle was over, and thus earned the, *sobriquet of the late*[82] *General Needham*. Whether the failure were really in this officer, or (as was alleged by his apologists) had been already preconcerted in the inconsistent orders issued to him by General Lake, with the covert intention, as many believe, of mercifully counteracting his own scheme of wholesale butchery, to this day remains obscure. The effect of that delay, in whatever way caused, was for once such as must win every body's applause. The action had commenced at seven o'clock in the morning; by half past eight, the whole rebel army was in flight; and, naturally making for the only point left unguarded, it escaped with no great slaughter (but leaving behind all its artillery, and a good deal of valuable plunder) through what was facetiously called ever afterwards *Needham's Gap*. After this capital rout of Vinegar Hill, the rebel army day by day mouldered away. A large body, however, of the fiercest and most desperate continued for some time to make flying marches in all directions, according to the positions of the king's forces and the momentary

---

[81] *"For quarter was not granted on either side."* —I repeat, as all along and necessarily I have repeated, that which orally I was told at the time, or which subsequently I have read in published accounts. But the reader is aware by this time of my steadfast conviction, that more easily might a camel go through the eye of a needle, than a reporter, fresh from a campaign blazing with partisanship, and that partisanship representing ancient and hereditary feuds, could by possibility cleanse himself from the *virus* of such a prejudice.

[82] The same jest was applied to Mr. Pitt's brother. When first lord of the Admiralty, people calling on him as late as even 10 or 11, P.M., were told that his lordship was riding in the park. On this account, partly, but more pointedly with a malicious reference to the contrast between his languor and the fiery activity of his father, the first earl, he was jocularly called, *the late Lord Chatham*.

favor of accidents. Once or twice they were brought to action by Sir James Duff and Sir Charles Asgill; and, ludicrously enough, once more they were suffered to escape by the eternal delays of the "late Needham." At length, however, after many skirmishes, and all varieties of local success, they finally dispersed upon a bog in the county of Dublin. Many desperadoes, however, took up their quarters for a long time in the dwarf woods of Killaughrim, near Enniscorthy, assuming the trade of marauders, but ludicrously designating themselves the Babes in the Wood. It is an inexplicable fact, that many deserters from the militia regiments, who had behaved well throughout the campaign, and adhered faithfully to their colors, now resorted to this confederation of the woods; from which it cost some trouble to dislodge them. Another party, in the woods and mountains of Wicklow, were found still more formidable, and continued to infest the adjacent country through the ensuing winter. These were not finally ejected from their lairs until after one of their chiefs had been killed in a night skirmish by a young man defending his house, and the other chief, weary of his savage life, had surrendered himself to transportation.

It diffused general satisfaction throughout Ireland, that, on the very day before the final engagement of Vinegar Hill, Lord Cornwallis made his entry into Dublin as the new lord lieutenant. A proclamation, issued early in July, of general amnesty to all who had shed no blood except on the field of battle, notified to the country the new spirit of policy which now distinguished the government; and, doubtless, that one merciful change worked marvels in healing the agitations of the land. Still it was thought necessary that severe justice should take its course amongst the most conspicuous leaders or agents in the insurrection. Martial law still prevailed; and under that law we know, through a speech of the Duke of Wellington's, how entirely the very elements of justice are dependent upon individual folly or caprice. Many of those who had shown the greatest generosity, and with no slight risk to themselves, were now selected to suffer. Bagenal Harvey, a Protestant gentleman, who had held the supreme command of the rebel army for some time with infinite vexation to himself, and taxed with no one instance of cruelty or excess, was one of those doomed to execution. He had possessed an estate of nearly three thousand per annum; and at the same time with him was executed another gentleman, of more than three times that estate, Cornelius Grogan. Singular it was, that men of this condition and property, men of feeling and refinement, should have staked the happiness of their families upon a contest so forlorn. Some there were, however, and possibly these gentlemen, who could have explained their motives intelligibly enough: they had been forced by persecution, and actually baited into the ranks of the rebels. One picturesque difference in the deaths of these two gentlemen was remarkable, as contrasted with their previous habits. Grogan was constitutionally timid; and yet he faced the scaffold and the trying preparations of the executioner with fortitude. On the other hand, Bagenal Harvey, who had fought several duels with coolness, exhibited considerable trepidation in his last moments. Perhaps, in both, the difference might be due entirely to some physical accident of health or momentary nervous derangement.[83]

[83] Perhaps also *not*. Possibly enough there may be no call for any such *exceptional* solution; for, after all, there may be nothing to solve—no *dignus vindice nodus*. As regards

Among the crowd, however, of persons who suffered death at this disastrous era, there were two that merit a special commemoration for their virtuous resistance, in disregard of all personal risk, to a horrid fanaticism of cruelty. One was a butcher, the other a seafaring man—both rebels. But they must have been truly generous, brave, and noble-minded men. During the occupation of Wexford by the rebel army, they were repeatedly the sole opponents, at great personal risk, to the general massacre then meditated by some few Popish bigots. And, finally, when all resistance seemed likely to be unavailing, they both demanded resolutely from the chief patron of this atrocious policy that he should fight themselves, armed in whatever way he might prefer, and, as they expressed it, "prove himself a man," before he should be at liberty to sport in this wholesale way with innocent blood.

One painful fact I will state in taking leave of this subject; and *that*, I believe, will be quite sufficient to sustain any thing I have said in disparagement of the government; by which, however, I mean, in justice, the local administration of Ireland. For, as to the supreme government in England, that body must be supposed, at the utmost, to have passively acquiesced in the recommendations of the Irish cabinet, even when it interfered so far. In particular, the scourgings and flagella-

---

the sudden interchange of characters on the scaffold,—the constitutionally brave man all at once becoming timid, and the timid man becoming brave,—it must be remembered, that the particular sort of courage applicable to duelling, when the danger is much more of a fugitive and momentary order than that which invests a battle lasting for hours, depends almost entirely upon a man's *confidence in his own luck*—a peculiarity of mind which exists altogether apart from native resources of courage, whether moral or physical: usually this mode of courage is but a transformed expression for a sanguine temperament. A man who is habitually depressed by a constitutional taint of despondency may carry into a duel a sublime principle of calm, self-sacrificing courage, as being possibly utterly without hope—a courage, therefore, which has to fight with internal resistance, to which there may be nothing corresponding in a cheerful temperament.

But there is another and separate agency through which the fear of death may happen to act as a disturbing force, and most irregularly as viewed in relation to moral courage and strength of mind. This anomalous force is the imaginative and shadowy terror with which different minds recoil from death—not considered as an agony or torment, but considered as a mystery, and, next after God, as the most infinite of mysteries. In a brave man this terror may happen to be strong; in a pusillanimous man, simply through inertness and original feebleness of imagination, may happen to be scarcely developed. This oscillation of horror, alternating between death as an agony and death as a mystery, not only exists with a corresponding set of consequences accordingly as one or other prevails, but is sometimes consciously contemplated and put into the scales of comparison and counter valuation. For instance, one of the early Csesars reviewed the case thus: "*Emori nolo; me esse mortuum nihil cestumo*: From death as the act and process of dying, I revolt; but as to death, viewed as a permanent state or condition, I don't value it at a straw." What this particular Caesar detested, and viewed with burning malice, was death the agony—death the physical torment. As to death the mystery, want of sensibility to the infinite and the shadowy had disarmed *that* of its terrors for him. Yet, on the contrary, how many are there who face the mere physical anguish of dying with stern indifference! But death the mystery,—death that, not satisfied with changing our objective, may attack even the roots of our subjective,—*there* lies the mute, ineffable, voiceless horror before which all human courage is abashed, even as all human resistance becomes childish when measuring itself against gravitation.

tions resorted to in Wexford and Kildare, &c., must have been originally suggested by minds familiar with the habits of the Irish aristocracy in the treatment of dependants. Candid Irishmen will admit that the habit of kicking, or threatening to kick, waiters in coffee houses or other menial dependants,—a habit which, in England, would be met instantly by defiance and menaces of action for assault and battery, —is not yet altogether obsolete in Ireland.[84] Thirty years ago it was still more prevalent, and presupposed that spirit and temper in the treatment of menial dependants, out of which, doubtless, arose the practice of judicial (*i.e.*, tentative) flagellations. Meantime, that fact with which I proposed to close my recollections of this great tumult, and which seems to be a sufficient guaranty for the very severest reflections on the spirit of the government, is expressed significantly in the terms, used habitually by Roman Catholic gentlemen, in prudential exculpation of themselves, when threatened with inquiry for their conduct during these times of agitation: "I thank my God that no man can charge me justly with having saved the life of any Protestant, or his house from pillage, by my intercession with the rebel chiefs." How! Did men boast of collusion with violence and the spirit of massacre! What did *that* mean? It meant this: Some Roman Catholics had pleaded, and pleaded truly, as a reason for special indulgence to themselves, that any influence which might belong to them, on the score of religion or of private friendship, with the rebel authorities, had been used by them on behalf of persecuted Protestants, either in delivering them altogether, or in softening their doom. But, to the surprise of every body, this plea was so far from being entertained favorably by the courts of inquiry, that, on the contrary, an argument was built upon it, dangerous in the last degree to the pleader. "You admit, then," it was retorted, "having had this very considerable influence upon the rebel councils; your influence extended to the saving of lives; in that case we must suppose you to have been known privately as their friend and supporter." Thus to have delivered an innocent man from murder, argued that the deliverer must have been an accomplice of the murderous party. Readily it may be supposed that few would be disposed to urge such a vindication, when it became known in what way it was likely to operate. The government itself had made it perilous to profess humanity; and every man henceforward gloried publicly in his callousness and insensibility, as the one best safeguard to himself on a path so closely beset with rocks.

---

[84] *"Not yet altogether obsolete."* —Written in 1833.

CHAPTER X.

FRENCH INVASION OF IRELAND, AND SECOND REBELLION.

The decisive battle of Vinegar Hill took place at midsummer; and with that battle terminated the First Rebellion. Two months later, a French force, not making fully a thousand men, under the command of General Humbert, landed on the west coast of Ireland, and again roused the Irish peasantry to insurrection. This latter insurrection, and the invasion which aroused it, naturally had a peculiar interest for Lord Westport and myself, who, in our present abode of Westport House, were living in its local centre.

I, in particular, was led, by hearing on every side the conversation reverting to the dangers and tragic incidents of the era, separated from us by not quite two years, to make inquiries of every body who had personally participated in the commotions. Records there were on every side, and memorials even in our bed rooms, of this French visit; for, at one time, they had occupied Westport House in some strength. The largest town in our neighborhood was Castlebar, distant about eleven Irish miles. To this it was that the French addressed their very earliest efforts. Advancing rapidly, and with their usual style of theatrical confidence, they had obtained at first a degree of success which was almost surprising to their own insolent vanity, and which, long afterwards, became a subject of bitter mortification to our own army. Had there been at this point any energy at all corresponding to that of the enemy, or commensurate to the intrinsic superiority of our own troops in steadiness, the French would have been compelled to lay down their arms. The experience of those days, however, showed how deficient is the finest composition of an army, unless where its martial qualities have been developed by practice; and how liable is all courage, when utterly inexperienced to sudden panics. This gasconading advance, which would have foundered utterly against a single battalion of the troops which fought in 1812-13 amongst the Pyrenees, was here for the moment successful.

The bishop of this see, Dr. Stock, with his whole household, and, indeed, his whole pastoral charge, became, on this occasion, prisoners to the enemy. The republican head quarters were fixed for a time in the episcopal palace; and there it was that General Humbert and his staff lived in familiar intercourse with the bishop, who thus became well qualified to record (which he soon afterwards did in an anonymous pamphlet) the leading circumstances of the French incursion, and the consequent insurrection in Connaught, as well as the most striking features in the character and deportment of the republican officers. Riding over the scene of these transactions daily for some months, in company with Dr. Peter Browne, the Dean of Ferns, (an illegitimate son of the late Lord Altamont, and, therefore, half brother to the present,) whose sacred character had not prevented him from taking that military part which seemed, in those difficult moments, a duty of elementary patriotism laid upon all alike, I enjoyed many opportunities for checking the statements of the bishop. The small body of French troops which undertook this remote service had been detached in one half from the army of the Rhine; the other half had served under Napoleon in his first foreign campaign, viz., the Italian campaign of 1796, which accomplished the conquest of Northern Italy. Those from Germany showed, by their looks and their meagre condition, how much they had suffered; and some of them, in describing their hardships, told their Irish acquaintance that, during the seige of Metz, which had occurred in the previous winter of 1797, they had slept in holes made four feet below the surface of the snow. One officer declared solemnly that he had not once undressed, further than by taking off his coat, for a period of twelve months. The private soldiers had all the essential qualities fitting them for a difficult and trying service: "intelligence, activity, temperance, patience to a surprising degree, together with the exactest discipline." This is the statement of their candid and upright enemy. "Yet," says the bishop, "with all these martial qualities, if you except the grenadiers, they had nothing to catch the eye. Their stature, for the most part, was low, their complexion pale and yellow, their clothes much the worse for wear: to a superficial observer, they would have appeared incapable of enduring any hardship. These were the men, however, of whom it was presently observed, that they could be well content to live on bread or potatoes, to drink water, to make the stones of the street their bed, and to sleep in their clothes, with no covering but the canopy of heaven." "How vast," says Cicero, "is the revenue of Parsimony!" and, by a thousand degrees more striking, how celestial is the strength that descends upon the feeble through Temperance!

It may well be imagined in what terror the families of Killala heard of a French invasion, and the necessity of immediately receiving a republican army. As *sans culottes*, these men, all over Europe, had the reputation of pursuing a ferocious marauding policy; in fact, they were held little better than sanguinary brigands. In candor, it must be admitted that their conduct at Killala belied these reports; though, on the other hand, an obvious interest obliged them to a more pacific demeanor in a land which they saluted as friendly, and designed to raise into extensive insurrection. The French army, so much dreaded, at length arrived. The general and his staff entered the palace; and the first act of one officer, on coming into the dining room, was to advance to the sideboard, sweep all the plate into a basket, and deliver it to the bishop's butler, with a charge to carry it off to a place of security.[85]

---

[85] As this happened to be the truth, the bishop did right to report it. Otherwise, his lordship does not seem to have had much acquaintance with the French scenical mode of arranging their public acts for purposes of effect. Cynical people (like myself, when looking back to this anecdote from the year 1833) were too apt to remark that this plate and that basket were carefully numbered; that the episcopal butler (like Pharaoh's) was liable, alas!

The French officers, with the detachment left under their orders by the commander-in-chief, staid about one month at Killala. This period allowed opportunities enough for observing individual differences of character and the general tone of their manners. These opportunities were not thrown away upon the bishop; he noticed with a critical eye, and he recorded on the spot, whatever fell within his own experience. Had he, however, happened to be a political or courtier bishop, his record would, perhaps, have been suppressed; and, at any rate, it would have been colored by prejudice. As it was, I believe it to have been the honest testimony of an honest man; and, considering the minute circumstantiality of its delineations, I do not believe that, throughout the revolutionary war, any one document was made public which throws so much light on the quality and composition of the French republican armies. On this consideration I shall extract a few passages from the bishop's personal sketches.

The commander-in-chief of the French armament is thus delineated by the bishop:—

"Humbert, the leader of this singular body of men, was himself as extraordinary a personage as any in his army. Of a good height and shape, in the full vigor of life, prompt to decide, quick in execution, apparently master of his art, you could not refuse him the praise of a good officer, while his physiognomy forbade you to like him as a man. His eye, which was small and sleepy, cast a sidelong glance of insidiousness and even of cruelty; it was the eye of a cat preparing to spring upon her prey. His education and manners were indicative of a person sprung from the lower orders of society; though he knew how to assume, when it was convenient, the deportment of a gentleman. For learning, he had scarcely enough to enable him to write his name. His passions were furious; and all his behavior seemed marked with the character of roughness and insolence. A narrower observation of him, however, seemed to discover that much of this roughness was the result of art, being assumed with the view of extorting by terror a ready compliance with his commands. Of this truth the bishop himself was one of the first who had occasion to be made sensible."

The particular occasion here alluded to by the bishop arose out of the first attempts to effect the disembarkation of the military stores and equipments from the French shipping, as also to forward them when landed. The case was one of extreme urgency; and proportionate allowance must be made for the French general. Every moment might bring the British cruisers in sight,—two important expeditions had already been baffled in that way,—and the absolute certainty, known to all parties alike, that delay, under these circumstances, was tantamount to ruin; that upon a difference of ten or fifteen minutes, this way or that, might happen to hinge the whole issue of the expedition: such a consciousness gave unavoidably to every demur at this critical moment the color of treachery. Neither boats, nor carts, nor horses could be obtained; the owners most imprudently and selfishly retiring from that service. Such being the extremity, the French general made the

---

to be hanged in case the plate were not forthcoming on a summons from head quarters; and that the Killala "place of security" was kindly strengthened, under the maternal anxiety of the French republic, by doubling the French sentries.

bishop responsible for the execution of his orders; but the bishop had really no means to enforce this commission, and failed. Upon that, General Humbert threatened to send his lordship, together with his whole family, prisoners of war to France, and assumed the air of a man violently provoked. Here came the crisis for determining the bishop's weight amongst his immediate flock, and his hold upon their affections. One great bishop, not far off, would, on such a trial, have been exultingly consigned to his fate: that I well know; for Lord Westport and I, merely as his visitors, were attacked in the dusk so fiercely with stones, that we were obliged to forbear going out unless in broad daylight. Luckily the Bishop of Killala had shown himself a Christian pastor, and now he reaped the fruits of his goodness. The public selfishness gave way when the danger of the bishop was made known. The boats, the carts, the horses were now liberally brought in from their lurking-places; the artillery and stores were landed; and the drivers of the carts, &c., were paid in drafts upon the Irish Directory, which (if it were an aerial coin) served at least to mark an unwillingness in the enemy to adopt violent modes of hostility, and ultimately became available in the very character assigned to them by the French general; not, indeed, as drafts upon the rebel, but as claims upon the equity of the English government.

The officer left in command at Killala, when the presence of the commander-in-chief was required elsewhere, bore the name of Charost. He was a lieutenant colonel, aged forty-five years, the son of a Parisian watchmaker. Having been sent over at an early age to the unhappy Island of St. Domingo, with a view to some connections there by which he hoped to profit, he had been fortunate enough to marry a young woman who brought him a plantation for her dowry, which was reputed to have yielded him a revenue of £2000 sterling per annum. But this, of course, all went to wreck in one day, upon that mad decree of the French convention which proclaimed liberty, without distinction, without restrictions, and without gradations, to the unprepared and ferocious negroes.[86] Even his wife and daughter would have perished simultaneously with his property but for English protection, which delivered them from the black sabre, and transferred them to Jamaica. There, however, though safe, they were, as respected Colonel Charost, unavoidably captives; and "his eyes would fill," says the bishop," when he told the family that he had not seen these dear relatives for six years past, nor even had tidings of them for the last three years." On his return to France, finding that to have been a watchmaker's son was no longer a bar to the honors of the military profession, he had entered the army, and had risen by merit to the rank which he now held. "He had a plain, good understanding. He seemed careless or doubtful of revealed religion, but said that he believed in God; was inclined to think that there must be a future state; and was very sure that, while he lived in this world, it was his duty to do all the good to his fellow-creatures that he could. Yet what he did not exhibit in his own conduct he appeared to respect in others; for he took care that no noise or disturbance should be made in the castle (*i.e.*, the bishop's palace) on Sundays, while the family, and many Protestants from the town, were

---

[86] I leave this passage as it was written originally under an impression then universally current. But, from what I have since read on this subject, I beg to be considered as speaking very doubtfully on the true causes of the St. Domingo disasters.

assembled in the library at their devotions.

"Boudet, the next in command, was a captain of foot, twenty-eight years old. His father, he said, was still living, though sixty-seven years old when he was born. His height was six feet two inches. In person, complexion, and gravity, he was no inadequate representation of the Knight of La Mancha, whose example he followed in a recital of his own prowess and wonderful exploits, delivered in measured language and an imposing seriousness of aspect." The bishop represents him as vain and irritable, but distinguished by good feeling and principle. Another officer was Ponson, described as five feet six inches high, lively and animated in excess, volatile, noisy, and chattering *à l›outrance*. "He was hardy," says the bishop, "and patient to admiration of labor and want of rest." And of this last quality the following wonderful illustration is given: "A continued watching of *five days and nights together*, when the rebels were growing desperate for prey and mischief, *did not appear to sink his spirits in the smallest degree.*"

Contrasting with the known rapacity of the French republican army in *all* its ranks the severest honesty of these particular officers, we must come to the conclusion, either that they had been *selected* for their tried qualities of abstinence and self-control, or else that the perilous tenure of their footing in Ireland had coerced them into forbearance. Of this same Ponson, the last described, the bishop declares that "he was strictly honest, and could not bear the absence of this quality in others; so that his patience was pretty well tried by his Irish allies. "At the same time, he expressed his contempt for religion in a way which the bishop saw reason for ascribing to vanity—"the miserable affectation of appearing worse than he really was." One officer there was, named *Truc*, whose brutality recalled the impression, so disadvantageous to French republicanism, which else had been partially effaced by the manners and conduct of his comrades. To him the bishop (and not the bishop only, but many of my own informants, to whom Truc had been familiarly known) ascribes "a front of brass, an incessant fraudful smile, manners altogether vulgar, and in his dress and person a neglect of cleanliness, even beyond the affected negligence of republicans."

Truc, however, happily, was not leader; and the principles or the policy of his superiors prevailed. To them, not merely in their own conduct, but also in their way of applying that influence which they held over their most bigoted allies, the Protestants of Connaught were under deep obligations. Speaking merely as to property, the honest bishop renders the following justice to the enemy: "And here it would be an act of great injustice to the excellent discipline constantly maintained by these invaders while they remained in our town, not to remark, that, with every temptation to plunder, which the time and the number of valuable articles within their reach presented to them in the bishop's palace, from a sideboard of plate and glasses, a hall filled with hats, whips, and greatcoats, as well of the guests as of the family, not a single particular of private property was found to have been carried away, when the owners, after the first fright, came to look for their effects, which was not for a day or two after the landing." Even in matters of delicacy the same forbearance was exhibited: "Beside the entire use of other apartments, during the stay of the French in Killala, the attic story, containing a library and three bed chambers, continued sacred to the bishop and his family. And so scrupulous was the delicacy of the French not to disturb the female part of the house, that not one of them was ever seen to go higher than the middle floor, except on the evening of the success at Castlebar, when two officers begged leave to carry to the family the news of the battle; and seemed a little mortified that the news was received with an air of dissatisfaction." These, however, were not the weightiest instances of that eminent service which the French had it in their power to render on this occasion. The royal army behaved ill in every sense. Liable to continual panics in the field,—panics which, but for the overwhelming force accumulated, and the discretion of Lord Cornwallis, would have been fatal to the good cause,—the royal forces erred as unthinkingly, in the abuse of any momentary triumph. Forgetting that the rebels held many hostages in their hands, they once recommenced the old system practised in Wexford and Kildare—of hanging and shooting without trial, and without a thought of the horrible reprisals that might be adopted. These reprisals, but for the fortunate influence of the French commanders, and but for their great energy in applying that influence according to the exigencies of time and place, would have been made: it cost the whole weight of the French power, their influence was stretched almost to breaking, before they could accomplish their purpose of neutralizing the senseless cruelty of the royalists, and of saving the trembling Protestants. Dreadful were the anxieties of these moments; and I myself heard persons, at a distance of nearly two years, declare that their lives hung at that time by a thread; and that, but for the hasty approach of the lord lieutenant by forced marches, that thread would have snapped. "We heard with panic," said they, "of the madness which characterized the proceedings of our *soi-disant* friends; and, for any chance of safety, unavoidably we looked only to our nominal enemies—the staff of the French army."

One story was still current, and very frequently repeated, at the time of my own residence upon the scene of these transactions. It would not be fair to mention it, without saying, at the same time, that the bishop, whose discretion was so much impeached by the affair, had the candor to blame himself most heavily, and always applauded the rebel for the lesson he had given him. The case was this: Day after day the royal forces had been accumulating upon military posts in the neighborhood of Killala, and could be descried from elevated stations in that town. Stories travelled simultaneously to Killala, every hour, of the atrocities which marked their advance; many, doubtless, being fictions, either of blind hatred, or of that ferocious policy which sought to make the rebels desperate, by tempting them into the last extremities of guilt, but, unhappily, too much countenanced as to their general outline, by excesses on the royal part, already proved, and undeniable. The ferment and the anxiety increased every hour amongst the rebel occupants of Killala. The French had no power to protect, beyond the moral one of their influence as allies; and, in the very crisis of this alarming situation, a rebel came to the bishop with the news that the royal cavalry was at that moment advancing from Sligo, and could be traced along the country by the line of blazing houses which accompanied their march. The bishop doubted this, and expressed his doubt. "Come with me," said the rebel. It was a matter of policy to yield, and his lordship went. They ascended together the Needle Tower Hill, from the summit of which the bishop now discovered that the fierce rebel had spoken but too truly. A line of smoke and fire ran over the country in the rear of a strong patrol detached from the king's forces. The moment was critical; the rebel's eye expressed the unsettled state of his feelings; and, at that instant, the imprudent bishop utterred a sentiment which, to his dying day, he could not forget. "They," said he, meaning the ruined houses, "are only wretched cabins." The rebel mused, and for a few moments seemed in self-conflict—a dreadful interval to the bishop, who became sensible of his own extreme imprudence the very moment after the words had escaped him. However, the man contented himself with saying, after a pause, "A poor man's cabin is to him as dear as a palace." It is probable that this retort was far from expressing the deep moral indignation at his heart, though his readiness of mind failed to furnish him with any other more stinging; and, in such cases, all depends upon the first movement of vindictive feeling being broken. The bishop, however, did not forget the lesson he had received; nor did he fail to blame himself most heavily, not so much for his imprudence as for his thoughtless adoption of a language expressing an aristocratic hauteur that did not belong to his real character. There was, indeed, at that moment no need that fresh fuel should be applied to the irritation of the rebels; they had already declared their intention of plundering the town; and, as they added, "in spite of the French," whom they now regarded, and openly denounced, as "abetters of the Protestants," much more than as their own allies.

Justice, however, must be done to the rebels as well as to their military associates. If they were disposed to plunder, they were found generally to shrink from bloodshed and cruelty, and yet from no want of energy or determination. "The peasantry never appeared to want animal courage," says the bishop, "for they flocked together to meet danger whenever it was expected. Had it pleased Heaven to be as liberal to them of brains as of hands, it is not easy to say to what length of mischief they might have proceeded; but they were all along unprovided with leaders of any ability." This, I believe, was true; and yet it would be doing poor justice to the Connaught rebels, nor would it be drawing the moral truly as respects this aspect of the rebellion, if their abstinence from mischief, in its worst form, were to be explained out of this defect in their leaders. Nor is it possible to suppose *that* the bishop's meaning, though his words seem to tend that way. For he himself elsewhere notices the absence of all wanton bloodshed as a feature of this Connaught rebellion most honorable in itself to the poor misguided rebels, and as distinguishing it very remarkably from the greater insurrection so recently crushed in the centre and the east. "It is a circumstance," says he, "worthy of particular notice, that, during the whole time of this civil commotion, not a single drop of blood was shed by the Connaught rebels, except in the field of war. It is true, the example and influence of the French went a great way to prevent sanguinary excesses. But it will not be deemed fair to ascribe to this cause alone the forbearance of which we were witnesses, when it is considered what a range of country lay at the mercy of the rebels for several days after the French power was known to be at an end."

To what, then, *are* we to ascribe the forbearance of the Connaught men, so singularly contrasted with the hideous excesses of their brethren in the east? Solely to the different complexion (so, at least, I was told) of the policy pursued by government. In Wexford, Kildare, Meath, Dublin, &c., it had been judged advisable to adopt, as a sort of precautionary policy, not for the punishment, but for the discovery of rebellious purposes, measures of the direst severity; not merely free quarterings of the soldiery, with liberty (or even an express commission) to commit outrages and insults upon all who were suspected, upon all who refused to countenance such measures, upon all who presumed to question their justice, but even, under color of martial law, to inflict croppings, and pitch cappings, half hangings, and the torture of "picketings;" to say nothing of houses burned, and farms laid waste—things which were done daily, and under military orders; the purpose avowed being either vengeance for some known act of insurrection, or the determination to extort confessions. Too often, however, as may well be supposed, in such utter disorganization of society, private malice, either personal or on account of old family feuds, was the true principle at work. And many were thus driven, by mere frenzy of just indignation, or, perhaps, by mere desperation, into acts of rebellion which else they had not meditated. Now, in Connaught, at this time, the same barbarous policy was no longer pursued; and then it was seen, that, unless maddened by ill usage, the peasantry were capable of great self-control. There was no repetition of the Enniscorthy massacres; and it was impossible to explain honestly *why* there was none, without, at the same time, reflecting back upon that atrocity some color of palliation.

These things considered, it must be granted that there was a spirit of unjustifiable violence in the royal army on achieving their triumph. It is shocking, however, to observe the effect of panic to irritate the instincts of cruelty and sanguinary violence, even in the gentlest minds. I remember well, on occasion of the memorable tumults in Bristol, (autumn of 1831,) that I, for my part, could not read, without horror and indignation, one statement, (made, I believe, officially at that time,) which yet won the cordial approbation of some ladies who had participated in the panic. I allude to that part of the report which represents several of the dragoons as having dismounted, resigned the care of their horses to persons in the street, and pursued the unhappy fugitives, criminals, undoubtedly, but no longer dangerous, up stairs and down stairs, to the last nook of their retreat. The worst criminals could not be known and identified as such; and even in a case where they could, vengeance so hellish and so unrelenting was not justified by houses burned or by momentary panics raised. Scenes of the same description were beheld upon the first triumph of the royal cause in Connaught; and but for Lord Cornwallis, equally firm before his success and moderate in its exercise, they would have prevailed more extensively. The poor rebels were pursued with a needless ferocity on the recapture of Killala. So hotly, indeed, did some of the conquerors hang upon the footsteps of the fugitives, that both rushed almost simultaneously—pursuers and pursued—into the terror-stricken houses of Killala; and, in some instances, the ball meant for a rebel told with mortal effect upon a royalist. Here, indeed, as in other cases of this rebellion, in candor it should be mentioned, that the royal army was composed chiefly of militia regiments. Not that militia, or regiments composed chiefly of men who had but just before volunteered for the line, have not often made unexceptionable soldiers; but in this case there was no reasonable proportion of veterans, or men who had seen any service. The Bishop of Killala was assured by an intelligent officer of the king's army that the victors were within a trifle of being beaten. I was myself told by a gentlemen who rode as a volunteer on that day, that, to the best of his belief, it was merely a mistaken order of the rebel chiefs causing a false application of a select reserve at a very critical moment, which had saved his own party from a ruinous defeat. It may be added, upon almost universal testimony, that the recapture of Killala was abused, not only as respected the defeated rebels, but also as respected the royalists of that town. "The regiments that came to their assistance, being all militia, seemed to think that they had a right to take the property they had been the means of preserving, and to use it as their own whenever they stood in need of it. Their rapacity differed in no respect from that of the rebels, except that they seized upon things with less of ceremony and excuse, and that his majesty's soldiers were incomparably superior to the Irish traitors in dexterity at stealing. In consequence, the town grew very weary of their guests, and were glad to see them march off to other quarters."

The military operations in this brief campaign were discreditable, in the last degree, to the energy, to the vigilance, and to the steadiness of the Orange army. Humbert had been a leader against the royalists of La Vendée, as well as on the Rhine; consequently he was an ambidextrous enemy—fitted equally for partisan warfare, and for the tactics of regular armies. Keenly alive to the necessity, under *his* circumstances, of vigor and despatch, after occupying Killala on the evening of the 22d August, (the day of his disembarkation,) where the small garrison of 50 men (yeomen and fencibles) had made a tolerable resistance, and after other trifling affairs, he had, on the 26th, marched against Castlebar with about 800 of his own men, and perhaps 1200 to 1500 of the rebels. Here was the advanced post of the royal army. General Lake (the Lord Lake of India) and Major General Hutchinson (the Lord Hutchinson of Egypt) had assembled upon this point a respectable force; some say upwards of 4000, others not more than 1100. The disgraceful result is well known: the French, marching all night over mountain roads, and through one pass which was thought impregnable, if it had been occupied by a battalion instead of a captain's guard, surprised Castlebar on the morning of the 27th. *Surprised*, I say, for no word short of that can express the circumstances of the case. About two o'clock in the morning, a courier had brought intelligence of the French advance; but from some unaccountable obstinacy, at head quarters, such as had proved fatal more than either once or twice in the Wexford campaign, his news was disbelieved; yet, if disbelieved, why therefore neglected? Neglected, however, it was; and at seven, when the news proved to be true, the royal army was drawn out in hurry and confusion to meet the enemy. The French, on their part, seeing our strength, looked for no better result to themselves than summary surrender; more especially as our artillery was well served, and soon began to tell upon their ranks. Better hopes first arose, as they afterwards declared, upon observing that many of the troops fired in a disorderly way, without waiting for the word of command; upon this they took new measures: in a few minutes a panic arose; General Lake ordered a retreat; and then, in spite of all that could be done by the indignant officers, the flight became irretrievable. The troops reached Tuam, thirty miles distant, on that same day; and one small party of mounted men actually pushed on to Athlone, which is above sixty miles from the field of battle. Fourteen pieces of artillery were lost on this occasion. However, it ought to be mentioned that some serious grounds appeared afterwards for suspecting treachery; most of those who had been reported "missing" having been afterwards observed in the ranks of the enemy, where it is remarkable enough (or perhaps not so remarkable, as simply implying how little they were trusted by their new allies, and for that reason how naturally they were put forward on the most dangerous services) that these deserters perished to a man. Meantime, the new lord lieutenant, having his foot constantly in the stirrup, marched from Dublin without a moment's delay. By means of the grand canal, he made a forced march of fifty-six English miles in two days; which brought him to Kilbeggan on the 27th. Very early on the following morning, he received the unpleasant news from Castlebar. Upon this he advanced to Athlone, meeting every indication of a routed and panic-struck army. Lord Lake was retreating upon that town, and thought himself *(it is said)* so little secure, even at this distance from the enemy, that the road from Tuam was covered with strong patrols. On the other hand, in ludicrous contrast to these demonstrations of alarm, (*supposing them to be related without exaggeration,*) the French had never stirred from Castlebar. On the 4th of September, Lord Cornwallis was within fourteen miles of that place. Humbert, however, had previously dislodged towards the county of Longford. His motive for this movement was to cooperate with an insurrection in that quarter, which had just then broken out in strength. He was now, however, hemmed in by a large army of perhaps 25,000 men, advancing from all points; and a few moves were all that remained of the game, played with whatever skill. Colonel Vereker, with about 300 of the Limerick militia, first came up with him, and skirmished very creditably (September 6) with part, or (as the colonel always maintained) with the whole of the French army. Other affairs of trivial importance followed; and at length, on the 8th of September, General Humbert surrendered with his whole army, now reduced to 844 men, of whom 96 were officers; having lost since their landing at Killala exactly 288 men. The rebels were not admitted to any terms; they were pursued and cut down without mercy. However, it is pleasant to know, that, from their agility in escaping, this cruel policy was defeated: not much above 500 perished; and thus were secured to the royal party the worst results of vengeance the fiercest, and of clemency the most undistinguishing, without any one advantage of either. Some districts, as Laggan and Eris, were treated with martial rigor; the cabins being burned, and their unhappy tenants driven out into the mountains for the winter. Rigor, therefore, there was; for the most humane politicians, erroneously, as one must believe, fancied it necessary for the army to leave behind some impressions of terror amongst the insurgents. It is certain, however, that, under the counsels of Lord Cornwallis, the standards of public severity were very much lowered, as compared with the previous examples in Wexford.

The tardiness and slovenly execution of the whole service, meantime, was well illustrated in what follows:—

Killala was not delivered from rebel hands until the 23rd of September, notwithstanding the general surrender had occurred on the 8th; and then only in consequence of an express from the bishop to General Trench, hastening his march. The situation of the Protestants was indeed critical. Humbert had left three French officers to protect the place, but their influence gradually had sunk to a shadow. And plans of pillage, with all its attendant horrors, were daily debated. Under these circumstances, the French officers behaved honorably and courageously. "Yet," says the bishop, "the poor commandant had no reason to be pleased with the treatment he had received immediately after the action. He had returned to the castle for his sabre, and advanced with it to the gate, in order to deliver it up to some English officer, when it was seized and forced from his hand by a common soldier of Fraser's. He came in, got another sword, which he surrendered to an officer, and turned to reenter the hall. At this moment a second Highlander burst through the gate, in spite of the sentinel placed there by the general, and fired at the commandant with an aim that was near proving fatal, for the ball passed under his arm, piercing a very thick door entirely through, and lodging in the jamb. Had we lost the worthy man by such an accident, his death would have spoiled the whole relish of our present enjoyment. He complained, and received an apology for the soldier's behavior from his officer. Leave was immediately granted to the three French officers (left behind by Humbert at Killala) to keep their swords, their effects, and even their bed chambers in the house."

* * * * *

Note applying generally to this chapter on the Second Irish Rebellion. — Already in 1833, when writing this 10th chapter, I felt a secret jealously (intermittingly recurring) that possibly I might have fallen under a false bias at this point of my youthful memorials. I myself had seen reason to believe — indeed, sometimes I knew for certain — that, in the *personalities* of Irish politics from Grattan downwards, a spirit of fiery misrepresentation prevailed, which made it hopeless to seek for any thing resembling truth. If in any quarter you found candor and liberality, *that* was because no interest existed in any thing Irish, and consequently no real information. Find out any man that could furnish you with information such as presupposed an interest in Ireland, and inevitably he turned out a bigoted partisan. There cannot be a stronger proof of this than the ridiculous libels and literary caricatures current even in England, through one whole generation, against the late Lord Londonderry — a most able and faithful manager of our English foreign interests in times of unparalleled difficulty. Already in the closing years of the last century, his Irish policy had been inextricably falsified: subsequently, when he came to assume a leading part in the English Parliament, the efforts to calumniate him became even more intense; and it is only within the last five years that a reaction of public opinion on this subject has been strong enough to reach even those among his enemies who were enlightened men. Liberal journals (such, *e. g.*, as the "North British Review") now recognize his merits. Naturally it was impossible that the civil war of 1798 in Ireland, and the persons conspicuously connected with it, should escape this general destiny of Irish politics. I wrote, therefore, originally under a jealousy that partially I might have been duped. At present, in reviewing what I had written twenty years ago, I feel this jealousy much more keenly. I shrink from the bishop's malicious portraitures of our soldiers, sometimes of their officers, as composing a licentious army, without discipline, without humanity, without even steady courage. Has any man a right to ask our toleration for pictures so romantic as these? Duped perhaps I was myself: and it was natural that I should be so under the overwhelming influences oppressing any right that I *could* have at my early age to a free, independent judgment. But I will not any longer assist in duping the reader; and I will therefore suggest to him two grounds of vehement suspicion against all the insidious colorings given to his statements by the bishop:—

1st. I beg to remind the reader that this army of Mayo, in 1798, so unsteady and so undisciplined, if we believe the bishop, was in part the army of Egypt in the year 1801: how would the bishop have answered *that*?

2dly. The bishop allows great weight in treating any allegations whatever against the English army or the English government, to the moderation, equity, and self-control claimed for the Irish peasantry as notorious elements in their character. Meantime he forgets this doctrine most conspicuously at times; and represents the safety of the Protestants against pillage, or even against a spirit of massacre, as entirely dependent on the influence of the French. Whether for property or life, it was to the French that the Irish Protestants looked for protection: not I it is, but the bishop, on whom that representation will be found to rest.

CHAPTER XI.

TRAVELLING.

It was late in October, or early in November, that I quitted Connaught with Lord Westport; and very slowly, making many leisurely deviations from the direct route, travelled back to Dublin. Thence, after some little stay, we recrossed St. George's Channel, landed at Holyhead, and then, by exactly the same route as we had pursued in early June, we posted through Bangor, Conway, Llanrwst, Llangollen, until once again we found ourselves in England, and, as a matter of course, making for Birmingham. But why making for Birmingham? Simply because Birmingham, under the old dynasty of stage coaches and post chaises, was the centre of our travelling system, and held in England something of that rank which the golden milestone of Rome held in the Italian peninsula.

At Birmingham it was (which I, like myriads beside, had traversed a score of times without ever yet having visited it as a *terminus ad quem*) that I parted with my friend Lord Westport. His route lay through Oxford; and stopping, therefore, no longer than was necessary to harness fresh horses,—an operation, however, which was seldom accomplished in less than half an hour at that era,—he went on directly to Stratford. My own destination was yet doubtful. I had been directed, in Dublin, to inquire at the Birmingham post office for a letter which would guide my motions. There, accordingly, upon sending for it, lay the expected letter from my mother; from which I learned that my sister was visiting at Laxton, in Northamptonshire, the seat of an old friend, to which I also had an invitation. My route to this lay through Stamford. Thither I could not go by a stage coach until the following day; and of necessity I prepared to make the most of my present day in gloomy, noisy, and, at that time, dirty Birmingham.

Be not offended, compatriot of Birmingham, that I salute your natal town with these disparaging epithets. It is not my habit to indulge rash impulses of contempt towards any man or body of men, wheresoever collected, far less towards a race of high-minded and most intelligent citizens, such as Birmingham has exhibited to the admiration of all Europe. But as to the noise and the gloom which I ascribe to you, those features of your town will illustrate what the Germans mean by a *one-sided*[87] (ein-seitiger) judgment. There are, I can well believe, thousands to whom Birmingham is another name for domestic peace, and for a reasonable share of sunshine. But in my case, who have passed through Birmingham a hun-

[87] It marks the rapidity with which new phrases float themselves into currency under our present omnipresence of the press, that this word, *now* (viz., in 1853) familiarly used in every newspaper, *then* (viz., in 1833) required a sort of apology to warrant its introduction.

dred times, it always happened to rain, except once; and that once the Shrewsbury mail carried me so rapidly away, that I had not time to examine the sunshine, or see whether it might not be some gilt Birmingham counterfeit; for you know, men of Birmingham, that you *can* counterfeit—such is your cleverness—all things in heaven and earth, from Jove's thunderbolts down to a tailor's bodkin. Therefore, the gloom is to be charged to my bad luck. Then, as to the noise, never did I sleep at that enormous *Hen and Chickens*[88] to which usually my destiny brought me, but I had reason to complain that the discreet hen did not gather her vagrant flock to roost at less variable hours. Till two or three, I was kept waking by those who were retiring; and about three commenced the morning functions of the porter, or of "boots," or of "underboots," who began their rounds for collecting the several freights for the Highflyer, or the Tally-ho, or the Bang-up, to all points of the compass, and too often (as must happen in such immense establishments) blundered into my room with that appalling, "Now, sir, the horses are coming out." So that

---

[88] A well-known hotel, and also a coach inn, which we English in those days thought colossal. It was in fact, according to the spirit of Dr. Johnson's itty reply to Miss Knight, big enough for an island. But our transatlantic brothers, dwelling upon so mighty a continent, have gradually enlarged their scale of inns as of other objects into a size of commensurate grandeur. In two separate New York journals, which, by the kindness of American friends, are at this moment (April 26) lying before me, I read astounding illustrations of this. For instance: (1.) In "Putnam's Monthly" for April, 1853, the opening article, a very amusing one, entitled "New York daguerreotyped," estimates the hotel population of that vast city as "not much short of ten thousand;" and one individual hotel, apparently far from being the most conspicuous, viz., the *Metropolitan*, reputed to have "more than twelve miles of water and gas pipe, and two hundred and fifty servants," offers "accommodations for one thousand guests." (2.) Yet even this Titanic structure dwindles by comparison with *The Mount Vernon Hotel* at Cape May, N. J., (meant, I suppose, for New Jersey,) which advertises itself in the "New York Herald," of April 12, 1853, under the authority of Mr. J. Taber, its aspiring landlord, as offering accommodations, from the 20th of next June, to the romantic number of *three thousand five hundred* guests. The Birmingham Hen and Chickens undoubtedly had slight pretensions by the side of these behemoths and mammoths. And yet, as a street in a very little town may happen to be quite as noisy as a street in London, I can testify that any single gallery in this Birmingham hotel, if measured in importance by the elements of discomfort which it could develop, was entitled to an American rating. But alas! *Fuit Ilium;* I have not seen the ruins of this ancient hotel; but an instinct tells me that the railroad has run right through it; that the hen has ceased to lay golden eggs, and that her chickens are dispersed. (3.) As another illustration, I may mention that, in the middle of March, 1853, I received, as a present from New York, the following newspaper. Each page contained eleven columns, whereas our London "Times" contains only six. It was entitled "The New York Journal of Commerce," and was able to proclaim itself with truth the largest journal in the world. For 25-1/2 years it had existed in a smaller size, but even in this infant stage had so far outrun all other journals in size (measuring, from the first, 816 square inches) as to have earned the name of *"the blanket sheet:"* but this thriving baby had continued to grow, until at last, on March 1, 1853, it came out in a sheet "comprising an area of 2057-1/4 square inches, or 16- 2/3 square feet." This was the monster sent over the Atlantic to myself; and I really felt it as some relief to my terror, when I found the editor protesting that the monster should not be allowed to grow any more. I presume that it was meant to keep the hotels in countenance; for a journal on the old scale could not expect to make itself visible in an edifice that offered accommodations to an army.

rarely, indeed, have I happened to *sleep* in Birmingham. But the dirt!—*that* sticks a little with you, friend of Birmingham. How do I explain away *that*? Know, then, reader, that at the time I speak of, and in the way I speak of, viz., in streets and inns, all England was dirty.

* * * * *

Being left therefore alone for the whole of a rainy day in Birmingham, and Birmingham being as yet the centre of our travelling system, I cannot do better than spend my Birmingham day in reviewing the most lively of its reminiscences.

The revolution in the whole apparatus, means, machinery, and dependences of that system—a revolution begun, carried through, and perfected within the period of my own personal experience—merits a word or two of illustration in the most cursory memoirs that profess any attention at all to the shifting scenery and moving forces of the age, whether manifested in great effects or in little. And these particular effects, though little, when regarded in their separate details, are *not* little in their final amount. On the contrary, I have always maintained, that under a representative government, where the great cities of the empire must naturally have the power, each in its proportion, of reacting upon the capital and the councils of the nation in so conspicious a way, there is a result waiting on the final improvements of the arts of travelling, and of transmitting intelligence with velocity, such as cannot be properly appreciated in the absence of all historical experience. Conceive a state of communication between the centre and the extremities of a great people, kept up with a uniformity of reciprocation so exquisite as to imitate the flowing and ebbing of the sea, or the systole and diastole of the human heart; day and night, waking and sleeping, not succeeding to each other with more absolute certainty than the acts of the metropolis and the controlling notice of the provinces, whether in the way of support or of resistance. Action and reaction from every point of the compass being thus perfect and instantaneous, we should then first begin to understand, in a practical sense, what is meant by the unity of a political body, and we should approach to a more adequate appreciation of the powers which are latent in organization. For it must be considered that hitherto, under the most complex organization, and that which has best attained its purposes, the national will has never been able to express itself upon one in a thousand of the public acts, simply because the national voice was lost in the distance, and could not collect itself through the time and the space rapidly enough to connect itself immediately with the evanescent measure of the moment. But, as the system of intercourse is gradually expanding, these bars of space and time are in the same degree contracting, until finally we may expect them altogether to vanish; and then every part of the empire will react upon the whole with the power, life, and effect of immediate conference amongst parties brought face to face. Then first will be seen a political system truly *organic*—*i.e.*, in which each acts upon all, and all react upon each; and a new earth will arise from the indirect agency of this merely physical revolution. Already, in this paragraph, written twenty years ago, a prefiguring instinct spoke within me of some great secret yet to come in the art of distant communication. At present I am content to regard the electric telegraph as the oracular response to that prefiguration. But I still look for some higher and transcendent response.

The reader whose birth attaches him to this present generation, having known only macadamized roads, cannot easily bring before his imagination the antique and almost aboriginal state of things which marked our travelling system down to the end of the eighteenth century, and nearly through the first decennium of the present. A very few lines will suffice for some broad notices of our condition, in this respect, through the last two centuries. In the Parliament war, (1642-6,) it is an interesting fact, but at the same time calculated to mislead the incautious reader, that some officers of distinction, on both sides, brought close carriages to head quarters; and sometimes they went even upon the field of battle in these carriages, not mounting on horseback until the preparations were beginning for some important manoeuvre, or for a general movement. The same thing had been done throughout the Thirty Years' war, both by the Bavarian, imperial, and afterwards by the Swedish officers of rank. And it marks the great diffusion of these luxuries about this era, that on occasion of the reinstalment of two princes of Mecklenburg, who had been violently dispossessed by Wallenstein, upwards of eighty coaches mustered at a short notice, partly from the territorial nobility, partly from the camp. Precisely, however, at military head quarters, and on the route of an army, carriages of this description were an available and a most useful means of transport. Cumbrous and unweildy they were, as we know by pictures; and they could not have been otherwise, for they were built to meet the roads. Carriages of our present light and *reedy* (almost, one might say, *corky*) construction would, on the roads of Germany or of England, in that age, have foundered within the first two hours. To our ancestors, such carriages would have seemed playthings for children. Cumbrous as the carriages of that day were, they could not be more so than artillery or baggage wagons: where these could go, coaches could go. So that, in the march of an army, there was a perpetual guaranty to those who had coaches for the possibility of their transit. And hence, and not because the roads were at at all better than they have been generally described in those days, we are to explain the fact, that both in the royal camp, in Lord Manchester's, and afterwards in General Fairfax's and Cromwell's, coaches were an ordinary part of the camp equipage. The roads, meantime, were as they have been described, viz., ditches, morasses, and sometimes channels for the course of small brooks. Nor did they improve, except for short reaches, and under peculiar local advantages, throughout that century. Spite of the roads, however, publick carriages began to pierce England, in various lines, from the era of 1660. Circumstantial notices of these may be found in Lord Auckland's (Sir Frederic Eden's) large work on the poor laws. That to York, for example, (two hundred miles,) took a fortnight in the journey, or about fourteen miles a day. But Chamberlayne, who had a personal knowledge of these public carriages, says enough to show that, if slow, they were cheap; half a crown being the usual rate for fifteen miles, (*i.e.*, 2 *d.* a mile.) Public conveyances, multiplying rapidly, could not but diffuse a general call for improved roads; improved both in dimensions and also in the art of construction. For it is observable, that, so early as Queen Elizabeth's days, England, the most equestrian of nations, already presented to its inhabitants a general system of decent bridle roads. Even at this day, it is doubtful whether any man, taking all hinderances into account, and having laid no previous relays of horses, could much exceed the exploit of Carey, (afterwards Lord Monmouth,) a younger son of the first Lord Hunsden, a cousin of Queen Elizabeth. Yet we must not forget that the particular road concerned in this exploit was the Great North Road, (as it is still called by way of distinction,) lying through Doncaster and York, between the northern and southern capitals of the island. But roads less frequented were tolerable as bridle roads; whilst all alike, having been originally laid down with no view to the broad and ample coaches, from 1570 to 1700, scratched the panels on each side as they crept along. Even in the nineteenth century, I have known a case in the sequestered district of Egremont, in Cumberland, where a post chaise, of the common narrow dimensions, was obliged to retrace its route of fourteen miles, on coming to a bridge built in some remote age, when as yet post chaises were neither known nor anticipated, and, unfortunately, too narrow by three or four inches. In all the provinces of England, when the soil was deep and adhesive, a worse evil beset the stately equipage. An Italian of rank, who has left a record of his perilous adventure, visited, or attempted to visit, Petworth, near London, (then a seat of the Percys, now of Lord Egremont,) about the year 1685. I forget how many times he was overturned within one particular stretch of five miles; but I remember that it was a subject of gratitude (and, upon meditating a return by the same route a subject of pleasing hope) to dwell upon the softlying which was to be found in that good-natured morass. Yet this was, doubtless, a pet road, (sinful punister! dream not that I glance at *Pet* worth,) and an improved road. Such as this, I have good reason to think, were most of the roads in England, unless upon the rocky strata which stretch northwards from Derbyshire to Cumberland and Northumberland. The public carriages were the first harbingers of a change for the better; as these grew and prospered, slender lines of improvement began to vein and streak the map. And Parliament began to show their zeal, though not always a corresponding knowledge, by legislating backwards and forwards on the breadth of wagon wheel tires, &c. But not until our cotton system began to put forth blossoms, not until our trade and our steam engines began to stimulate the coal mines, which in *their* turn stimulated *them*, did any great energy apply itself to our roads. In my childhood, standing with one or two of my brothers and sisters at the front windows of my mother's carriage, I remember one unvarying set of images before us. The postilion (for so were all carriages then driven) was employed, not by fits and starts, but always and eternally, in *quartering*[89] *i.e.*, in crossing from side to side—according to the casualties of the ground. Before you stretched a wintry length of lane, with ruts deep enough to fracture the leg of a horse, filled to the brim with standing pools of rain water; and the collateral chambers of these ruts kept from becoming confluent by thin ridges, such as the Romans called *lirae*, to maintain the footing upon which *lirae*, so as not to swerve, (or, as the Romans would say, *delirare*,) was a trial of some skill both for the horses and their postilion. It was, indeed, next to impossible for any horse, on such a narrow crust of separation, not to grow *delirious* in the Roman metaphor; and the nervous anxiety, which haunted me when a child, was much fed by this very image so often before my eye, and the sympathy with which I followed the

---

[89] Elsewhere I have suggested, as the origin of this term, the French word *cartayer*, to manoeuvre so as to evade the ruts.

motion of the docile creature's legs. Go to sleep at the beginning of a stage, and the last thing you saw—wake up, and the first thing you saw—was the line of wintry pools, the poor off-horse planting his steps with care, and the cautious postilion gently applying his spur, whilst manoeuvring across this system of grooves with some sort of science that looked like a gypsy's palmistry; so equally unintelligible to me were his motions, in what he sought and in what he avoided.

I may add, by way of illustration, and at the risk of gossiping, which, after all, is not the worst of things, a brief notice of my very first journey. I might be then seven years old. A young gentleman, the son of a wealthy banker, had to return home for the Christmas holidays to a town in Lincolnshire, distant from the public school where he was pursuing his education about a hundred miles. The school was in the neighborhood of Greenhay, my father's house. There were at that time no coaches in that direction; now (1833) there are many every day. The young gentleman advertised for a person to share the expense of a post chaise. By accident, I had an invitation of some standing to the same town, where I happened to have some female relatives of mature age, besides some youthful cousins. The two travellers elect soon heard of each other, and the arrangement was easily completed. It was my earliest migration from the paternal roof; and the anxieties of pleasure, too tumultuous, with some slight sense of undefined fears, combined to agitate my childish feelings. I had a vague, slight apprehension of my fellow-traveller, whom I had never seen, and whom my nursery maid, when dressing me, had described in no very amiable colors. But a good deal more I thought of Sherwood Forest, (the forest of Robin Hood,) which, as I had been told, we should cross after the night set in. At six o'clock I descended, and not, as usual, to the children's room, but, on this special morning of my life, to a room called the breakfast room: where I found a blazing fire, candles lighted, and the whole breakfast equipage, as if for my mother, set out, to my astonishment, for no greater personage than myself. The scene being in England, and on a December morning, I need scarcely say that it rained: the rain beat violently against the windows, the wind raved; and an aged servant, who did the honors of the breakfast table, pressed me urgently to eat. I need not say that I had no appetite: the fulness of my heart, both from busy anticipation, and from the parting which was at hand, had made me incapable of any other thought or attention but such as pointed to the coming journey. All circumstances in travelling, all scenes and situations of a representative and recurring character, are indescribably affecting, connected, as they have been, in so many myriads of minds, more especially in a land which is sending off forever its flowers and blossoms to a clime so remote as that of India, with heart-rending separations, and with farewells never to be repeated. But, amongst them all, none cleaves to my own feelings more indelibly, from having repeatedly been concerned, either as witness or as a principal party in its little drama, than the early breakfast on a wintry morning long before the darkness has given way, when the golden blaze of the hearth, and the bright glitter of candles, with female ministrations of gentleness more touching than on common occasions, all conspire to rekindle, as it were for a farewell gleam, the holy memorials of household affections. And many have, doubtless, had my feelings; for, I believe, few readers will ever forget the beautiful manner in which Mrs. Inchbald has treated such a scene in winding up the first part of her "Simple Story," and the power with which she has invested it.

Years, that seem innumerable, have passed since that December morning in my own life to which I am now recurring; and yet, even to this moment, I recollect the audible throbbing of heart, the leap and rushing of blood, which suddenly surprised me during a deep lull of the wind, when the aged attendant said, without hurry or agitation, but with something of a solemn tone, "That is the sound of wheels. I hear the chaise. Mr. H— — will be here directly." The road ran, for some distance, by a course pretty nearly equidistant from the house, so that the groaning of the wheels continued to catch the ear, as it swelled upon the wind, for some time without much alteration. At length a right-angled turn brought the road continually and rapidly nearer to the gates of the grounds, which had purposely been thrown open. At this point, however, a long career of raving arose; all other sounds were lost; and, for some time, I began to think we had been mistaken, when suddenly the loud trampling of horses' feet, as they whirled up the sweep below the windows, followed by a peal long and loud upon the bell, announced, beyond question, the summons for my departure. The door being thrown open, steps were heard loud and fast; and in the next moment, ushered by a servant, stalked forward, booted and fully equipped, my travelling companion—if such a word can at all express the relation between the arrogant young blood, just fresh from assuming the *toga virilis*, and a modest child of profound sensibilities, but shy and reserved beyond even English reserve. The aged servant, with apparently constrained civility, presented my mother's compliments to him, with a request that he would take breakfast. This he hastily and rather peremptorily declined. Me, however, he condescended to notice with an approving nod, slightly inquiring if I were the young gentleman who shared his post chaise. But, without allowing time for an answer, and striking his boot impatiently with a riding whip, he hoped I was ready. "Not until he has gone up to my mistress," replied my old protectress, in a tone of some asperity. Thither I ascended. What counsels and directions I might happen to receive at the maternal toilet, naturally I have forgotten. The most memorable circumstance to me was, that I, who had never till that time possessed the least or most contemptible coin, received, in a network purse, six glittering guineas, with instructions to put three immediately into Mr. H— —'s hands, and the others when he should call for them.

The rest of my mother's counsels, If deep, were not long; she, who had always something of a Roman firmness, shed more milk of roses, I believe, upon my cheeks than tears; and why not? What should there be to *her* corresponding to an ignorant child's sense of pathos, in a little journey of about a hundred miles? Outside her door, however, there awaited me some silly creatures, women of course, old and young, from the nursery and the kitchen, who gave, and who received, those fervent kisses which wait only upon love without awe and without disguise. Heavens! what rosaries might be strung for the memory of sweet female kisses, given without check or art, before one is of an age to value them! And again, how sweet is the touch of female hands as they array one for a journey! If any thing needs fastening, whether by pinning, tying, or any other contrivance, how perfect is one's confidence in female skill; as if, by mere virtue of her sex and feminine instinct, a woman could not possibly fail to know the best and readiest way of adjusting every case that could arise in dress. Mine was hastily completed amongst them: each had a pin to draw from her bosom, in order to put something to rights about my throat or hands; and a chorus of "God bless hims!" was arising, when, from below, young Mephistopheles murmured an impatient groan, and perhaps the horses snorted. I found myself lifted into the chaise; counsels about the night and the cold flowing in upon me, to which Mephistopheles listened with derision or astonishment. I and he had each our separate corner; and, except to request that I would draw up one of the glasses, I do not think he condescended to address one word to me until dusk, when we found ourselves rattling into Chesterfield, having barely accomplished four stages, or forty or forty-two miles, in about nine hours. This, except on the Bath or great north roads, may be taken as a standard amount of performance, in 1794, (the year I am recording,) and even ten years later.[90] In these present hurrying and tumultuous days, whether time is really of more value, I cannot say; but all people on the establishment of inns are required to suppose it of the most awful value. Nowadays, (1833,) no sooner have the horses stopped at the gateway of a posting house than a summons is passed down to the stables; and in less than one minute, upon a great road, the horses next in rotation, always ready harnessed when expecting to come on duty, are heard trotting down the yard. "Putting to" and transferring the luggage, (supposing your conveyance a common post chaise,) once a work of at least thirty minutes, is now easily accomplished in three. And scarcely have you paid the ex- postilion before his successor is mounted; the hostler is standing ready with the steps in his hands to receive his invariable sixpence; the door is closed; the representative waiter bows his acknowledgment for the house, and you are off at a pace never less than ten miles an hour; the total detention at each stage not averaging above four minutes. Then, (*i.e.*, at the latter end of the eighteenth and beginning of the nineteenth century,) half an hour was the minimum of time spent at each change of horses. Your arrival produced a great bustle of unloading and unharnessing; as a matter of course, you alighted and went into the inn; if you sallied out to report progress, after waiting twenty minutes, no signs appeared of any stir about the stables. The most choleric person could not much expedite preparations, which loitered not so much from any indolence in the attendants, as from faulty arrangements and total defect of forecasting. The pace was such as the roads of that day allowed; never so much as six miles an hour, except upon a very great road, and then only by extra payment to the driver. Yet, even under this comparatively miserable system, how superior was England, as a land for the traveller, to all the rest of the world, Sweden only excepted! Bad as were the roads, and defective as were all the arrangements, still you had these advantages: no town so insignificant, no posting house so solitary, but that at all seasons, except a contested election, it could furnish horses without delay, and without license to distress the neighboring farmers. On the worst road, and on a winter's day, with no more than a single pair of horses, you generally

---

[90] It appears, however, from the Life of Hume, by my distinguished friend Mr. Hill Burton, that already, in the middle of the last century, the historian accomplished without difficulty six miles an hour with only a pair of horses. But this, it should be observed, was on the great North Road.

made out sixty miles; even if it were necessary to travel through the night, you could continue to make way, although more slowly; and finally, if you were of a temper to brook delay, and did not exact from all persons the haste or energy of Hotspurs, the whole system in those days was full of respectability and luxurious ease, and well fitted to renew the image of the home you had left, if not in its elegances, yet in all its substantial comforts. What cosy old parlors in those days! low roofed, glowing with ample fires, and fenced from the blasts of doors by screens, whose foldings were, or seemed to be, infinite. What motherly landladies! won, how readily, to kindness the most lavish, by the mere attractions of simplicity and youthful innocence, and finding so much interest in the bare circumstance of being a traveller at a childish age. Then what blooming young handmaidens! how different from the knowing and worldly demireps of modern high roads! And sometimes gray-headed, faithful waiters, how sincere and how attentive, by comparison with their flippant successors, the eternal "coming, sir, coming," of our improved generation!

Such an honest, old, butler-looking servant waited on us during dinner at Chesterfield, carving for me, and urging me to eat. Even Mephistopheles found his pride relax under the influence of wine; and when loosened from this restraint, his kindness was not deficient. To me he showed it in pressing wine upon me, without stint or measure. The elegances which he had observed in such parts of my mother's establishment as could be supposed to meet his eye on so hasty a visit, had impressed him perhaps favorably towards myself; and could I have a little altered my age, or dismissed my excessive reserve, I doubt not that he would have admitted me, in default of a more suitable comrade, to his entire confidence for the rest of the road. Dinner finished, and myself at least, for the first time in my childish life, somewhat perhaps overcharged with wine, the bill was called for, the waiter paid in the lavish style of antique England, and we heard our chaise drawing up under the gateway,—the invariable custom of those days,—by which you were spared the trouble of going into the street; stepping from the hall of the inn right into your carriage. I had been kept back for a minute or so by the landlady and her attendant nymphs, to be dressed and kissed; and, on seating myself in the chaise, which was well lighted with lamps, I found my lordly young principal in conversation with the landlord, first upon the price of oats,—which youthful horsemen always affect to inquire after with interest,—but, secondly, upon a topic more immediately at his heart—viz., the reputation of the road. At that time of day, when gold had not yet disappeared from the circulation, no traveller carried any other sort of money about him; and there was consequently a rich encouragement to highwaymen, which vanished almost entirely with Mr. Pitt's act of 1797 for restricting cash payments. Property which could be identified and traced was a perilous sort of plunder; and from that time the free trade of the road almost perished as a regular occupation. At this period it did certainly maintain a languishing existence; here and there it might have a casual run of success; and, as these local ebbs and flows were continually shifting, perhaps, after all, the trade might lie amongst a small number of hands. Universally, however, the landlords showed some shrewdness, or even sagacity, in qualifying, according to the circumstances of the inquirer, the sort of credit which they allowed to the exaggerated ill fame of the roads. Returning on this very road, some months after, with a timid female relative, who put her questions with undisguised and distressing alarm, the very same people, one and all, assured her that the danger was next to nothing. Not so at present: rightly presuming that a haughty cavalier of eighteen, flushed with wine and youthful blood, would listen with disgust to a picture too amiable and pacific of the roads before him, Mr. Spread Eagle replied with the air of one who knew more than he altogether liked to tell; and looking suspiciously amongst the strange faces lit up by the light of the carriage lamps—"Why, sir, there have been ugly stories afloat; I cannot deny it; and sometimes, you know, sir,"—winking sagaciously, to which a knowing nod of assent was returned,—"it may not be quite safe to tell all one knows. But you can understand me. The forest, you are well aware, sir, *is* the forest: it never was much to be trusted, by all accounts, in my father's time, and I suppose will not be better in mine. But you must keep a sharp lookout; and, Tom," speaking to the postilion, "mind, when you pass the third gate, to go pretty smartly by the thicket." Tom replied in a tone of importance to this professional appeal. General valedictions were exchanged, the landlord bowed, and we moved off for the forest. Mephistopheles had his travelling case of pistols. These he began now to examine; for sometimes, said he, I have known such a trick as drawing the charge whilst one happened to be taking a glass of wine. Wine had unlocked his heart,—the prospect of the forest and the advancing night excited him,—and even of such a child as myself he was now disposed to make a confidant. "Did you observe," said he, "that ill-looking fellow, as big as a camel, who stood on the landlord's left hand? "Was it the man, I asked timidly, who seemed by his dress to be a farmer? "Farmer, you call him! Ah! my young friend, that shows your little knowledge of the world. He is a scoundrel, the bloodiest of scoundrels. And so I trust to convince him before many hours are gone over our heads." Whilst saying this, he employed himself in priming his pistols; then, after a pause, he went on thus: "No, my young friend, this alone shows his base purposes—his calling himself a farmer. Farmer he is not, but a desperate highwayman, of which I have full proof. I watched his malicious glances whilst the landlord was talking; and I could swear to his traitorous intentions." So speaking, he threw anxious glances on each side as we continued to advance: we were both somewhat excited; he by the spirit of adventure, I by sympathy with him—and both by wine. The wine, however, soon applied a remedy to its own delusions; six miles from the town we had left, both of us were in a bad condition for resisting highwaymen with effect—being fast asleep. Suddenly a most abrupt halt awoke us,—Mephistopheles felt for his pistols,—the door flew open, and the lights of the assembled group announced to us that we had reached Mansfield. That night we went on to Newark, at which place about forty miles of our journey remailed. This distance we performed, of course, on the following day, between breakfast and dinner. But it serves strikingly to illustrate the state of roads in England, whenever your affairs led you into districts a little retired from the capital routes of the public travelling, that, for one twenty-mile stage,—viz. from Newark to Sleaford,—they refused to take us forward with less than four horses. This was neither a fraud, as our eyes soon convinced us, (for even four horses could scarcely extricate the chaise from the deep sloughs which occasionally seamed the road through tracts of two or three miles in succession,) nor was it an accident of the weather. In all seasons the same demand was enforced, as my female protectress found in conducting me back at a fine season of the year, and had always found in traversing the same route. The England of that date (1794) exhibited many similar cases. At present I know of but one stage in all England where a traveller, without regard to weight, is called upon to take four horses; and that is at Ambleside, in going by the direct road to Carlisle. The first stage to Patterdale lies over the mountain of Kirkstone, and the ascent is not only toilsome, (continuing for above three miles, with occasional intermissions,) but at times is carried over summits too steep for a road by all the rules of engineering, and yet too little frequented to offer any means of repaying the cost of smoothing the difficulties.

It was not until after the year 1715 that the main improvement took place in the English travelling system, so far as regarded speed. It is, in reality, to Mr. Macadam that we owe it. All the roads in England, within a few years, were remodelled, and upon principles of Roman science. From mere beds of torrents and systems of ruts, they were raised universally to the condition and appearance of gravel walks in private parks or shrubberies. The average rate of velocity was, in consequence, exactly doubled—ten miles an hour being now generally accomplished, instead of five. And at the moment when all further improvement upon this system had become hopeless, a new prospect was suddenly opened to us by railroads; which again, considering how much they have already exceeded the *maximum* of possibility, as laid down by all engineers during the progress of the Manchester and Liverpool line, may soon give way to new modes of locomotion still more astonishing to our preconceptions.

One point of refinement, as regards the comfort of travellers, remains to be mentioned, in which the improvement began a good deal earlier, perhaps by ten years, than in the construction of the roads. Luxurious as was the system of English travelling at all periods, after the general establishment of post chaises, it must be granted that, in the circumstance of cleanliness, there was far from being that attention, or that provision for the traveller's comfort, which might have been anticipated from the general habits of the country. I, at all periods of my life a great traveller, was witness, to the first steps and the whole struggle of this revolution. Maréchal Saxe professed always to look under his bed, applying his caution chiefly to the attempts of robbers. Now, if at the greatest inns of England you had, in the days I speak of, adopted this marshal's policy of reconnoitring, what would you have seen? Beyond a doubt, you would have seen what, upon all principles of seniority, was entitled to your veneration, viz., a dense accumulation of dust far older than yourself. A foreign author made some experiments upon the deposition of dust, and the rate of its accumulation, in a room left wholly undisturbed. If I recollect, a century would produce a stratum about half an inch in depth. Upon this principle, I conjecture that much dust which I have seen in inns, during the first four or five years of the present century, must have belonged to the reign of George II. It was, however, upon travellers by coaches that the full oppression of the old vicious system operated. The elder Scaliger mentions, as a characteristic of the English in his day, (about 1530,) a horror of cold water; in which, however, there must have been some mistake.[91] Nowhere could he and his foreign companions obtain the luxury of cold water for washing their hands either before or after dinner. One day he and his party dined with the lord chancellor; and now, thought he, for very shame they will allow us some means of purification. Not at all; the chancellor viewed this outlandish novelty with the same jealousy as others. However, on the earnest petition of Scaliger, he made an order that a basin or other vessel of cold water should be produced. His household bowed to this judgment, and a slop basin was cautiously introduced. "What!" said Scaliger, "only one, and we so many?" Even that one contained but a teacup full of water: but the great scholar soon found that he must be thankful for what he had got. It had cost the whole strength of the English chancery to produce that single cup of water; and, for that day, no man in his senses could look for a second. Pretty much the same struggle, and for the same cheap reform, commenced about the year 1805-6. Post-chaise travellers could, of course, have what they liked; and generally they asked for a bed room. It is of coach travellers I speak. And the particular innovation in question commenced, as was natural, with the mail coach, which, from the much higher scale of its fares, commanded a much more select class of company. I was a party to the very earliest attempts at breaking ground in this alarming revolution. Well do I remember the astonishment of some waiters, the indignation of others, the sympathetic uproars which spread to the bar, to the kitchen, and even to the stables, at the first opening of our extravagant demands. Sometimes even the landlady thought the case worthy of her interference, and came forward to remonstrate with us upon our unheard-of conduct. But gradually we made way. Like Scaliger, at first we got but one basin amongst us, and that one was brought into the breakfast room; but scarcely had two years revolved before we began to see four, and all appurtenances, arranged duly in correspondence to the number of inside passengers by the mail; and, as outside travelling was continually gaining ground amongst the wealthier classes, more comprehensive arrangements were often made; though, even to this day, so much influence survives, from the original aristocratic principle upon which public carriages were constructed, that on the mail coaches there still prevails the most scandalous inattention to the comfort, and even to the security, of the outside passengers: a slippery glazed roof frequently makes the sitting a matter of effort and anxiety, whilst the little iron side rail of four inches in height serves no one purpose but that of bruising the thigh. Concurrently with these reforms in the system of personal cleanliness, others were silently making way through all departments of the household economy. Dust, from the reign of George II., became scarcer; gradually it came to bear an antiquarian value: basins lost their grim appearance, and looked as clean as in gentlemen's houses. And at length the whole system was so thoroughly ventilated and purified, that all good inns, nay, generally speaking, even second-rate inns, at this day, reflect the best features, as to cleanliness and neatness, of well-managed

[91] *Some mistake.*—The mistake was possibly this: what little water for ablution, and what little rags called towels, a foreigner ever sees at home will at least be always within reach, from the continental practice of using the bed room for the sitting room. But in England our plentiful means of ablution are kept in the background. Scaliger should have asked for a bed room: the surprise was, possibly, not at his wanting water, but at his wanting it in a dining room.

private establishments.

CHAPTER XII.

MY BROTHER.

The reader who may have accompanied me in these wandering memorials of my own life and casual experiences, will be aware, that in many cases the neglect of chronological order is not merely permitted, but is in fact to some degree inevitable: there are cases, for instance, which, as a whole, connect themselves with my own life at so many different eras, that, upon any chronological principle of position, it would have been difficult to assign them a proper place; backwards or forwards they must have leaped, in whatever place they had been introduced; and in their entire compass, from first to last, never could have been represented as properly belonging to any one *present* time, whensoever that had been selected: belonging to every place alike, they would belong, according to the proverb, to no place at all; or, (reversing that proverb,) belonging to no place by preferable right, they would, in fact, belong to every place, and therefore to this place.

The incidents I am now going to relate come under this rule; for they form part of a story which fell in with my own life at many different points. It is a story taken from the life of my own brother; and I dwell on it with the more willingness, because it furnishes an indirect lesson upon a great principle of social life, now and for many years back struggling for its just supremacy—the principle that all corporal punishments whatsoever, and upon whomsoever inflicted, are hateful, and an indignity to our common nature, which (with or without our consent) is enshrined in the person of the sufferer. Degrading *him*, they degrade *us*. I will not here add one word upon the general thesis, but go on to the facts of this case; which, if all its incidents could now be recovered, was perhaps as romantic as any that ever yet has tried the spirit of fortitude and patience in a child. But its moral interest depends upon this—that, simply out of one brutal chastisement, arose naturally the entire series of events which so very nearly made shipwreck of all hope for one individual, and did in fact poison the tranquility of a whole family for seven years.

My next brother, younger by about four years than myself, (he, in fact, that caused so much affliction to the Sultan Amurath,) was a boy of exquisite and delicate beauty—delicate, that is, in respect to its feminine elegance and bloom; for else (as regards constitution) he turned out remarkably robust. In such excess did his beauty flourish during childhood, that those who remember him and myself at the public school at Bath will also remember the ludicrous molestation in the streets (for to him it *was* molestation) which it entailed upon him—ladies stopping constantly to kiss him. On first coming up to Bath from Greenhay, my mother occupied the very appartments on the North Parade just quitted by Edmund Burke, then in a decaying condition, though he did not die (I believe) till 1797. That state of Burkes's health, connected with the expectation of finding him still there, brought for some weeks crowds of inquirers, many of whom saw the childish Adonis, then scarcely seven years old, and inflicted upon him what he viewed as the martyrdom of their caresses. Thus began a persecution which continued as long as his years allowed it. The most brilliant complexion that could be imagined, the features of an Antinous, and perfect symmetry of figure at that period of his life, (afterwards he lost it,) made him the subject of never-ending admiration to the whole female population, gentle and simple, who passed him in the streets. In after days, he had the grace to regret his own perverse and scornful coyness. But, at that time, so foolishly insensible was he to the honor, that he used to kick and struggle with all his might to liberate himself from the gentle violence which was continually offered; and he renewed the scene (so elaborately painted by Shakspeare) of the conflicts between Venus and Adonis. For two years this continued a subject of irritation the keenest on the one side, and of laughter on the other, between my brother and his plainer school-fellows. Not that we had the slightest jealousy on the subject—far from it; it struck us all (as it generally does strike boys) in the light of an attaint upon the dignity of a male, that he should be subjected to the caresses of women, without leave asked; this was felt to be a badge of childhood, and a proof that the object of such caressing tenderness, so public and avowed, must be regarded in the light of a baby—not to mention that the very foundation of all this distinction, a beautiful face, is as a male distinction regarded in a very questionable light by multitudes, and often by those most who are the possessors of that distinction. Certainly that was the fact in my brother's case. Not one of us could feel so pointedly as himself the ridicule of his situation; nor did he cease, when increasing years had liberated him from that female expression of delight in his beauty, to regard the beauty itself as a degradation; nor could he bear to be flattered upon it; though, in reality, it did him service in after distresses, when no other endowment whatsoever would have been availing. Often, in fact, do men's natures sternly contradict the promise of their features; for no person would have believed that, under the blooming loveliness of a Narcissus, lay shrouded a most heroic nature; not merely an adventurous courage, but with a capacity of patient submission to hardship, and of wrestling with calamity, such as is rarely found amongst the endowments of youth. I have reason, also, to think that the state of degradation in which he believed himself to have passed his childish years, from the sort of public petting which I have described, and his strong recoil from it as an insult, went much deeper than was supposed, and had much to do in his subsequent conduct, and in nerving him to the strong resolutions he adopted. He seemed to resent, as an original insult of nature, the having given him a false index of character in his feminine beauty, and to take a pleasure in contradicting it. Had it been in his power, he would have spoiled it. Certain it is, that, from the time he reached his eleventh birthday, he had begun already to withdraw himself from the society of all other boys,—to fall into long fits of abstraction,—and to throw himself upon his own resources in a way neither usual nor necessary. Schoolfellows of his own age and standing—those, even, who were the most amiable—he shunned; and, many years after his disappearance, I found, in his handwriting, a collection of fragments, couched in a sort of wild lyrical verses, presenting, unquestionably, the most extraordinary evidences of a proud, self-sustained mind, consciously concentrating his own hopes in himself, and abjuring the rest of the world, that can ever have emanated from so young a person; since, upon the largest allowance, and supposing them to have been written on the eve of his quitting England, they must have been written at the age of twelve. I have often speculated on the subject of these mysterious compositions; they were of a nature to have proceeded rather from some mystical quietist, such as Madame Guyon, if with this rapt devotion one can suppose the union of a rebellious and murmuring ambition. Passionate apostrophes there were to nature and the powers of nature; and what seemed strangest of all was, that, in style, not only were they free from all tumor and inflation which might have been looked for in so young a writer, but were even wilfully childish and colloquial in a pathetic degree—in fact, in point of tone, allowing for the difference between a narrative poem and a lyrical, they somewhat resemble that beautiful poem[92] of George Herbert, entitled LOVE UN-KNOWN, in which he describes symbolically to a friend, under the form of treacherous ill usage he had experienced, the religious processes by which his soul had been weaned from the world. The most obvious solution of the mystery would be, to suppose these fragments to have been copied from some obscure author; but, besides that no author could have remained obscure in this age of elaborate research, who had been capable of sighs (for such I may call them) drawn up from such well-like depths of feeling, and expressed with such fervor and simplicity of language, there was another testimony to their being the productions of him who owned the penmanship; which was, that some of the papers exhibited the whole process of creation and growth, such as erasures, substitutions, doubts expressed as to this and that form of expression, together with references backwards and forwards. Now, that the handwriting was my brother's, admitted of no doubt whatsoever. I go on with his story. In 1800, my visit to Ireland, and visits to other places subsequently, separated me from him for above a year. In 1801, we were at very different schools—I in the highest class of a great public school, he at a very sequestered parsonage on a wild moor (Horwich Moor) in Lancashire. This situation, probably, fed and cherished his melancholy habits; for he had no society except-that of a younger brother, who would give him no disturbance at all. The development of our national resources had not yet gone so far as absolutely to exterminate from the map of England everything like a heath, a breezy down, (such as gave so peculiar a character to the counties of Wilts, Somerset, Dorset, &c.,) or even a village common. Heaths were yet to be found in England, not so spacious, indeed, as the *landes* of France, but equally wild and romantic. In such a situation my brother lived, and under the tuition of a clergyman, retired in his habits, and even ascetic, but gentle in his manners. To that I can speak myself; for in the winter of 1801 I dined with him, and found that his yoke was, indeed, a mild one; since, even to my youngest brother H., a headstrong child of seven, he used no stronger remonstrance, in urging him to some essential point of duty, than *"Do be persuaded, sir."* On another occasion I, accompanied by a friend, slept at Mr. J.'s:

---

[92] This poem, from great admiration of its mother English, and to illustrate some ideas upon style, Mr. Coleridge republished in his "Biographia Literaria."

we were accidentally detained there through the greater part of the following day by snow; and, to the inexpressible surprise of my companion, a mercantile man from Manchester, for a considerable time after breakfast the reverend gentleman persisted in pursuing my brother from room to room, and at last from the ground floor up to the attics, holding a book open, (which turned out to be a Latin grammar;) each of them (pursuer and pursued) moving at a tolerably slow pace, my brother H. silent; but Mr. J., with a voice of adjuration, solemn and even sad, yet kind and conciliatory, singing out at intervals, "Do be persuaded, sir!" "It is *your* welfare I seek!" "Let your own interest, sir, plead in this matter between us!" And so the chase continued, ascending and descending, up to the very garrets, down to the very cellars, then steadily revolving from front to rear of the house; but finally with no result at all. The spectacle reminded me of a groom attempting to catch a coy pony by holding out a sieve containing, or pretending to contain, a bribe of oats. Mrs. J., the reverend gentleman's wife, assured us that the same process went on at intervals throughout the week; and in any case it was clearly good as a mode of exercise. Now, such a master, though little adapted for the headstrong H., was the very person for the thoughtful and too sensitive R. Search the island through, there could not have been found another situation so suitable to my brother's wayward and haughty nature. The clergyman was learned, quiet, absorbed in his studies; humble and modest beyond the proprieties of his situation, and treating my brother in all points as a companion; whilst, on the other hand, my brother was not the person to forget the respect due, by a triple title, to a clergyman, a scholar, and his own preceptor—one, besides, who so little thought of exacting it. How happy might all parties have been— what suffering, what danger, what years of miserable anxiety might have been spared to all who were interested—had the guardians and executors of my father's will thought fit to "let *well* alone"! But, *"per star meglio"*[93] they chose to remove my brother from this gentle recluse to an active, bustling man of the world, the very anti-pole in character. What might be the pretensions of this gentleman to scholarship, I never had any means of judging; and, considering that he must now, (if living at all,) at a distance of thirty-six years, be gray headed, I shall respect his age so far as to suppress his name. He was of a class now annually declining (and I hope rapidly) to extinction. Thanks be to God, in this point at least, for the dignity of human nature, that, amongst the many, many cases of reform destined eventually to turn out chimerical, this one, at least, never can be defeated, injured, or eclipsed. As man grows more intellectual, the power of managing him by his intellect and his moral nature, in utter contempt of all appeals to his mere animal instincts of pain, must go on *pari passu*. And, if a *"Te Deum,"* or an *"O, Jubilate!"* were to be celebrated by all nations and languages for any one advance and absolute conquest over wrong and error won by human nature in our times,—yes, not excepting

> "The bloody writing by all nations torn"—

the abolition of the commerce in slaves,—to my thinking, that festival should be for the mighty progress made towards the suppression of brutal, bestial modes

---

[93] From the well-known Italian epitaph—*"Stava bene; ma per star meglio, sto qui"*—I was well; but, because I would be better than well, I am—where you see.

of punishment. Nay, I may call them worse than bestial; for a man of any goodness of nature does not willingly or needlessly resort to the spur or the lash with his horse or with his hound. But, with respect to man, if he will not be moved or won over by conciliatory means,—by means that presuppose him a reasonable creature,—then let him die, confounded in his own vileness; but let not me, let not the man (that is to say) who has him in his power, dishonor himself by inflicting punishments, violating that grandeur of human nature which, not in any vague rhetorical sense, but upon a religious principle of duty, (viz., the scriptural doctrine that the human person is "the temple of the Holy Ghost,") ought to be a consecrated thing in the eyes of all good men; and of this we may be assured,—this is more sure than day or night,—that, in proportion as man is honored, exalted, trusted, in that proportion will he become more worthy of honor, of exaltation, of trust.

This schoolmaster had very different views of man and his nature. He not only thought that physical coercion was the one sole engine by which man could be managed, but—on the principle of that common maxim which declares that, when two schoolboys meet, with powers at all near to a balance, no peace can be expected between them until it is fairly settled *which* is the master—on that same principle he fancied that no pupil could adequately or proportionably reverence his master until he had settled the precise proportion of superiority in animal powers by which his master was in advance of himself. Strength of blows only could ascertain *that*; and, as he was not very nice about creating his opportunities, as he plunged at once "*in medias res*," and more especially when he saw or suspected my rebellious tendencies, he soon picked a quarrel with my unfortunate brother. Not, be it observed, that he much cared for a well-looking or respectable quarrel. No. I have been assured that, even when the most fawning obsequiousness ad appealed to his clemency, in the person of some timorous new-comer, appalled by the reports he had heard, even in such cases, (deeming it wise to impress, from the beginning, a salutary awe of his Jovian thunders) he made a practice of doing thus: He would speak loud, utter some order, not very clearly, perhaps, as respected the sound, but with *perfect* perplexity as regarded the sense, to the timid, sensitive boy upon whom he intended to fix a charge of disobedience. "Sir, if you please, what was it that you said?" "What was it that I said? What! playing upon my words? Chopping logic? Strip, sir; strip this instant." Thenceforward this timid boy became a serviceable instrument in his equipage. Not only was he a proof, even without coöperation on the master's part, that extreme cases of submission could not insure mercy, but also he, this boy, in his own person, breathed forth, at intervals, a dim sense of awe and worship—the religion of fear—towards the grim Moloch of the scene. Hence, as by electrical conductors, was conveyed throughout every region of the establishment a tremulous sensibility that vibrated towards the centre. Different, O Rowland Hill! are the laws of thy establishment; far other are the echoes heard amid the ancient halls of Bruce.[94] There it is possible for the timid child to be happy—for the child destined to an early grave to reap his brief

[94] This was not meant assuredly as any advertisement of an establishment, which could not by all reports need any man's praise, but was written under a very natural impulse derived from a recent visit to the place, and under an unaffected sympathy with the spirit of freedom and enjoyment that seemed to reign amongst the young people.

harvest in peace. Wherefore were there no such asylums in those days? Man flourished then, as now, in beauty and in power. Wherefore did he not put forth his power upon establishments that might cultivate happiness as well as knowledge? Wherefore did no man cry aloud, in the spirit of Wordsworth,—

> "Ah, what avails heroic deed?
> What liberty? if no defence
> Be won for feeble innocence.
> Father of all! though wilful manhood read
> His punishment in soul distress
> Grant to the *morn* of life its natural blessedness"?

Meantime, my brother R., in an evil hour, having been removed from that most quiet of human sanctuaries, having forfeited that peace which possibly he was never to retrieve, fell (as I have said) into the power of this Moloch. And this Moloch upon him illustrated the laws of his establishment; him also, the gentle, the beautiful, but, also the proud, the haughty, the beat, kicked, trampled on!

In two hours from that time, my brother was on the road to Liverpool. Painfully he made out his way, having not much money, and with a sense of total abandonment which made him feel that all he might have would prove little enough for his purposes.

My brother went to an inn, after his long, long journey to Liverpool, footsore—(for he had walked through four days, and, from ignorance of the world, combined with excessive shyness,—O, how shy do people become from pride!—had not profited by those well-known incidents upon English high roads—return post chaises, stage coaches, led horses, or wagons)—footsore, and eager for sleep. Sleep, supper, breakfast in the morning,—all these he had; so far his slender finances reached; and for these he paid the treacherous landlord; who then proposed to him that they should take a walk out together, by way of looking at the public buildings and the docks. It seems the man had noticed my brother's beauty, some circumstances about his dress inconsistent with his mode of travelling, and also his style of conversation. Accordingly, he wiled him along from street to street, until they reached the Town Hall. "Here *seems* to be a fine building," said this Jesuitical guide,—as if it had been some new Pompeii, some Luxor or Palmyra, that he had unexpectedly lit upon amongst the undiscovered parts of Liverpool,—"here seems to be a fine building; shall we go in and ask leave to look at it?" My brother, thinking less of the spectacle than the spectator, whom, in a wilderness of man, naturally he wished to make his friend, consented readily. In they went; and, by the merest accident, Mr. Mayor and the town council were then sitting. To them the insidious landlord communicated privately an account of his suspicions. He himself conducted my brother, under pretence of discovering the best station for picturesque purposes, to the particular box for prisoners at the bar. This was not suspected by the poor boy, not even when Mr. Mayor began to question him. He still thought it an accident, though doubtless he blushed excessively on being questioned, and questioned so impertinently, in public. The object of the mayor and of other Liverpool gentlemen then present was, to ascertain my brother's real rank and family; for he persisted in representing himself as a poor wandering boy. Various means were vainly tried to elicit this information; until at length—like the wily Ulysses, who mixed with his peddler's budget of female ornaments and attire a few arms, by way of tempting Achilles to a self-detection in the court of Lycomedes—one gentleman counselled the mayor to send for a Greek Testament. This was done; the Testament was presented open at St. John's Gospel to my brother, and he was requested to say whether he knew in what language that book was written; or whether, perhaps, he could furnish them with a translation from the page before him. R., in his confusion, did not read the meaning of this appeal, and fell into the snare; construed a few verses; and immediately was consigned to the care of a gentleman, who won from him by kindness what he had refused to importunities or menaces. His family he confessed at once, but not his school. An express was therefore forwarded from Liverpool to our nearest male relative—a military man, then by accident on leave of absence from India. He came over, took my brother back, (looking upon the whole as a boyish frolic of no permanent importance,) made some stipulations in his behalf for indemnity from punishment, and immediately returned home. Left to himself, the grim tyrant of the school easily evaded the stipulations, and repeated his brutalities more fiercely than before—now acting in the double spirit of tyranny and revenge.

In a few hours, my brother was again on the road to Liverpool. But not on this occasion did he resort to any inn, or visit any treacherous hunter of the picturesque. He offered himself to no temptations now, nor to any risks. Right onwards he went to the docks, addressed himself to a grave, elderly master of a trading vessel, bound upon a distant voyage, and instantly procured an engagement. The skipper was a good and sensible man, and (as it turned out) a sailor accomplished in all parts of his profession. The ship which he commanded was a South Sea whaler, belonging to Lord Grenville—whether lying at Liverpool or in the Thames at that moment, I am not sure. However, they soon afterwards sailed.

For somewhat less than three years my brother continued under the care of this good man, who was interested by his appearance, and by some resemblance which he fancied in his features to a son whom he had lost. Fortunate, indeed, for the poor boy was this interval of fatherly superintendence; for, under this captain, he was not only preserved from the perils which afterwards beseiged him, until his years had made him more capable of confronting them, but also he had thus an opportunity, which he improved to the utmost, of making himself acquainted with the two separate branches of his profession—navigation and seamanship, qualifications which are not very often united.

After the death of his captain, my brother ran through many wild adventures; until at length, after a severe action, fought off the coast of Peru, the armed merchant-man in which he then served was captured by pirates. Most of the crew were massacred. My brother, on account of the important services he could render, was spared; and with these pirates, cruising under a black flag, and perpetrating unnumbered atrocities, he was obliged to sail for the next two years; nor could he, in all that period, find any opportunity for effecting his escape.

During this long expatriation, let any thoughtful reader imagine the perils of every sort which beseiged one so young, so inexperienced, so sensitive, and so haughty; perils to his life; (but these it was the very expression of his unhappy situation, were the perils least to be mourned for;) perils to his good name, going the length of absolute infamy—since, if the piratical ship had been captured by a British man-of-war, he might have found it impossible to clear himself of a voluntary participation in the bloody actions of his shipmates; and, on the other hand, (a case equally probable in the regions which they frequented,) supposing him to have been captured by a Spanish *guarda costa,* he would scarcely have been able, from his ignorance of the Spanish language, to draw even a momentary attention to the special circumstances of his own situation; he would have been involved in the general presumptions of the case, and would have been executed in a summary way, upon the *prima facie* evidence against him, that he did not appear to be in the condition of a prisoner; and, if his name had ever again reached his country, it would have been in some sad list of ruffians, murderers, traitors to their country; and even these titles, as if not enough in themselves, aggravated by the name of pirate, which at once includes them all, and surpasses them all. These were perils sufficiently distressing at any rate; but last of all came others even more appalling—the perils of moral contamination, in that excess which might be looked for from such associates; not, be it recollected, a few wild notions or lawless principles adopted into his creed of practical ethics, but that brutal transfiguration of the entire character, which occurs, for instance, in the case of the young gypsy son of Effie Deans; a change making it impossible to rely upon the very holiest instincts of the moral nature, and consigning its victim to hopeless reprobation. Murder itself might have lost its horrors to one who must have been but too familiar with the spectacle of massacre by wholesale upon unresisting crews, upon passengers enfeebled by sickness, or upon sequestered villagers, roused from their slumbers by the glare of conflagration, reflected from gleaming cutlasses and from the faces of demons. This fear it was—a fear like this, as I have often thought—which must, amidst her other woes, have been the Aaron woe that swallowed up all the rest to the unhappy Marie Antoinette. This must have been the sting of death to her maternal heart, the grief paramount, the "crowning" grief—the prospect, namely, that her royal boy would not be dismissed from the horrors of royalty to peace and humble innocence; but that his fair cheek would be ravaged by vice as well as sorrow; that he would be tempted into brutal orgies, and every mode of moral pollution; until, like poor Constance with her young Arthur, but for a sadder reason, even if it were possible that the royal mother should see her son in "the courts of heaven," she would not know again one so fearfully transfigured. This prospect for the royal Constance of revolutionary France was but too painfully fulfilled, as we are taught to guess even from the faithful records of the Duchesse d'Angoulême. The young dauphin, (*it has been said,* 1837,) to the infamy of his keepers, was so trained as to become loathsome for coarse brutality, as well as for habits of uncleanliness, to all who approached him—one purpose of his guilty tutors being to render royalty and august descent contemptible in his person. And, in fact, they were so far likely to succeed in this purpose, for the moment, and to the extent of an individual case, that, upon that account alone, but still more for the sake of the poor child, the most welcome news with respect to *him*—him whose birth[95] had

---

[95] To those who are open to the impression of omens, there is a most striking one on

record with respect to the birth of this ill-fated prince, not less so than the falling off of the head from the cane of Charles I. at his trial, or the same king's striking a medal, bearing an oak tress, (prefiguring the oak of *Boscobel*,) with this prophetic inscription, *"Seris nepotibus umbram."* At the very moment when (according to immemorial usage) the birth of a child was in the act of annunciation to the great officers of state assembled in the queen's bed chamber, and when a private signal from a lady had made known the glad tidings that it was a dauphin, (the first child having been a princess, to the signal disappointment of the nation; and the second, who was a boy, having died,) the whole frame of carved woodwork at the back of the queen's bed, representing the crown and other regalia of France, with the Bourbon lilies, came rattling down in ruins. There is another and more direct ill omen connected, apparently, with the birth of this prince; in fact, a distinct prophecy of his ruin, —a prophecy that he should survive his father, and yet no reign, —which is so obscurely told, that one knows not in what light to view it; and especially since Louis XVIII., who is the original authority for it, obviously confounds the first dauphin, who died before the calamities of his family commenced, with the second. As to this second, who is of course the prince concerned in the references of the text, a new and most extraordinary interest has begun to invest his tragical story in this very month of April, 1853; at least, it is now first brought before universal Christendom. In the monthly journal of Putnam, (published in New York,) the No. for April contains a most interesting memoir upon the subject, signed T. H. Hanson. Naturally, it indisposed most readers to put faith in any fresh pretensions of this nature, that at least one false dauphin had been pronounced such by so undeniable a judge of the Duchesse d'Angoulême. Meantime, it is made probably enough by Mr Hanson that the true dauphin did not die in the year 1795 at the Temple, but was personated by a boy unknown; that two separate parties had an equal interest in sustaining the fraud, and *did* sustain it; but one would hesitate to believe whether at the price of murdering a celebrated physician; that they had the prince conveyed secretly to an Indian settlement in Lower Canada, as a situation in which French, being the prevailing language, would attract no attention, as it must have done in most other parts of North America; that the boy was educated and trained as a missionary clergyman; and finally, that he is now acting in that capacity under the name of Eleazar Williams— perfectly aware of the royal pretensions put forward on his behalf, but equally, through age (being about 69) and through absorption in spiritual views, indifferent to these pretensions. It is admitted on all hands that the Prince de Joinville had an interview with Eleazar Williams a dozen years since—the prince alleges through mere accident; but this seems improbable; and Mr Hanson is likely to be right in supposing this visit to have been a pre-concerted one, growing out of some anxiety to test the reports current, so far as they were grounded upon resemblances in Mr. Williams's features to those of the Bourbon and Austrian families. The most pathetic fact is that of the idiocy common to the dauphin and Mr. Eleazar Williams. It is clear from all the most authentic accounts of the young prince that idiocy was in reality stealing over him—due, doubtless, to the stunning nature of the calamities that overwhelmed his family; to the removal from him by tragical deaths, in so rapid a succession, of the Princesse de Lamballe, of his aunt, of his father, of his mother, and others whom most he had loved; to his cruel separation from his sister; and to the astounding (for him naturally incomprehensible) change that had come over the demeanor and the language of nearly all the people placed about the persons of himself and his family. An idiocy resulting from what must have seemed a causeless and demoniac conspiracy would be more likely to melt away under the sudden transfer to kindness and the gayety of forest life than any idiocy belonging to original organic imbecility. Mr. Williams describes his own confusion of mind as continuing up to his fourteenth year, and all things which had happened in earlier years as gleaming through clouds of oblivion, and as painfully perplexing; but otherwise he shows no desire to strengthen the pretensions made for himself by any reminiscences piercing these clouds that could point specially to France drawn anthems of exultation from twenty-five millions of men—was the news of his death. And what else can well be expected for children suddenly withdrawn from parental tenderness, and thrown upon their own guardianship at such an age as nine or ten, and under the wilful misleading of perfidious guides? But, in my brother's case, all the adverse chances, overwhelming as they seemed, were turned aside by some good angel; all had failed to harm him; and from the fiery furnace he came out unsinged.

I have said that he would not have appeared to any capturing ship as standing in the situation of prisoner amongst the pirates, nor was he such in the sense of being confined. He moved about, when on board ship, in freedom; but he was watched, never trusted on shore, unless under very peculiar circumstances; and tolerated at all only because one accomplishment made him indispensable to the prosperity of the ship. Amongst the various parts of nautical skill communicated to my brother by his first fatherly captain, was the management of chronometers. Several had been captured, some of the highest value, in the many prizes, European or American. My brother happened to be perfect in the skill of managing them; and, fortunately for him, no other person amongst them had that skill, even in its lowest degree. To this one qualification, therefore, (and ultimately to this only,) he was indebted for, both safety and freedom; since, though he might have been spared in the first moments of carnage from other considerations, there is little doubt that, in some one of the innumerable brawls which followed through the years of his captivity, he would have fallen a sacrifice to hasty impulses of anger or wantonness, had not his safety been made an object of interest and vigilance to those in command, and to all who assumed any care for the general welfare. Much, therefore, it was that he owed to this accomplishment. Still, there is no good thing without its alloy; and this great blessing brought along with it something worse than a dull duty—the necessity, in fact, of facing fears and trials to which the sailor's heart is preeminently sensible. All sailors, it is notorious, are superstitious; partly, I suppose, from looking out so much upon the wilderness of waves, empty of all human life; for mighty solitudes are generally fear-haunted and fear-peopled; such, for instance, as the solitudes of forests, where, in the absence of human forms and ordinary human sounds, are discerned forms more dusky and vague, not referred by the eye to any known type, and sounds imperfectly intelligible. And, therefore, are all German coal burners, woodcutters, &c., superstitious. Now, the sea is often peopled, amidst its ravings, with what seem innumerable human voices—such voices, or as ominous, as what were heard by Kubla Khan—"ancestral voices prophesying war;" oftentimes laughter mixes, from a distance, (seeming to come also from distant times, as well as distant places,) with the uproar of waters; and doubtless shapes of fear, or shapes of beauty not less awful, are at times seen upon the waves by the diseased eye of the sailor, in other cases besides the somewhat rare one of calenture. This vast solitude of the sea being taken, therefore, as one condition of the superstitious fear found so commonly among sailors, a second may be the perilous insecurity of their own lives, or (if the lives of sailors, after all, by means of large immunities from danger in other shapes are *not* so insecure as is supposed, though, by the way, it is enough for this result that to

or to royal experiences.

themselves they seem so) yet, at all events, the insecurity of the ships in which they sail. In such a case, in the case of battle, and in others where the empire of chance seems absolute, there the temptation is greatest to dally with supernatural oracles and supernatural means of consulting them. Finally, the interruption habitually of all ordinary avenues to information about the fate of their dearest relatives; the consequent agitation which must often possess those who are reëntering upon home waters; and the sudden burst, upon stepping ashore, of heart-shaking news in long accumulated arrears, — these are circumstances which dispose the mind to look out for relief towards signs and omens as one way of breaking the shock by dim anticipations. Rats leaving a vessel destined to sink, although the political application of it as a name of reproach is purely modern, must be ranked among the oldest of omens; and perhaps the most sober-minded of men might have leave to be moved with any augury of an ancient traditional order, such as had won faith for centuries, applied to a fate so interesting as that of the ship to which he was on the point of committing himself. Other causes might be assigned, causative of nautical superstition, and tending to feed it. But enough. It is well known that the whole family of sailors *is* superstitious. My brother, poor Pink, (this was an old household name which he retained amongst us from an incident of his childhood,) was so in an immoderate degree. Being a great reader, (in fact, he had read every thing in his mother tongue that was of general interest,) he was pretty well aware how general was the ridicule attached in our times to the subject of ghosts. But this—nor the reverence he yielded otherwise to some of those writers who had joined in that ridicule—any more had unsettled his faith in their existence than the submission of a sailor in a religious sense to his spiritual counsellor upon the false and fraudulent pleasures of luxury can ever disturb his remembrance of the virtues lodged in rum or tobacco. His own unconquerable, unanswerable experience, the blank realities of pleasure and pain, put to flight all arguments whatsoever that anchor only in his understanding. Pink used, in arguing the case with me, to admit that ghosts might be questionable realities in our hemisphere; but "it's a different thing to the *suthard* of the line." And then he would go on to tell me of his own fearful experience; in particular of one many times renewed, and investigated to no purpose by parties of men communicating from a distance upon a system of concerted signals, in one of the Gallapagos Islands. These islands, which were visited, and I think described, by Dampier, and therefore must have been an asylum to the buccaneers and flibustiers[96] in the latter part of the seventeenth century, were so still to their more desperate successors, the pirates, at the beginning of the nineteenth; and for the same reason — the facilities they offer (rare in those seas) for procuring wood and water. Hither, then, the black flag often resorted; and here, amidst these romantic solitudes, — islands untenanted by man, — oftentimes it lay furled up for weeks together; rapine and murder had rest for a season, and the bloody cutlass slept within its scabbard. When this happened, and when it became

---

[96] "*Flibustiers.*" — This word, which is just now revolving upon us in connection with the attempts on Cuba, &c., is constantly spelt by our own and the American journals as *fillibustiers* and fillibusteros. But the true word of nearly two centuries back amongst the old original race of sea robbers (French and English) that made irregular war upon the Spanish shipping and maritime towns was that which I have here retained.

known beforehand that it *would* happen, a tent was pitched on shore for my brother, and the chronometers were transported thither for the period of their stay.

The island selected for this purpose, amongst the many equally open to their choice, might, according to circumstances, be that which offered the best anchorage, or that from which the reëmbarkation was easiest, or that which allowed the readiest access to wood and water. But for some, or all these advantages, the particular island most generally honored by the piratical custom and "good will" was one known to American navigators as "The Woodcutter's Island." There was some old tradition—and I know not but it was a tradition dating from the times of Dampier—that a Spaniard or an Indian settler in this island (relying, perhaps, too entirely upon the protection of perfect solitude) had been murdered in pure wantonness by some of the lawless rovers who frequented this solitary archipelago. Whether it were from some peculiar atrocity of bad faith in the act, or from the sanctity of the man, or the deep solitude of the island, or with a view to the peculiar edification of mariners in these semi-Christian seas, so, however, it was, and attested by generations of sea vagabonds, (for most of the armed roamers in these ocean Zaaras at one time were of a suspicious order,) that every night, duly as the sun went down and the twilight began to prevail, a sound arose—audible to other islands, and to every ship lying quietly at anchor in that neighborhood—of a woodcutter's axe. Sturdy were the blows, and steady the succession in which they followed: some even fancied they could hear that sort of groaning respiration which is made by men who use an axe, or by those who in towns ply the "three-man beetle" of Falstaff, as paviers; echoes they certainly heard of every blow, from the profound woods and the sylvan precipices on the margin of the shores; which, however, should rather indicate that the sounds were *not* supernatural, since, if a visual object, falling under hyper-physical or cata-physical laws, loses its shadow, by parity of argument, an audible object, in the same circumstances, should lose its echo. But this was the story; and amongst sailors there is as little variety of versions in telling any true sea story as there is in a log book, or in "The Flying Dutchman:" *literatim* fidelity is, with a sailor, a point at once of religious faith and worldly honor. The close of the story was—that after, suppose, ten or twelve minutes of hacking and hewing, a horrid crash was heard, announcing that the tree, if tree it were, that never yet was made visible to daylight search, had yielded to the old woodman's persecution. It was exactly the crash, so familiar to many ears on board the neighboring vessels, which expresses the harsh tearing asunder of the fibres, caused by the weight of the trunk in falling; beginning slowly, increasing rapidly, and terminating in one rush of rending. This over,—one tree felled "towards his winter store,"—there was an interval; man must have rest; and the old woodman, after working for more than a century, must want repose. Time enough to begin again after a quarter of an hour's relaxation. Sure enough, in that space of time, again began, in the words of Comus, "the wonted roar amid the woods." Again the blows became quicker, as the catastrophe drew nearer; again the final crash resounded; and again the mighty echoes travelled through the solitary forests, and were taken up by all the islands near and far, like Joanna's laugh amongst the Westmoreland hills, to the astonishment of the silent ocean. Yet, wherefore should the ocean be astonished?—he that had heard this nightly tumult, by all accounts, for more than a century. My brother, however, poor Pink, *was* astonished, in good earnest, being, in that respect, of the *genus attonitorum*; and as often as the gentlemen pirates steered their course for the Gallapagos, he would sink in spirit before the trials he might be summoned to face. No second person was ever put on shore with Pink, lest poor Pink and he might become jovial over the liquor, and the chronometers be broken or neglected; for a considerable quantity of spirits was necessarily landed, as well as of provisions, because sometimes a sudden change of weather, or the sudden appearance of a suspicious sail, might draw the ship off the island for a fortnight. My brother could have pleaded his fears without shame; but he had a character to maintain with the sailors: he was respected equally for his seamanship and his shipmanship.[97] By the way, when it is considered that one half of a sailor's professional science refers him to the stars, (though it is true the other half refers him to the sails and shrouds of a ship,) just as, in geodesical operations, one part is referred to heaven and one to earth, when this is considered, another argument arises for the superstition of sailors, so far as it is astrological. They who know (but know the *oti* without knowing the *dia ti*) that the stars have much to do in guiding their own movements, which are yet so far from the stars, and, to all appearance, so little connected with them, may be excused for supposing that the stars are connected astrologically with human destinies. But this by the way. The sailors, looking to Pink's double skill, and to his experience on shore, (more astonishing than all beside, being experience gathered amongst ghosts,) expressed an admiration which, to one who was also a sailor, had too genial a sound to be sacrificed, if it could be maintained at any price. Therefore it was that Pink still clung, in spite of his terrors, to his shore appointment. But hard was his trial; and many a time has he described to me one effect of it, when too long continued, or combined with darkness too intense. The woodcutter would begin his operations soon after the sun had set; but uniformly, at that time, his noise was less. Three hours after sunset it had increased; and generally at midnight it was greatest, but not always. Sometimes the case varied thus far: that it greatly increased towards three or four o'clock in the morning; and, as the sound grew louder, and thereby seemed to draw nearer, poor Pink's ghostly panic grew insupportable; and he absolutely crept from his pavilion, and its luxurious comforts, to a point of rock—a promontory—about half a mile off, from which he could see the ship. The mere sight of a human abode, though an abode of ruffians, comforted his panic. With the approach of daylight, the mysterious sounds ceased. Cockcrow there happened to be none, in those islands of the Gallapagos, or none in that particular island; though many cocks are heard crowing in the woods of America, and these,

---

[97] *"Seamanship and shipmanship"* — These are two functions of a sailor seldom, separated in the mind of a landsman. The conducting a ship (causing her to *choose* a right path) through the ocean; that is one thing. Then there is the management of the ship within herself, the trimming of her sails, &c., (causing her to *keep* the line chosen;) that is another thing. The first is called seamanship; the second might be called shipmanship, but is, I believe, called navigation. They are perfectly distinct; one man rarely has both in perfection. Both may be illustrated from the rudder. The question is, suppose at the Cape of Good Hope, to steer for India: trust the rudder to him, as a seaman, who knows the passage whether within or without Madagascar. The question is to avoid a sunk rock: trust the rudder to him, as a navigator, who understands the art of steering to a nicety.

perhaps, might be caught by spiritual senses; or the woodcutter may be supposed, upon Hamlet's principle, either scenting the morning air, or catching the sounds of Christian matin bells, from some dim convent, in the depth of American forests. However, so it was; the woodcutter's axe began to intermit about the earliest approach of dawn; and, as light strengthened, it ceased entirely. At nine, ten, or eleven o'clock in the forenoon the whole appeared to have been a delusion; but towards sunset it revived in credit; during twilight it strengthened; and, very soon afterwards, superstitious panic was again seated on her throne. Such were the fluctuations of the case. Meantime, Pink, sitting on his promontory in early dawn, and consoling his terrors by looking away from the mighty woods to the tranquil ship, on board of which (in spite of her secret black flag) the whole crew, murderers and all, were sleeping peacefully—he, a beautiful English boy, chased away to the antipodes from one early home by his sense of wounded honor, and from his immediate home by superstitious fear, recalled to my mind an image and a situation that had been beautifully sketched by Miss Bannerman in "Basil," one of the striking (though, to rapid readers, somewhat unintelligible) metrical tales published early in this century, entitled "Tales of Superstition and Chivalry." Basil is a "rude sea boy," desolate and neglected from infancy, but with feelings profound from nature, and fed by solitude. He dwells alone in a rocky cave; but, in consequence of some supernatural terrors connected with a murder, arising in some way (not very clearly made out) to trouble the repose of his home, he leaves it in horror, and rushes in the gray dawn to the seaside rocks; seated on which, he draws a sort of consolation for his terrors, or of sympathy with his wounded heart, from that mimicry of life which goes on forever amongst the raving waves.

From the Gallapagos, Pink went often to Juan (or, as he chose to call it, after Dampier and others, *John*) Fernandez. Very lately, (December, 1837,) the newspapers of America informed us, and the story was current for full nine days, that this fair island had been swallowed up by an earthquake; or, at least, that in some way or other it had disappeared. Had that story proved true, one pleasant bower would have perished, raised by Pink as a memorial expression of his youthful feelings either towards De Foe, or his visionary creature, Robinson Crusoe—but rather, perhaps, towards the substantial Alexander Selkirk; for it was raised on some spot known or reputed by tradition to have been one of those most occupied as a home by Selkirk. I say, "rather towards Alexander Selkirk;" for there is a difficulty to the judgment in associating Robinson Crusoe with this lovely island of the Pacific, and a difficulty even to the fancy. *Why*, it is hard to guess, or through what perverse contradiction to the facts, De Foe chose to place the shipwreck of Robinson Crusoe upon the *eastern* side of the American continent. Now, not only was this in direct opposition to the realities of the case upon which he built, as first reported (I believe) by Woodes Rogers, from the log book of the Duke and Duchess,—(a privateer fitted out, to the best of my remembrance, by the Bristol merchants, two or three years before the peace of Utrecht,) and so far the mind of any man acquainted with these circumstances was staggered, in attempting to associate this eastern wreck of Crusoe with this western island,—but a worse obstacle than that, because a moral one, is this, that, by thus perversely transferring the scene from the Pacific to the Atlantic, De Foe has transferred it from a quiet and sequestered to a populous and troubled sea,—the Fleet Street or Cheapside of the navigating world, the great throughfare of nations,—and thus has prejudiced the moral sense and the fancy against his fiction still more inevitably than his judgment, and in a way that was perfectly needless; for the change brought along with it no shadow of compensation.

My brother's wild adventures amongst these desperate sea rovers were afterwards communicated in long letters to a female relative; and, even as letters, apart from the fearful burden of their contents, I can bear witness that they had very extraordinary merit. This, in fact, was the happy result of writing from his heart; feeling profoundly what he communicated, and anticipating the profoundest sympathy with all that he uttered from her whom he addressed. A man of business, who opened some of these letters, in his character of agent for my brother's five guardians, and who had not any special interest in the affair, assured me that, throughout the whole course of his life, he had never read any thing so affecting, from the facts they contained, and from the sentiments which they expressed; above all, the yearning for that England which he remembered as the land of his youthful pleasures, but also of his youthful degradations. Three of the guardians were present at the reading of these letters, and were all affected to tears, not-withstanding they had been irritated to the uttermost by the course which both myself and my brother had pursued—a course which seemed to argue some defect of judgment, or of reasonable kindness, in themselves. These letters, I hope, are still preserved, though they have been long removed from my control. Thinking of them, and their extraordinary merit, I have often been led to believe that every post town (and many times in the course of a month) carries out numbers of beautifully-written letters, and more from women than from men; not that men are to be supposed less capable of writing good letters,—and, in fact, amongst all the celebrated letter writers of past or present times, a large overbalance happens to have been men,—but that more frequently women write from their hearts; and the very same cause operates to make female letters good which operated at one period to make the diction of Roman ladies more pure than that of orators or professional cultivators of the Roman language—and which, at another period, in the Byzantine court, operated to preserve the purity of the mother idiom within the nurseries and the female drawing rooms of the palace, whilst it was corrupted in the forensic standards and the academic—in the standards of the pulpit and the throne.

With respect to Pink's yearning for England, that had been partially gratified in some part of his long exile: twice, as we learned long afterwards, he had landed in England; but such was his haughty adherence to his purpose, and such his consequent terror of being discovered and reclaimed by his guardians, that he never attempted to communicate with any of his brothers or sisters. There he was wrong; me they should have cut to pieces before I would have betrayed him. I, like him, had been an obstinate recusant to what I viewed as unjust pretensions of authority; and, having been the first to raise the standard of revolt, had been taxed by my guardians with having seduced Pink by my example. But that was untrue; Pink acted for himself. However, he could know little of all this; and he traversed

England twice, without making an overture towards any communication with his friends. Two circumstances of these journeys he used to mention; both were from the port of London (for he never contemplated London but as a port) to Liverpool; or, thus far I may be wrong, that one of the two might be (in the return order) from Liverpool to London. On the first of these journeys, his route lay through Coventry; on the other, through Oxford and Birmingham. In neither case had he started with much money; and he was going to have retired from the coach at the place of supping on the first night, (the journey then occupying two entire days and two entire nights,) when the passengers insisted on paying for him: that was a tribute to his beauty—not yet extinct. He mentioned this part of his adventures somewhat shyly, whilst going over them with a sailor's literal accuracy; though, as a record belonging to what he viewed as childish years, he had ceased to care about it. On the other journey his experience was different, but equally testified to the spirit of kindness that is every where abroad. He had no money, on this occasion, that could purchase even a momentary lift by a stage coach: as a pedestrian, he had travelled down to Oxford, occupying two days in the fifty-four or fifty-six miles which then measured the road from London, and sleeping in a farmer's barn, without leave asked. Wearied and depressed in spirits, he had reached Oxford, hopeless of any aid, and with a deadly shame at the thought of asking it. But, somewhere in the High Street,—and, according to his very accurate sailor's description of that noble street, it must have been about the entrance of All Souls' College,—he met a gentleman, a gownsman, who (at the very moment of turning into the college gate) looked at Pink earnestly, and then gave him a guinea, saying at the time, "I know what it is to be in your situation. You are a schoolboy, and you have run away from your school. Well, I was once in your situation, and I pity you." The kind gownsman, who wore a velvet cap with a silk gown, and must, therefore, have been what in Oxford is called a gentleman commoner, gave him an address at some college or other, (Magdalen, he fancied, in after years,) where he instructed him to call before he quitted Oxford. Had Pink done this, and had he frankly communicated his whole story, very probably he would have received, not assistance merely, but the best advice for guiding his future motions. His reason for not keeping the appointment was simply that he was nervously shy, and, above all things, jealous of being entrapped by insidious kindness into revelations that might prove dangerously circumstantial. Oxford had a mayor; Oxford had a corporation; Oxford had Greek Testaments past all counting; and so, remembering past experiences, Pink held it to be the wisest counsel that he should pursue his route on foot to Liverpool. That guinea, however, he used to say, saved him from despair.

One circumstance affected me in this part of Pink's story. I was a student in Oxford at that time. By comparing dates, there was no doubt whatever that I, who held my guardians in abhorrence, and, above all things, admired my brother for his conduct, might have rescued him at this point of his youthful trials, four years before the fortunate catastrophe of his case, from the calamities which awaited him. This is felt generally to be the most distressing form of human blindness—the case when accident brings two fraternal hearts, yearning for reunion, into almost touching neighborhood, and then, in a moment after, by the difference, perhaps, of three inches in space, or three seconds in time, will separate them again, unconscious of their brief neighborhood, perhaps forever. In the present case, however, it may be doubted whether this unconscious rencontre and unconscious parting in Oxford ought to be viewed as a misfortune. Pink, it is true, endured years of suffering, four, at least, that might have been saved by this seasonable rencontre; but, on the other hand, by travelling through his misfortunes with unabated spirit, and to their natural end, he won experience and distinctions that else he would have missed. His further history was briefly this:—

Somewhere in the River of Plate he had effected his escape from the pirates; and a long time after, in 1807, I believe, (I write without books to consult,) he joined the storming party of the English at Monte Video. Here he happened fortunately to fall under the eye of Sir Home Popham; and Sir Home forthwith rated my brother as a midshipman on board his own ship, which was at that time, I think, a fifty-gun ship—the Diadem. Thus, by merits of the most appropriate kind, and without one particle of interest, my brother passed into the royal navy. His nautical accomplishments were now of the utmost importance to him; and, as often as he shifted his ship, which (to say the truth) was far too often,—for his temper was fickle and delighting in change,—so often these accomplishments were made the basis of very earnest eulogy. I have read a vast heap of certificates vouching for Pink's qualifications as a sailor in the highest terms, and from several of the most distinguished officers in the service. Early in his career as a midshipman, he suffered a mortifying interruption of the active life which had long since become essential to his comfort. He had contrived to get appointed on board a fire ship, the Prometheus, (chiefly with a wish to enlarge his experience by this variety of naval warfare,) at the time of the last Copenhagen expedition, and he obtained his wish; for the Prometheus had a very distinguished station assigned her on the great night of bombardment, and from her decks, I believe, was made almost the first effectual trial of the Congreve rockets. Soon after the Danish capital had fallen, and whilst the Prometheus was still cruising in the Baltic, Pink, in company with the purser of his ship, landed on the coast of Jutland, for the purpose of a morning's sporting. It seems strange that this should have been allowed upon a hostile shore; and perhaps it was *not* allowed, but might have been a thoughtless abuse of some other mission shorewards. So it was, unfortunately; and one at least of the two sailors had reason to rue the sporting of that day for eighteen long months of captivity. They were perfectly unacquainted with the localities, but conceived themselves able at any time to make good their retreat to the boat, by means of fleet heels, and arms sufficient to deal with any opposition of the sort they apprehended. Venturing, however, too far into the country, they became suddenly aware of certain sentinels, posted expressly for the benefit of chance English visitors. These men did not pursue, but they did worse, for they fired signal shots; and, by the time our two thoughtless Jack tars had reached the shore, they saw a detachment of Danish cavalry trotting their horses pretty coolly down in a direction for the boat. Feeling confident of their power to keep ahead of the pursuit, the sailors amused themselves with various sallies of nautical wit; and Pink, in particular, was just telling them to present his dutiful respects to the crown prince, and assure him that, but for this lubberly interruption, he trusted to have improved his royal dinner by a brace of birds, when—O sight of blank confusion!—all at once they became aware that between themselves and their boat lay a perfect network of streams, deep watery holes, requiring both time and local knowledge to unravel. The purser hit upon a course which enabled him to regain the boat; but I am not sure whether he also was not captured. Poor Pink *was*, at all events; and, through seventeen or eighteen months, bewailed this boyish imprudence. At the end of that time there was an exchange of prisoners, and he was again serving on board various and splendid frigates. Wyborg, in Jutland, was the seat of his Danish captivity; and such was the amiableness of the Danish character, that, except for the loss of his time, to one who was aspiring to distinction and professional honor, none of the prisoners who were on parole could have had much reason for complaint. The street mob, excusably irritated with England at that time, (for, without entering on the question of right or of expedience as regarded that war, it is notorious that such arguments as we had for our unannounced hostilities could not be pleaded openly by the English cabinet, for fear of compromising our private friend and informant, the King of Sweden,) the mob, therefore, were rough in their treatment of the British prisoners: at night, they would pelt them with stones; and here and there some honest burgher, who might have suffered grievously in his property, or in the person of his nearest friends, by the ruin inflicted upon the Danish commercial shipping, or by the dreadful havoc made in Zealand, would show something of the same bitter spirit. But the great body of the richer and more educated inhabitants showed the most hospitable attention to all who justified that sort of notice by their conduct. And their remembrance of these English friendships was not fugitive; for, through long years after my brother's death, I used to receive letters, written in the Danish, (a language which I had attained in the course of my studies, and which I have since endeavored to turn to account in a public journal, for some useful purposes of research,) from young men as well as women in Jutland—letters couched in the most friendly terms, and recalling to his remembrance scenes and incidents which sufficiently proved the terms of fraternal affection upon which he had lived amongst these public enemies; and some of them I have preserved to this day, as memorials that do honor, on different considerations, to both parties alike.[98]

---

[98] For this little parenthetical record of my brother's early history the exact chronology of the several items in the case may possible be now irrecoverable; but any error must be of trivial importance. His two pedestrian journeys between London and Liverpool occurred, I believe, in the same year—viz., after the death of the friendly captain, and during the last visit of his ship to England. The capture of Pink by the pirates took place after the ship's return to the Pacific.

CHAPTER XIII.

PREMATURE MANHOOD.

My last two chapters, very slenderly connected with Birmingham, are yet made to rise out of it; the one out of Birmingham's own relation to the topic concerned, (viz., *Travelling*,) and the other (viz., *My Brother*) out of its relation to all possible times in my earlier life, and, therefore, why not to all possible places? *Any where* introduced, the chapter was partially out of its place; as well then to introduce it in Birmingham as elsewhere. Somewhat arbitrary episodes, therefore, are these two last chapters; yet still endurable as occurring in a work confessedly rambling, and whose very duty lies in the pleasant paths of vagrancy. Pretending only to amuse my reader, or pretending chiefly to *that*, however much I may have sought, or *shall* seek, to interest him occasionally through his profounder affections, I enjoy a privilege of neglecting harsher logic, and connecting the separate sections of these sketches, not by ropes and cables, but by threads of aerial gossamer.

This present chapter, it may seem, promises something of the same episodical or parenthetic character. But in reality it does not. I am now returning into the main current of my narrative, although I may need to linger for a moment upon a past anecdote. I have mentioned already, that, on inquiring at the Birmingham post office for a letter addressed to myself, I found one directing me to join my sister Mary at Laxton, a seat of Lord Carbery's in Northamptonshire, and giving me to understand, that, during my residence at this place, some fixed resolution would be taken and announced to me in regard to the future disposal of my time, during the two or three years before I should be old enough on the English system for matriculating at Oxford or Cambridge. In the poor countries of Europe, where they cannot afford double sets of scholastic establishments,—having, therefore, no splendid schools, such as are, in fact, peculiar to England,—they are compelled to throw the duties of such schools upon their universities; and consequently you see boys of thirteen and fourteen, or even younger, crowding such institutions, which, in fact, they ruin for all higher functions. But England, whose regal establishments of both classes emancipate her from this dependency, sends her young men to college not until they have ceased to be boys—not earlier, therefore, than eighteen.

But when, by what test, by what indication, does manhood commence? Physically by one criterion, legally by another, morally by a third, intellectually by a fourth—and all indefinite. Equator, absolute equator, there is none. Between the two spheres of youth and age, perfect and imperfect manhood, as in all analogous cases, there is no strict line of bisection. The change is a large process, accomplished within a large and corresponding space; having, perhaps, some central or equatorial line, but lying, like that of our earth, between certain tropics, or limits widely separated. This *intertropical* region may, and generally does, cover a number of years; and, therefore, it is hard to say, even for an assigned case, by any tolerable approximation, at what precise era it would be reasonable to describe the individual as having ceased to be a boy, and as having attained his inauguration as a man. Physically, we know that there is a very large latitude of differences, in the periods of human maturity, not merely between individual and individual, but also between nation and nation; differences so great, that, in some southern regions of Asia, we hear of matrons at the age of twelve. And though, as Mr. Sadler rightly insists, a romance of exaggeration has been built upon the facts, enough remains behind of real marvel to irritate the curiosity of the physiologist as to its efficient, and, perhaps, of the philosopher as to its final cause. Legally and politically, that is, conventionally, the differences are even greater on a comparison of nations and eras. In England we have seen senators of mark and authority, nay, even a prime minister, the haughtiest,[99] the most despotic, and the most irresponsible of his times, at an age which, in many states, both ancient and modern, would have operated as a ground of absolute challenge to the candidate for offices the meanest. Intellectually speaking, again, a very large proportion of men *never* attain maturity. Nonage is their final destiny; and manhood, in this respect, is for them a pure idea. Finally, as regards the moral development,—by which I mean the whole system and economy of their love and hatred, of their admirations and contempts, the total organization of their pleasures and their pains,—hardly any of our species ever attain manhood. It would be unphilosophic to say that intellects of the *highest* order were, or could be, developed fully without a corresponding development of the whole nature. But of such intellects there do not appear above two or three in a thousand years. It is a fact, forced upon one by the whole experience of life, that almost all men are children, more or less, in their tastes and admirations. Were it not for man's latent tendencies,—were it not for that imperishable grandeur which exists by way of germ and ultimate possibility in his nature, hidden though it is, and often all but effaced,—how unlimited would be the contempt amongst all the wise for his species! and misanthropy would, but for the angelic ideal buried and imbruted in man's sordid race, become amongst the noble fixed, absolute, and deliberately cherished.

But, to resume my question, how, under so variable a standard, both natural and conventional, of every thing almost that can be received for a test or a presumption of manhood, shall we seize upon any characteristic feature, sufficiently universal to serve a *practical* use, as a criterion of the transition from the childish mind to the dignity (relative dignity at least) of that mind which belongs to conscious maturity? One such criterion, and one only, as I believe, there is—all others are variable and uncertain. It lies in the reverential feeling, sometimes suddenly developed, towards woman, and the idea of woman. From that moment when

---

[99] *"The haughtiest."* —Which, however, is very doubtful. Such, certainly, was the popular impression. But people who knew Mr. Pitt intimately have always ascribed to him a nature the most amiable and social, under an unfortunate reserve of manner. Whilst, on the contrary, Mr. Fox, ultra democratic in his principles and frank in his address, was repulsively aristocratic in his temper and sympathies.

women cease to be regarded with carelessness, and when the ideal of woman-hood, in its total pomp of loveliness and purity, dawns like some vast aurora upon the mind, boyhood has ended; childish thoughts and inclinations have passed away forever; and the gravity of manhood, with the self-respecting views of man-hood, have commenced.

> "Mentemque priorem
> Expulit, atque hominem toto sibi cedere jussit Pectore." —*Lucan*.

These feelings, no doubt, depend for their development in part upon physical causes; but they are also determined by the many retarding or accelerating forces enveloped in circumstances of position, and sometimes in pure accident. For my-self, I remember most distinctly the very day— the scene and its accidents—when that mysterious awe fell upon me which belongs to woman in her ideal portrait; and from that hour a profounder gravity colored all my thoughts, and a "beauty still more beauteous" was lit up for me in this agitating world. Lord Westport and myself had been on a visit to a noble family about fifty miles from Dublin; and we were returning from Tullamore by a public passage boat, on the splendid canal which connects that place with the metropolis. To avoid attracting an unpleasant attention to ourselves in public situations, I observed a rule of never addressing Lord Westport by his title: but it so happened that the canal carried us along the margin of an estate belonging to the Earl (now Marquis) of Westmeath; and, on turning an angle, we came suddenly in view of this nobleman taking his morning lounge in the sun. Somewhat loftily he reconnoitred the miscellaneous party of clean and unclean beasts, crowded on the deck of our ark, ourselves amongst the number, whom he challenged gayly as young acquaintances from Dublin; and my friend he saluted more than once as "My lord." This accident made known to the assembled mob of our fellow-travellers Lord Westport's rank, and led to a scene rather too broadly exposing the spirit of this world. Herded together on the deck (or roof of that den denominated the "*state* cabin") stood a party of young ladies, headed by their governess. In the cabin below was mamma, who as yet had not condescended to illuminate our circle, for she was an awful personage—a wit, a bluestocking, (I call her by the name then current,) and a leader of *ton* in Dublin and Belfast. The fact, however, that a young lord, and one of great expecta-tions, was on board, brought her up. A short cross examination of Lord Westport's French valet had confirmed the flying report, and at the same time (I suppose) put her in possession of my defect in all those advantages of title, fortune, and expectation which so brilliantly distinguished my friend. Her admiration of him, and her contempt for myself, were equally undisguised. And in the ring which she soon cleared out for public exhibition, she made us both fully sensible of the very equitable stations which she assigned to us in her regard. She was neither very brilliant, nor altogether a pretender, but might be described as a showy woman, of slight but popular accomplishments. Any woman, however has the advantage of possessing the ear of any company; and a woman of forty, with such tact and ex-perience as she will naturally have gathered in a talking practice of such duration, can find little difficulty in mortifying a boy, or sometimes, perhaps, in tempting him to unfortunate sallies of irritation. Me it was clear that she viewed in the light

of a humble friend, or what is known in fashionable life by the humiliating name
of a "toad-eater." Lord Westport, full of generosity in what regarded his own pretensions, and who never had violated the perfect equality which reigned in our
deportment to each other, colored with as much confusion as myself at her coarse
insinuations. And, in reality, our ages scarcely allowed of that relation which she
supposed to exist between us. Possibly she did *not* suppose it; but it is essential to
the wit and the display of some people that it should have a foundation in malice.
A victim and a sacrifice are indispensable conditions in every exhibition. In such a
case, my natural sense of justice would generally have armed me a hundred fold
for retaliation; but at present, chiefly, perhaps, because I had no effectual ally, and
could count upon no sympathy in my audience, I was mortified beyond the power of retort, and became a passive butt to the lady's stinging contumely and the
arrowy sleet of her gay rhetoric. The narrow bounds of our deck made it not easy
to get beyond talking range; and thus it happened, that for two hours I stood the
worst of this bright lady's feud. At length the tables turned. Two ladies appeared
slowly ascending from the cabin, both in deepest mourning, but else as different in
aspect as summer and winter. The elder was the Countess of Errol, then mourning
an affliction which had laid her life desolate, and admitted of no human consolation. Heavier grief—grief more self-occupied and deaf to all voice of sympathy—I
have not happened to witness. She seemed scarcely aware of our presence, except
it were by placing herself as far as was possible from the annoyance of our odious
conversation. The circumstances of her loss are now forgotten; at that time they
were known to a large circle in Bath and London, and I violate no confidence in
reviewing them. Lord Errol had been privately intrusted by Mr. Pitt with an official secret, viz., the outline and principal details of a foreign expedition; in which,
according to Mr. Pitt's original purpose, his lordship was to have held a high
command. In a moment of intoxication, the earl confided this secret to some false
friend, who published the communication and its author. Upon this, the unhappy
nobleman, under too keen a sense of wounded honor, and perhaps with an exaggerated notion of the evils attached to his indiscretion, destroyed himself. Months
had passed since that calamity when we met his widow; but time appeared to
have done nothing in mitigating her sorrow. The younger lady, on the other hand,
who was Lady Errol's sister,— Heavens! what a spirit of joy and festal pleasure
radiated from her eyes, her step, her voice, her manner! She was Irish, and the very
impersonation of innocent gayety, such as we find oftener, perhaps, amongst Irish
women than those of any other country. Mourning, I have said, she wore; from
sisterly consideration, the deepest mourning; that sole expression there was about
her of gloom or solemn feeling, —

> "But all things else about her drawn
> From May time and the cheerful dawn."

Odious bluestocking[100] of Belfast and Dublin! as some would call you, how
I hated you up to that moment! half an hour after, how grateful I felt for the hos-

[100] I have sometimes had occasion to remark, as a noticeable phenomenon of our
present times, that the order of ladies called *bluestockings*, by way of reproach, has become
totally extinct amongst us, except only here and there with superannuated clingers to obsolete remembrances. The reason of this change is interesting; and I do not scruple to call

it honorable to our intellectual progress. In the last (but still more in the penultimate) generation, any tincture of literature, of liberal curiosity about science, or of ennobling interest in books, carried with it an air of something unsexual, mannish, and (as it was treated by the sycophantish satirists that for ever humor the prevailing folly) of something ludicrous. This mode of treatment was possible so long as the literary class of ladies formed a feeble minority. But now, when two vast peoples, English and American, counting between them forty-nine millions, when the leaders of transcendent civilization (to say nothing of Germany and France) behold their entire educated class, male and female alike, calling out, not for *Panem et circenses,* (Give us this day our daily bread and our games of the circus,) but for *Panem et literas,* (Give us this day our daily bread and literature,) the universality of the call has swept away the very name of *bluestocking;* the very possibility of the ridicule has been undermined by stern realities; and the verbal expression of the reproach is fast becoming, not simply obsolete, but even unintelligible to our juniors. By the way, the origin of this term *bluestocking* has never been satisfactorily accounted for, unless the reader should incline to think *my* account satisfactory. I incline to that opinion myself. Dr. Bisset (in his Life of Burke) traces it idly to a *sobriquet* imposed by Mrs. Montagu, and the literary ladies of her circle, upon a certain obscure Dr. Stillingfleet, who was the sole masculine assistant at their literary sittings in Portman Square, and chose, upon some inexplicable craze, to wear blue stockings. The translation, however, of this name from the doctor's legs to the ladies' legs is still unsolved. That great *hiatus* needs filling up. I, therefore, whether erroneously or not, in reviewing a German historical work of some pretensions, where this problem emerges, rejected the Portman Square doctor altogether, and traced the term to an old Oxford statute—one of the many which meddle with dress, and which charges it as a point of conscience upon loyal scholastic students that they shall wear cerulean socks. Such socks, therefore, indicated scholasticism: worn by females, they would indicate a self-dedication to what for them would be regarded as pedantic studies. But, says an objector, no rational *female* would wear cerulean socks. Perhaps not, female taste being too good. But as such socks would symbolize such a profession of pedantry, so, inversely, any profession of pedantry, by whatever signs expressed, would be symbolized reproachfully by the imputation of wearing cerulean socks. It classed a woman, in effect, as a scholastic pedant. Now, however, when the vast diffusion of literature as a sort of daily bread has made all ridicule of female literary culture not less ridiculous than would be the attempt to ridicule that same daily bread, the whole phenomenon, thing and word, substance and shadow, is melting away from amongst us. Something of the same kind has happened in the history of silver forks. Forks of any kind, as is well known, were first introduced into Italy; thence by a fantastic (but, in this instance, judicious) English traveller *immediately* (and not *mediately through France*) were introduced into England. This elegant revolution occurred about 240 years ago; and never since that day have there been wanting English protesters against the infamy of eating without forks; and for the last 160 years, at least, against the paganism of using *steel forks;* or, 2dly, two- pronged forks; or, 3dly, of putting the knife into the mouth. At least 120 years ago, the Duchess of Queensberry, (Gay's duchess,) that leonine woman, used to shriek out, on seeing a hyperborean squire conveying peas to his abominable mouth on the point of a knife. "O, stop him, stop him! that man's going to commit suicide." This anecdote argues silver forks as existing much more than a century back, else the squire had a good defence. Since then, in fact, about the time of the French revolution, silver forks have been recognized as not less indispensable appendages to any elegant dinner table than silver spoons; and, along with silver forks, came in the explosion of that anti-Queensberry brutalism which forks first superseded—viz., the fiendish practice of introducing the knife between the lips. But, in defiance of all these facts, certain select hacks of the daily press, who never had an opportunity of seeing a civilized dinner, and fancying that their own obscene modes of feeding prevailed every where, got up the name of the *Silver-fork* School, tility which had procured me such an alliance! One minute sufficed to put the quick-witted young Irish woman in possession of our little drama and the several parts we were playing. To look was to understand, to wish was to execute, with this ardent child of nature. Like Spenser's Bradamant, with martial scorn she couched her lance on the side of the party suffering wrong. Her rank, as sister-in-law to the constable of Scotland, gave her some advantage for winning a favorable audience; and throwing her aegis over me, she extended that benefit to myself. Road was now made perforce for me also; my replies were no longer stifled in noise and laughter. Personalities were banished; literature was extensively discussed; and that is a subject which, offering little room to argument, offers the widest to eloquent display. I had immense reading; vast command of words, which somewhat diminished as ideas and doubts multiplied; and, speaking no longer to a deaf audience, but to a generous and indulgent protectress, I threw out, as from a cornucopia, my illustrative details and recollections; trivial enough, perhaps, as I might now think, but the more intelligible to my present circle. It might seem too much the case of a storm in a slop basin, if I were to spend any words upon the revolution which ensued. Suffice it, that I remained the lion of that company which had previously been most insultingly facetious at my expense; and the intellectual lady finally declared the air of the deck unpleasant.

Never, until this hour, had I thought of women as objects of a possible interest or of a reverential love. I had known them either in their infirmities and their unamiable aspects, or else in those sterner relations which made them objects of ungenial and uncompanionable feelings. Now first it struck me that life might owe half its attractions and all its graces to female companionship. Gazing, perhaps, with too earnest an admiration at this generous and spirited young daughter of Ireland, and in that way making her those acknowledgments for her goodness which I could not properly clothe in words, I was aroused to a sense of my indecorum by seeing her suddenly blush. I believe that Miss Bl— — interpreted my admiration rightly; for she was not offended, but, on the contrary, for the rest of the day, when not attending to her sister, conversed almost exclusively, and in a confidential way, with Lord Westport and myself. The whole, in fact, of this conversation must have convinced her that I, mere boy as I was, (viz., about fifteen,) could not have presumed to direct my admiration to *her*, a fine young woman of twenty, in any other character than that of a generous champion, and a very adroit mistress in the dazzling fence of colloquial skirmish. My admiration had, in reality, been addressed to her moral qualities, her enthusiasm, her spirit, and her generosity. Yet that blush, evanescent as it was,—the mere possibility that I, so very a child, should have called up the most transitory sense of bashfulness or confusion (which should have indicated the school of decency,) as representing some ideal school of fantastic or ultra refinement. At length, however, when cheap counterfeits of silver have made the decent four-pronged fork cheaper than the two-pronged steel barbarism, what has followed? Why, this—that the universality of the diffusion has made it hopeless any longer to banter it. There is, therefore, this strict analogy between "the silver fork" reproach and "the bluestocking" reproach—that in both cases alike a recognition, gradually becoming universal, of the thing itself, as a social necessity, has put down forever all idle attempts to throw ridicule upon it—upon literature, in the one case, as a most appropriate female ornament; and upon silver forks, on the other, as an element of social decorum.

upon any female cheek, first,—and suddenly, as with a flash of lightning, penetrating some utter darkness, illuminated to my own startled consciousness, never again to be obscured, the pure and powerful ideal of womanhood and womanly excellence. This was, in a proper sense, a *revelation*; it fixed a great era of change in my life; and this new-born idea, being agreeable to the uniform tendencies of my own nature,—that is, lofty and aspiring,—it governed my life with great power, and with most salutary effects. Ever after, throughout the period of youth, I was jealous of my own demeanor, reserved and awe-struck, in the presence of women; reverencing, often, not so much *them* as my own ideal of woman latent in them. For I carried about with me the idea, to which often I seemed to see an approximation, of

> "A perfect woman, nobly planned,
> To warn, to comfort, to command."

And from this day I was an altered creature, never again relapsing into the careless, irreflective mind of childhood.

At the same time I do not wish, in paying my homage to the other sex, and in glorifying its possible power over ours, to be confounded with those thoughtless and trivial rhetoricians who flatter woman with a false lip worship; and, like Lord Byron's buccaneers, hold out to them a picture of their own empire, built only upon sensual or upon shadowy excellences. We find continually a false enthusiasm, a mere bacchanalian inebriation, on behalf of woman, put forth by modern verse writers, expressly at the expense of the other sex, as though woman could be of porcelain, whilst man was of common earthern ware. Even the testimonies of Ledyard and Park are partly false (though amiable) tributes to female excellence; at least they are merely one-sided truths—aspects of one phasis, and under a peculiar angle. For, though the sexes differ characteristically, yet they never fail to reflect each other; nor can they differ as to the general amount of development; never yet was woman in one stage of elevation, and man (of the same community) in another. Thou, therefore, daughter of God and man, all-potent woman! reverence thy own ideal; and in the wildest of the homage which is paid to thee, as also in the most real aspects of thy wide dominion, read no trophy of idle vanity, but a silent indication of the possible grandeur enshrined in thy nature; which realize to the extent of thy power,—

> "And show us how divine a thing
> A woman may become."

For what purpose have I repeated this story? The reader may, perhaps, suppose it introductory to some tale of boyish romantic passion for some female idol clothed with imaginary perfections. But in that case he will be mistaken. Nothing of the kind was possible to me. I was preoccupied by other passions. Under the disease—for disease it was—which at that time mastered me, one solitary desire, one frenzy, one demoniac fascination, stronger than the fascinations of calenture, brooded over me as the moon over the tides—forcing me day and night into speculations upon great intellectual problems, many times beyond my strength, as indeed often beyond all human strength, but not the less provoking me to pursue them. As a prophet in days of old had no power to resist the voice which, from hidden worlds, called him to a mission, sometimes, perhaps, revolting to his human sensibilities, as he must deliver, was under a coercion to deliver the burning word that spoke within his heart,—or as a ship on the Indian Ocean cannot seek rest by anchoring, but *must* run before the wrath of the monsoon,—such in its fury, such in its unrelentingness, was the persecution that overmastered me. School tasks under these circumstances, it may well be supposed, had become a torment to me. For a long time they had lost even that slight power of stimulation which belongs to the irritation of difficulty. Easy and simple they had now become as the elementary lessons of childhood. Not that it is possible for Greek studies, if pursued with unflinching sincerity, ever to fall so far into the rear as a *palaestra* for exercising both strength and skill; but, in a school where the exercises are pursued, in common by large classes, the burden must be adapted to the powers of the weakest, and not of the strongest. And, apart from that objection, at this period, the hasty unfolding of far different intellectual interests than such as belong to mere literature had, for a time, dimmed in my eyes the lustre of classical studies, pursued at whatsoever depth and on whatsoever scale. For more than a year, every thing connected with schools and the business of schools had been growing more and more hateful to me. At first, however, my disgust had been merely the disgust of weariness and pride. But now, at this crisis, (for crisis it was virtually to me,) when a premature development of my whole mind was rushing in like a cataract, forcing channels for itself and for the new tastes which it introduced, my disgust was no longer simply intellectual, but had deepened into a *moral* sense as of some inner dignity continually violated. Once the petty round of school tasks had been felt as a molestation; but now, at last, as a degradation. Constant conversation with grown-up men for the last half year, and upon topics oftentimes of the gravest order,—the responsibility that had always in some slight degree settled upon myself since I had become the eldest surviving son of my family, but of late much more so when circumstances had thrown me as an English stranger upon the society of distinguished Irishmen,—more, however, than all beside, the inevitable rebound and counter-growth of internal dignity from the everlasting commerce with lofty speculations, these agencies in constant operation had imbittered my school disgust, until it was travelling fast into a mania. Precisely at this culminating point of my self-conflict did that scene occur which I have described with Miss Bl— —. In that hour another element, which assuredly was not wanted, fell into the seething caldron of new-born impulses, that, like the magic caldron of Medea, was now transforming me into a new creature. Then first and suddenly I brought powerfully before myself the change which was worked in the aspects of society by the presence of woman—woman, pure, thoughtful, noble, coming before me as a Pandora crowned with perfections. Right over against this ennobling spectacle, with equal suddenness, I placed the odious spectacle of schoolboy society—no matter in what region of the earth; schoolboy society, so frivolous in the matter of its disputes, often so brutal in the manner; so foolishly careless, and yet so revoltingly selfish; dedicated ostensibly to learning, and yet beyond any section of human beings so conspicuously ignorant. Was it indeed *that* heavenly which I was soon to exchange for *this* earthly? It seemed to me, when contemplating the possibility that I could yet have nearly three years to pass in such society as this, that I heard some irresistible voice saying, Lay aside thy fleshly robes of humanity, and enter for a season into some brutal incarnation. But what connection had this painful prospect with Laxton? Why should it press upon my anxieties in approaching that mansion, more than it had done at Westport? Naturally enough, in part, because every day brought me nearer to the horror from which I recoiled: my return to England would recall the attention of my guardians to the question, which as yet had slumbered; and the knowledge that I had reached Northamptonshire would precipitate their decision. Obscurely, besides, through a hint which had reached me, I guessed what this decision was likely to be, and it took the very worst shape it could have taken. All this increased my agitation from hour to hour. But all this was quickened and barbed by the certainty of so immediately meeting Lady Carbery. To her it was, and to her only, that I could look for any useful advice or any effectual aid. She over my mother, as in turn my mother over *her*, exercised considerable influence; whilst my mother's power was very seldom disturbed by the other guardians. The mistress of Laxton it was, therefore, whose opinion upon the case would virtually be decisive; since, if *she* saw no reasonable encouragement to any contest with my guardians, I felt too surely that my own uncountenanced and unaided energies drooped too much for such an effort. Who Lady Carbery was, I will explain in my next chapter, entitled *Laxton*. Meantime, to me, individually, she was the one sole friend that ever I could regard as entirely fulfilling the offices of an honorable friendship. She had known me from infancy: when I was in my first year of life, she, an orphan and a great heiress, was in her tenth or eleventh; and on her occasional visits to "the Farm," (a rustic old house then occupied by my father,) I, a household pet, suffering under an ague, which lasted from my first year to my third, naturally fell into her hands as a sort of superior toy, a toy that could breathe and talk. Every year our intimacy had been renewed, until her marriage interrupted it. But, after no very long interval, when my mother had transferred her household to Bath, in that city we frequently met again; Lord Carbery liking Bath for itself, as well as for its easy connection with London, whilst Lady Carbery's health was supposed to benefit by the waters. Her understanding was justly reputed a fine one; but, in general, it was calculated to win respect rather than love, for it was masculine and austere, with very little toleration for sentiment or romance. But to myself she had always been indulgently kind; I was protected in her regard, beyond any body's power to dislodge me, by her childish remembrances; and of late years she had begun to entertain the highest opinion of my intellectual promises. Whatever could be done to assist my views, I most certainly might count upon her doing; that is to say, within the limits of her conscientious judgment upon the propriety of my own plans. Having, besides, so much more knowledge of the world than myself, she might see cause to dissent widely from my own view of what was expedient as well as what was right; in which case I was well assured that, in the midst of kindness and unaffected sympathy, she would firmly adhere to the views of my guardians. In any circumstances she would have done so. But at present a new element had begun to mix with the ordinary influences which governed her estimates of things: she had, as I knew from my sister's report, become religious; and her new opinions were of a gloomy cast, Calvinistic, in fact, and tending to what is *now* technically known in England as "Low Church," or "Evangelical Christianity." These views, being adopted in a great measure from my mother, were naturally the same as my mother's; so that I could form some guess as to the general spirit, if not the exact direction, in which her counsels would flow. It is singular that, until this time, I had never regarded Lady Carbery under any relation whatever to female intellectual society. My early childish knowledge of her had shut out that mode of viewing her. But now, suddenly, under the new-born sympathies awakened by the scene with Miss Bl——, I became aware of the distinguished place she was qualified to fill in such society. In that Eden—for such it had now consciously become to me—I had no necessity to cultivate an interest or solicit an admission; already, through Lady Carbery's too flattering estimate of my own pretensions, and through old, childish memories, I held the most distinguished place. This Eden, she it was that lighted up suddenly to my new-born powers of appreciation in all its dreadful points of contrast with the killing society of schoolboys. She it was, fitted to be the glory of such an Eden, who probably would assist in banishing me for the present to the wilderness outside. My distress of mind was inexpressible. And, in the midst of glittering saloons, at times also in the midst of society the most fascinating, I—contemplating the idea of that gloomy academic dungeon to which for three long years I anticipated too certainly a sentence of exile—felt very much as in the middle ages must have felt some victim of evil destiny, inheritor of a false, fleeting prosperity, that suddenly, in a moment of time, by signs blazing out past all concealment on his forehead, was detected as a leper; and in that character, as a public nuisance and universal horror, was summoned instantly to withdraw from society; prince or peasant, was indulged with no time for preparation or evasion; and, from the midst of any society, the sweetest or the most dazzling, was driven violently to take up his abode amid the sorrow-haunted chambers of a lazar house.

The author has exerted himself every where to keep the text accurate; and he is disposed to believe that his own care, combined with the general accuracy of the press, must have enabled him to succeed in that object. But if it should appear that any errors have after all escaped him, he must request his readers to excuse them, after explaining that he suffers under the oppression of a nervous distraction, which renders all labors exacting any energy of attention inexpressibly painful.

Lector House believes that a society develops through a two-fold approach of continuous learning and adaptation, which is derived from the study of classic literary works spread across the historic timeline of literature records. Therefore, we aim at reviving, repairing and redeveloping all those inaccessible or damaged but historically as well as culturally important literature across subjects so that the future generations may have an opportunity to study and learn from past works to embark upon a journey of creating a better future.

This book is a result of an effort made by Lector House towards making a contribution to the preservation and repair of original ancient works which might hold historical significance to the approach of continuous learning across subjects.

HAPPY READING & LEARNING!

LECTOR HOUSE LLP
E-MAIL: lectorpublishing@gmail.com